GOVERNMENT
FOR THE PEOPLE

ALSO BY ALAN PIFER

Our Aging Society: Paradox and Promise (co-editor)

GOVERNMENT FOR THE PEOPLE

The Federal Social Role:
What It Is, What It Should Be

FORREST CHISMAN

and

ALAN PIFER

W · W · NORTON & COMPANY
New York · *London*

Published simultaneously in Canada by Penguin Books Canada Ltd.,
2801 John Street, Markham, Ontario L3R 1B4.
Printed in the United States of America.

The text of this book is composed in Times Roman,
with display type set in Perpetua.
Composition and Manufacturing by The Maple-Vail Book Manufacturing Group.
Book design by Jacques Chazaud.

First Edition

ISBN 0-393-02491-1

W. W. Norton & Company, Inc., 500 Fifth Avenue, New York, N.Y. 10110
W. W. Norton & Company Ltd., 37 Great Russell Street, London WC1B 3NU

1 2 3 4 5 6 7 8 9 0

For Victoria and Erica

Contents

FOREWORD   *9*

1:   A Time for Reassessment   *17*

2:   The Activist Tradition   *29*

3:   The American Style of Activism   *47*

4:   Dimensions of the Social Role   *59*

5:   Myths and Realities   *85*

6:   In Arrears   *119*

7:   National Purpose and the American Style   *133*

8:   Prospects for Reform   *155*

9:   Driving Forces I: Economic Change   *169*

10:   Driving Forces II: Social Change   *195*

11:   Priorities for the Social Role   *219*

12:   Measures   *239*

13:   The Near Term   *263*

14:   Government for the People   *277*

NOTES   *285*

INDEX   *299*

Foreword

by ALAN PIFER

I n the spring of 1982 I was asked to address the annual meeting, in Boston, of the National Conference on Social Welfare. The subject was "the social role of government in a free enterprise society." I thought I would adhere fairly closely to the traditional social welfare role, what could be described as the American version of the welfare state. But as I prepared the speech, I was intrigued to realize that there were many other activities of our national government that, directly or indirectly, affect the social welfare of Americans, especially efforts to maintain employment by keeping the economy strong. These activities, it seemed, easily could be included in a functional definition of the government's social role.

This was the heyday of myths about the federal social role—that it was a vast conspiracy foisted on the nation by "liberal do-gooders," that it was the principal cause of inflation and an inhibitor of economic growth, that its programs were ineffective and, in the case of the poor, actually did more harm than good, that it discouraged efforts by states, localities, the voluntary and business sectors, and so on. It was not easy to puncture these ridiculous claims, so often had they been repeated.

A few months later, the NCSW asked me to set up a commission that would review the federal social role and make recommendations as to how much of it should be preserved and strengthened. I knew that such an undertaking, done properly, would require a substantial sum of money to carry out. But in talks with a few foundation leaders, I soon saw that skepticism about the value of commission exercises had become so great that funds of this magnitude were going to be extremely difficult to raise. Nevertheless, several foundations said they would put up small grants to enable me to carry out a six-month feasibility study.

My first step was to search for a director of the project, someone who would initially help me determine whether a study of the federal social role was really needed and, if so, what form the investigation should take. I was enormously fortunate in being able to enlist Forrest Chisman for this task.

From January to June of 1983, Mr. Chisman and I toured the nation, talking about the idea with some three hundred well-informed, experienced individuals of all political persuasions—members of Congress, current and former government administrators, governors, members of state legislatures, mayors, university scholars, staff members of research institutes, businessmen, journalists, and others. We received a ringing endorsement of the idea of a study and many offers of help, but general skepticism that setting up a commission of public figures was the way to go about our job. We were simply advised to carry out the study ourselves and to issue our findings in our own names.

Understandably, we were somewhat diffident about accepting this advice. We felt that it might seem presumptuous, if not foolhardy, especially to the professional policy studies community. Nonetheless, no comprehensive examination of the federal social role in its present form had ever been attempted, and it seemed that explaining to ordinary Americans what this role is, how it arose, and what its real, as opposed to alleged, shortcomings are was much needed. Furthermore, our preliminary reconnaissance had shown that no one else was planning, or was likely, to take on this large task.

Accordingly, with the concurrence of the NCSW, we decided

to go ahead—on our own—with what we called the Project on the Federal Social Role. It was to be under the auspices of the NCSW, but to enjoy an autonomous status.

The project was based on the broad definition of the federal social role that had intrigued me earlier. Thus, it included not only the traditional social welfare role (the social insurance and income transfer programs) but also an extensive range of other activities designed to promote social well-being more generally, such as social and economic regulation, tax and credit incentives, economic management, and the enforcement of Constitutional guarantees. We hoped that this approach would yield new insights into the true nature of the federal social role—in particular, how it relates to traditional American ideas about government in general as these had been shaped by the nation's two centuries as an independent republic.

As we began planning in earnest, we came to the conclusion that we were not going to be able to raise enough money prior to launching the project to adopt the centralized, comprehensive approach we at first designed. We settled on an alternative, decentralized plan that would enable us to get the project underway while we raised the necessary funds in smaller amounts over a longer period of time. In a way, this was a fortunate development. It obliged us to seek out groups of scholars in universities and research institutes who, with limited financial support, would be willing to carry out important pieces of the study that would coincide with their own interests and competencies. This approach led us to establish working groups at Yale, Princeton, the University of Chicago, Columbia, the Georgetown University Law School, and the Urban Institute and to create a seventh, free-standing, bipartisan group we named the Committee on Federalism and National Purpose.

This committee, chaired by Republican Senator Daniel J. Evans of Washington and the then Democratic Governor of Virginia, Charles S. Robb, produced a powerful report on reform of the intergovernmental system, entitled, *To Form a More Perfect Union.* The six working groups have produced a set of distinguished, scholarly books now in process of publication by the Princeton

University Press.[1] The project itself has published two books and ten sets of working papers. It is encouraging that there exists in the academic world today a new generation of extremely able young scholars making significant contributions to understanding the history and present functioning of social policy in the United States. In all, more than 150 scholars and experienced practitioners participated actively in one part or another of the project.

From the outset of the project, in addition to generating a substantial output of scholarly publication, we planned to write a book about the federal social role for a broad, general audience. Such a book would bring to the public, on the two hundredth anniversary of the adoption of the Constitution, our assessment of what the role of government at the national level should be in promoting the social welfare of the American people. The book that follows is that volume. Its purpose is to enable more Americans to understand what the social role is, how and why it came into being, what shortcomings are to be found in it, and how it must be re-energized and redirected in the light of the great social problems the nation will be facing in the years ahead.

This is not a book for specialists. It intentionally omits many of the nuances of fact and detail that are rightly of such great value in the academic world. Our goal is simply to give the concerned general reader a glimpse behind the front pages at how the federal social role works and why it is so valuable.

In arguing for activist government at the federal level, we do not disparage the roles of state and local government, voluntary organizations, and the business sector. All have important parts to play, and their efforts, too, must be encouraged and strengthened. We have concentrated on the federal social role because it has been under heavy—though misdirected—attack for the past decade, because it is essential to the nation's future strength and well-being, and because it needs reform and redirection. What we advocate is a cooperative society in which every instrumentality for the common good plays its part, but in which national government has special responsibilities, simply because so many of our problems today are national in character.

Although large numbers of people have helped us develop the

material in this book through their contributions to the project at large, and we are grateful to them for that help, the opinions expressed in it are entirely personal and are the responsibility of no one but ourselves. The book, therefore, is not a final report on the project but, rather, a personal statement by Forrest Chisman and myself emanating from our work on it.

There are so many people to whom thanks are due that we cannot conceivably mention all of them. We do, however, express our special appreciation to our colleagues, past and present, for their loyalty to us, their devotion to the project, and their extraordinarily hard work. They include Carmelita Cooksey, Judith Golub, Rachael Lowder, Audrey Ryack, Michael Weaver, Felicity Skidmore, and Helen Noah.

Warm thanks also are due to the many people who participated so effectively in our seminars at universities and research institutes. We particularly wish to thank the directors: Theda Skocpol at the University of Chicago; Theodore Marmor, Jerry Mashaw, and Elizabeth Auld at Yale; Amy Gutmann at Princeton; Alfred Kahn and Sheila Kamerman at Columbia; Peter Edelman at Georgetown; and Lee Bawden and Isabel Sawhill at the Urban Institute.

Senator Daniel J. Evans and Governor Charles S. Robb deserve particular thanks for their effective and enthusiastic leadership of the Committee on Federalism and National Purpose; Stephen Farber, Jack Brizius, Harold Hovey, and Barry Van Lare for their excellent support work for the committee; and Arthur Singer for his determined and successful effort to secure funding from the Alfred P. Sloan Foundation.

We must express to A. Sidney Johnson and Theodora Ooms our thanks for their manuscript on family policy, Thomas Hopkins for his manuscript on social regulation, and Robert Lampman for his manuscript on social policy and economic performance.

Duira Ward, Bertram Beck, and Joyce Black, successive presidents of the National Conference on Social Welfare, have been consistently supportive and helpful to us, while at the same time scrupulously respectful of the project's autonomy. We are grateful, indeed, to them.

14   FOREWORD

The Project on the Federal Social Role would never have been possible without financial support from Carnegie Corporation of New York, The Edna McConnell Clark Foundation, The Commonwealth Fund, The Ford Foundation, The George Gund Foundation, The William and Flora Hewlett Foundation, Ittleson Foundation, Inc., The Joyce Foundation, The Henry J. Kaiser Family Foundation, The John D. and Catherine T. MacArthur Foundation, New York Community Trust, Rockefeller Brothers Fund, The Rockefeller Foundation, The Scherman Foundation, Inc., Alfred P. Sloan Foundation, van Ameringen Foundation, Inc., and without special help from Dr. and Mrs. Caryl Haskins and an individual donor who wishes to remain anonymous.

Also, very special thanks must go to Robert Ball, Samuel Beer, the late Wilbur Cohen, Stuart Eizenstat, Arthur Flemming, John Palmer, Thomas Troyer, Arthur Schlesinger, Jr., and Willard Wirtz for being unfailing sources of moral support, advice, and inspiration to us.

A final note is in order about the contents of this book. Unlike many recent works on public policy and social issues, it is not based on original data gathering or analysis. The data it contains are used for illustrative purposes—to indicate orders of magnitude—and except where otherwise indicated they are from government reports and other standard sources.

New York City
January 1987

GOVERNMENT
FOR THE PEOPLE

I

A Time for Reassessment

On August 31, 1910, in a speech at Osawatomie, Kansas, former President Theodore Roosevelt spelled out the essence of his political philosophy. "The national government belongs to the whole American people," he declaimed, "and where the whole American people are interested, that interest can be guarded effectively only by the national government."[1] Seventy years later Ronald Reagan began his presidency on a different note. "In this present crisis," he said, "government is not the solution to our problem; government is the problem."[2] In the gap between these two sentiments lies the central question of American politics today: What should be the federal social role?

For over a decade Americans have been engaged in a thoroughgoing reassessment of the purposes and directions of their national government. Scarcely a program, policy, or expenditure mandated by Washington has escaped the scrutiny of politicians, scholars, and the press. There have been heated debates over taxes, welfare, social security, regulation, and a host of other activities in which the federal government is involved.

As an exercise in public education, this national questioning has been a resounding success. Seldom have the innards of a complex modern government been placed so comprehensively on display. The average newspaper reader today knows more about how the federal government works than ever before.

But as an exercise in public policy, the current reassessment has been a disappointment. No clear directions for the future have emerged. The growth of the federal government may have slowed, but it has not stopped. Few programs or activities have been recast, eliminated, or greatly reduced. There are plenty of ideas for new initiatives, but most have remained in the talking stage. Despite all the debate, the elements of federal policy are pretty much the same as they were a decade ago. The net effect of reassessment has been to arrest the development of policy, not to launch it on any new course.

The Stakes

It may not be surprising that the American people should take a long time making up their minds about what they want their national government to do. The stakes involved are enormous. The current reassessment is taking place in the waning years of a century that has brought to the United States the greatest wave of material and social progress in the history of mankind. The nation that elected Ronald Reagan is vastly freer, more affluent, and more secure than the nation that elected Theodore Roosevelt, and the federal government can take a large part of the credit.

In this century government at the national level has greased the wheels of industry and promoted the cause of agriculture with tariffs, subsidies, tax breaks, loans, contracts, scientific know-how, and measures to control the severity of economic downturns. It has curbed the excesses of business with standards and regulations. It has organized markets that were disorderly and policed markets to keep them competitive. It has taxed the increasing affluence that its policies have helped create. And it has used those tax dollars to provide a level of personal security that corporate America, voluntary associations, and most individuals acting on their own could never afford—against the hazards of old age, unemployment, disability, and other forms of hardship. It has helped to modernize our cities, build our homes, clean up our environment, and stretch our communications networks. And it has sought to end the centuries of injustice toward minorities and women.

All these and many more activities have been part of the federal social role. As a result, in this age of reassessment Americans, knowingly or unknowingly, are trying to decide whether policies and programs that have made an indispensable contribution to a century of national progress should be continued, recast, or set aside.

The Spirit of Activism

These stakes may seem large, but the issues raised by the current reassessment are larger still. During this century the federal social role has grown enormously, but that growth has taken place in a piecemeal fashion. Government at the national level has assumed responsibilities gradually in response to pressing issues of the times. Theodore Roosevelt's efforts to regulate business, Franklin Roosevelt's programs for economic security, and Lyndon Johnson's war on poverty and racism have been only the most memorable building blocks of the social role as we know it today.

But although the social role has been constructed out of many different initiatives in many different circumstances, each of its elements has been informed by a common philosophy. It is the philosophy of activist government that the first Roosevelt articulated so clearly at Osawatomie: the idea that in a democracy the people can and must use national government to solve their major common problems. It is really no more complicated than that. The key words are "in a democracy." Roosevelt and succeeding activist presidents believed that democratic government is the people's instrument. Americans have nothing to fear from it because it belongs to them and is controlled by them. They can safely use it to meet their needs, however and whenever they like. And in a complex modern society where none of us is completely the master of his fate, the need for activist government to solve common problems is bound to be great.

In Lincoln's words, democratic government is not only "government of the people" and "by the people," it is also "government for the people." The people can have a reasonable confidence that government will act in their interests, to the extent that those interests are made known. Or at least they can have confidence that its shortcomings are no greater than the frailties to which all human institutions are prone: the limited capacities and vision of even the best of men and women.

The federal social role, then, is more than just a collection of programs; it is also an idea and a tradition of government. Most of the current reassessment has focused piecemeal on particular programs that have developed equally piecemeal over many years. But because that reassessment has called into question virtually every aspect of the social role, it can be seen as a reconsideration of the philosophy underlying activist government as well.

Crystal Balls

Social critics of the right are among the first to agree that the current reassessment is, in fact, this radical. Many conservatives believe that it arises from a basic shift in public attitudes.[3] According to this theory, the American people have lost confidence in big government. They have concluded that it costs too much, that many of its programs are ineffective, and that it undermines both personal freedom and individual responsibility. For these and other reasons, they would prefer to rely more on "traditional" institutions, such as the family, voluntary associations, local government, and the private economy—rather than on government at the national level—to solve public problems.

These critics claim that changing public attitudes have brought about a "conservative revolution" in American politics. The public has elected leaders committed not only to stopping the growth of the federal social role but also to dismantling many of its parts. Subscribers to this theory believe we are witnessing a fundamental realignment in the nation's political life that is likely to continue for the indefinite future.

Critics of other political persuasions explain the current reassessment in terms of the institutional capacities of the federal government.[4] They believe that government at the national level has simply broken down under an overload of responsibilities. Even a brief listing of federal programs fills a thick book, and they are so closely interlinked that it takes a computer to understand how changes in one area resonate through the system as a whole. It is impossible for either government officials or the general public to oversee the present array of federal activities, let alone plan future initiatives.

According to this theory, the social role can only evolve if the federal government sheds some of its existing duties in favor of other tasks that have higher priority. Public policy has been stuck on a treadmill of reassessment, not because of any fundamental change in attitudes, but because of our inability to manage the present public agenda and our unwillingness to relinquish any part of it.

Still other observers believe that the current questioning of the federal role is only one phase in a great historical cycle. Historian Arthur M. Schlesinger, Jr., has remarked that periods of government activism in the United States occur with almost clockwork regularity every thirty years, and they are followed with the same regularity by periods of quietism and retrenchment.[5] The nation needs to catch its breath after bouts of political exertion. Schlesinger believes that today's reassessment is in many ways analogous to the conservatism of the 1920s and the 1950s. In due time, the nation will develop a new sense of urgency about its unmet needs, and it will demand a new surge of activist government, just as it has in the past.

Economist Albert Hirschman and political scientist Samuel Huntington have also developed cyclical views of American politics.[6] Hirschman believes the nation alternates between periods of public and private "involvements," and Huntington has identified recurrent tides of "creedal passions." Their theories, like

Schlesinger's, imply that government activism is not doomed; it is only resting.

Stalemate

Doubtless there is truth in all of these theories. But there is a far simpler view that is consistent both with them and with what we know about recent history and the actual views of the American public. It makes most sense to conclude that the American people and their leaders have been tied up in a prolonged reassessment because they are dissatisfied with many aspects of federal activism but don't quite know what to do.

Americans traditionally have been suspicious of large institutions, particularly government. Add to that suspicion the most salient events of our recent national experience and it becomes easy to understand why Americans would want to engage in a thorough stock-taking of the social role.

The trust in federal leadership that developed during the Great Depression and World War II and solidified during the Eisenhower years was shaken for more than one generation by Vietnam, Watergate, and other unpopular or unseemly events. In addition, the growth of federal activism has always been led by strong presidents. But of the last five American presidents, one was forced from office, one declined to seek reelection because of public discontent, two were defeated at the polls, and the fifth ran on a platform of dismantling the federal establishment.

During the years when these political events were taking place, many Americans also had a hard time economically. From the early 1970s through the early 1980s, the United States went through a prolonged period of high inflation and slow growth in real income. Big government is expensive, and these conditions undoubtedly made many people reluctant to pay the bill for an active social role.

Finally, some of the more ambitious goals enunciated for federal policy, particularly in the Johnson years, such as "curing poverty" and creating real equality of opportunity for minorities, did not meet with rushing success. And they generated deep hostility among other groups in the nation who felt that their interests were negatively affected.

In these circumstances, it is understandable that Americans have developed a skeptical attitude toward the wisdom and capacities of the federal government. Opinion polls show that trust in government as an institution has steadily declined in recent years. But the polls also show another pattern.[7] Respondents continue to express strong support for most of the policies that make up the federal social role and for many ideas that would extend its reach. The logical explanation for this seeming paradox is that Americans are recoiling from the shock of too many years of bad news traceable in one way or another to Washington. They don't reject the directions of activist government, but they are dissatisfied with leaders who seem unable to make it work, and they are vaguely suspicious that perhaps it can't be made to work at all. They have come to distrust government, not activism.

In a sense, the current reassessment has two faces: While the public supports the current directions of policy and is likely to resist efforts to undercut them, Americans are also looking for new leadership and critical views. In this climate of opinion, politicians maneuvering to catch the prevailing winds have found themselves becalmed. The people have not registered a conservative mandate or a liberal mandate; they have registered a vague mandate to "do something" without knowing exactly what that "something" should be. The reassessment of public policy is an understandable response to so vague a demand. Politicians have been systematically sorting through the federal social role, looking at each program from every possible point of view, in the hope of finding some workable response to popular discontent.

Collision

This dissection of social policy is perfectly healthy, up to a point. In a democracy everything that government does should be up for reassessment at all times. Nothing should be taken for granted. A period of prolonged public scrutiny can help to uncover latent problems that might otherwise go undetected until they erupt in crisis.

But beyond a certain point, reassessment becomes stalemate: an unproductive gnawing over of old political bones. It reduces government to little more than an accounting exercise—seeing what can be shaved or shifted to make the national books balance. This is the position we have reached in recent years. Not only has very little changed in the design of federal policy, but Congress and the administration have had the greatest difficulty even in agreeing on federal budgets that ratify the lack of change.

Prolonged stalemate in public policy is dangerous to the nation. In the first place, present federal programs are clearly inadequate to meet some of the nation's most pressing needs. Anyone can develop a long list of social problems widely regarded to be within the federal ambit that are poorly addressed by existing national policy. The "social safety net," which both liberals and conservatives agree should be maintained, fails to protect many of our most vulnerable citizens: children living in poverty, the elderly who are chronically ill, and many of the disabled. Our programs of regulation and public investment are often poorly targeted. Policies to address joblessness and the cost of health care are less effective than they should be. In short, we are only doing half the job in a great number of areas.

Even more important, the present reassessment is essentially a backward-looking exercise. While we continue to mull over policies of the past, we are on a collision course with the future. Although the basic array of federal programs may be pretty much the same as it was a decade ago, the needs of the nation have been changing for some time. Current policies fail to address many of the adverse effects of change, and as policy has ceased to evolve, those problems have become increasingly severe. Four major problem areas, in particular, have resulted from recent decades of social and economic change.

- *The Aging of the Population.* The increasing numbers of old and very old people in the Untied States and the decreasing proportion of children will create mounting problems for our economy, our health care system, our provisions for retirement, and many other aspects of our national well-being.

• *Threats to Employment.* The continuing decline of manufacturing as a source of jobs, the growth of the service sector, the increasing need for a more highly skilled work force, the growing pressure of international competition, and the greater international mobility of both capital and jobs pose serious threats to the future prospects for employment of many Americans, and possibly to our overall standard of living.

• *Threats to Families and Children.* Large-scale participation by women in the paid work force, a high divorce rate, the growing number of single-parent families, more frequent changes in employment and residence, and a staggering increase in personal debt are but a few of the changes that have stretched the capacities of families and other social support systems to their limits.

• *An Increasingly Hopeless Underclass.* A large number of poorly educated, rootless, unemployable young people find it increasingly hard to break out of a culture of poverty and are rapidly producing a successive generation with little or no chance of anything better.

These problems did not emerge overnight. They have been building for many years, and there is every reason to believe that they will continue to build. Collectively, they offer a powerful challenge to the present social policy stalemate because they are fundamentally altering virtually every function of the federal social role.

For example, the elderly whom we care for with public programs today are not the same elderly as twenty years ago. They are more numerous, they consume more health care, they contain larger numbers of the very old and the very frail, and they are less able to rely on either their personal savings or family supports. Likewise, a large portion of the unemployed today are not the unemployed of twenty years ago. Then they were largely prime-age industrial workers suffering layoffs due to periodic downturns in the economy. Today they are predominantly older workers, unskilled members of the underclass who have never held a job and have few resources to build on, or female single parents. Nor are the children of today the same as the children of twenty years ago. Fewer are being born. And among their smaller numbers are many more who come from broken homes, who live in poverty, or who spend their earliest years in the care of someone other than their parents.

The economy of today is not the economy of twenty years ago. America now must compete vigorously in the international market. And its success depends less on its resources of capital and raw materials and much more on the skills of its workers and innovations in technology to support them.

These changes pose life and death problems for the nation— economic and social advance or decline. The federal government is already committed to helping in some areas: for example, support for the elderly and the poor and stimulation of economic growth. But the policies in place were made for a society and economy of another era. That population and economy have changed dramatically, and they will continue to change. Some policies are doubtless sound, but others must be transformed to meet the challenges of the future.

The New Activism

The outstanding question the nation must answer is not, then, whether public policy should evolve. Public policy is already evolving as changes in our society cause old programs to miss their marks. The more relevant question is whether the nation simply will drift into the future or will face it with a clear sense of purpose by mobilizing the forces of activist government to meet the challenges that lie ahead.

Those challenges indicate definite directions for policy. In particular, they indicate that the social and economic well-being of the nation in the years to come will depend, above all else, on our ability to improve the skills, opportunities, and physical well-being of all our citizens. Activist government in the United States had its origins in the early days of our republic, when public leaders perceived that the nation was imperiled by a shortage of industrial capital and physical infrastructure. They used the federal government to mount a vigorous program of economic expansion. Today the peril comes from a shortage of human capital and social infrastructure, and an even more vigorous response is required.

The forces of change which require that response are already at work. The sooner we break the present stalemate and begin to develop a new framework for policy, the smaller the price of adaptation will be.

Argument

This book argues the case for activist government in the United States. The argument has three parts. The first part (Chapters 2 through 5) lays out the basic facts about the origins, functioning, dimensions, and effects of the federal social role. Despite a decade of critical reassessment, there is still widespread misunderstanding about these basic facts, and that misunderstanding is a major roadblock to future progress.

Chapter 2 explains how activism at the federal level developed in the United States and why. It shows that pragmatic activism has been the dominant political tradition during most of the two hundred years of our national life. And it shows how that tradition has evolved from our national circumstances and values.

Chapter 3 describes how Americans have adopted a distinctive style of handling public affairs and how that style affects the form that activist policies take.

Chapter 4 details the present dimensions of the social role. It shows that the system of social policy that has resulted from two centuries of activism in the American style is much more extensive than most people imagine.

Finally, Chapter 5 debunks a number of major myths about the effects of the social role on American society and on economic growth. Far too many public leaders as well as members of the general public wrongly believe that federal activism does serious harm to our social and economic life. Chapter 5 refutes these claims.

The middle part of this book is devoted to explaining the real, rather than imagined, defects of the social role in its present form. Chapters 6 and 7 describe the serious inadequacies of many current policies and trace those inadequacies to limits inherent in the American style of activism. Chapter 8 discusses the shortcomings of past proposals for improving the social role. Chapters 9 and 10 explore the future challenges that are certain to make current policies even more inadequate and to demand new directions for activism.

The final part of the book (Chapters 11 through 13) spells out the directions for future policy, centering on human resource development, that are mandated by both the nation's political traditions and its most urgent needs.

The last chapter draws all of these themes together, using them to indicate what the federal social role must be if the United States is to respond to problems of the future, as it has responded to problems of the past.

2

The Activist
Tradition

D ebate about the role of national government in the United
States is nothing new. To a remarkable extent, present-day
arguments are contemporary versions of a controversy that has
been going on since the earliest days of our republic. From that
controversy has emerged a distinctive tradition of government: a
tradition of pragmatic activism. In practice, this tradition provides the best answer Americans have found to questions about
what the federal role should be.

Voices from the Past

Two schools of thought have dominated debate about the role
of government throughout our history. Those who presume against
an extensive federal role rely on the old American tradition of
skepticism about the value of government in general and the federal government in particular. According to this view, government is, at best, a necessary evil. Ideally most of the work of
society could be performed by families, voluntary associations,
and businesses. These are "natural," congenial, and productive
institutions that support individual freedom and creativity. They

can easily be molded to the desires of ordinary members of society. Government is an impersonal, repressive, and unproductive institution that tends to run on its own agenda. It imposes a bland uniformity that stifles the freedom and creative energies of a large and diverse nation.

The only reason we have government, according to this view, is because other institutions are manifestly incapable of performing certain functions necessary to society—such as organizing for defense against foreign adversaries, maintaining public order, and providing for civil justice. For such functions we need public authority. But they should be kept as few as possible.

Accordingly, "That government governs best that governs least." If we must have government, we would do well to concentrate most of its authority at the state and local level, where ordinary people can keep an eye on it and where their opinions have most impact. National government is the most suspect of all institutions because it is both the most remote and, potentially, the most powerful. It must be carefully circumscribed by Constitutional guarantees, such as the Bill of Rights, and its functions should be kept to the bare minimum. The doctrine of "strict constructionism"—the idea that national government should perform only those functions explicitly mandated by the Constitution—is an important part of the limited government tradition. Another important part is aversion to both large federal surpluses and large national debts.

This American tradition of presuming against government in general, and national government in particular, is often associated with the philosophy of Thomas Jefferson. Although it may be unfair to ascribe so rigid an ideology to that complex and elusive man, Jefferson certainly did favor a limited federal role. "I own, I am not a friend of a very energetic government," he wrote. "It is always oppressive."[1] He was wary about the Constitution of 1787, fought for the Bill of Rights, advocated strict constructionism, opposed long-term national debt, and from time to time advocated the doctrine that states could nullify actions of the national government.

Jefferson believed that America's future should be to build a loosely organized rural society—a nation of small and medium-sized farmers minding their own affairs and conducting whatever mutual business they had through friendly local institutions and voluntary associations. He was particularly suspicious of a strong national government because its advocates were largely members of the merchant and banking classes who, he believed, would overthrow his Arcadian vision of America's future. Succinctly stated, Jefferson's ideal was "a wise and frugal government, which shall restrain men from injuring one another, which shall leave them otherwise free to regulate their own pursuits of industry and improvement, and shall not take from the mouth of labor the bread it has earned."[2]

But there is another American political tradition, which has proved even stronger than the Jeffersonian view. This tradition is usually associated with the ideas and politics of Alexander Hamilton. Looking at Jefferson's rural America, Hamilton saw not an ideal society but a backward, narrow-minded, and slothful culture that tolerated unseemly institutions such as slavery and squandered its resources on sterile activities such as land speculation. It had few common purposes, institutions, or activities. In fact, it was a nation in name only, and an underdeveloped nation at that. Hamilton's policies were based on the belief that there were certain common problems shared by all Americans, and that unless they mobilized their common resources to meet them our national experiment with independence would wither on the vine. In particular, he feared that the United States would succumb to internal divisiveness and fall prey to foreign powers unless it overcame its economic and social stagnation—unless it was transformed into an industrial and commercial power on a par with others.

To Hamilton it was "humiliating" for the United States to be so weak at home and abroad. America would not amount to much as a nation, in the eyes of its own citizens or other countries, unless its people became masters of their own fate in dealing with the major common problems of their times. He regarded government at the national level as the only possible instrument for accomplishing this. As Secretary of the Treasury, he used the new federal institutions to increase the stock of national capital and channel it into the business sector, to develop the rudiments of a nationwide infrastructure, and to establish a stable currency, a national banking system, customs houses, statistical agencies, scientific institutions, and other conveniences for the advancement of commerce.

To accomplish all of this, Hamilton created a large national debt and pushed the scope of the federal government well beyond the activities specifically mandated by the Constitution. He subscribed to the principle of "implied powers"—the idea that the Constitutional clause empowering the federal government to take any measures "necessary and proper" to carry out its mandated functions allows virtually any form of activism in the public interest. Without such leeway, he argued, any Constitution would be "a dead letter."

National government, according to Hamilton, is not a second-rate institution. It is a positive instrument for nation-building—for solving the common problems and seizing the common opportunities that any great nation encounters. Government is neither suspect nor wasteful. It is the natural and creative instrument for advancing the common interests that all members of a large and diverse community share—for promoting the common welfare. The great danger to America, he wrote, arises not from an overzealous government; rather, "It is that the common sovereign will not have power sufficient to unite the different members together, and direct the common forces to the interest and happiness of the whole."[3]

The Great Debate

As political antagonists, Hamilton and Jefferson were made for each other. Both were youthful prodigies: Jefferson drafted the Declaration of Independence at age thirty-three and Hamilton became Secretary of the Treasury at thirty-two. Both rose to fame from modest backgrounds: Hamilton as a soldier and New York lawyer; Jefferson as a lawyer, politician, and diplomat. Both were unusually well educated for their times, widely read, and steeped in the ideas of European philosophers. They were aloof, self-righteous men and exceptionally fine writers.

Rivalry between them was inevitable, particularly when both served as Cabinet members in the first administration under the Constitution of 1787. Given their different backgrounds, it was probably also inevitable that Jefferson should advocate the values of the more enlightened Virginia country gentlemen and Hamilton the values of the embryonic New York business community.

But the legacy they left far transcends personal differences. In the earliest days of our republic they established the terms of a great debate over activist government in the United States—a debate that has not changed greatly in its essentials to this day.

That debate has often been hard to follow, in part because the views of its protagonists have never been entirely opposed. "Our differences have been about measures only," Jefferson wrote. And he observed that "every difference of opinion is not a difference of principle."[4] Above all else Hamilton and Jefferson were patriots, dedicated to advancing the national welfare. More specifically, both believed that the fundamental objective of national government should be to advance the well-being of *all* the American people.

This may seem obvious today, but the founding fathers never tired of arguing that government in the United States was radically different from the European governments of their time. Governments in Europe were designed to serve the interests of privileged classes. The essence of the American Revolution was to establish a political system that would serve the welfare of all citizens—in Jefferson's words, to protect "life, liberty and the pursuit of happiness" for the American people as a whole.

Both Hamilton and Jefferson also held progressive views about how government should serve the general welfare. Obviously Hamilton's policies were progressive: government should be responsive to the most important problems and opportunities of the times. But there was a progressive side to Jefferson as well. Although he advocated limited government under the Constitution of 1787, he kept coming back to the idea that no form of government should be perpetuated indefinitely—that constitutions and laws should be remade by each generation to suit their conditions and ideals. What Hamilton sought by the continuing evolution of public policy, Jefferson would have sought by Constitutional revisions.

Where Hamilton and Jefferson differed most about the general welfare was in their emphasis on what problems and opportunities are of greatest concern for the United States and how the nation can best deal with them. The Hamiltonian tradition emphasizes problems and opportunities that are common to all Americans and argues that common problems require a common solution by the only institution capable of acting for the nation as a whole, the federal government. The Jeffersonian tradition contends that most of the important problems and opportunities of American life occur at the local level—within the compass of families, neighborhoods, or communities. Just because there are common national problems, we need not rush to common solutions: many common problems can be solved in different ways in different parts of the country without doing serious harm.

Hamilton and Jefferson also differed on the issue of individual freedom. Hamilton, who had never crossed the Atlantic, was trying to establish a European-style national government adapted to American conditions. Jefferson had lived abroad and seen the nation-states of Europe in action. That experience reinforced his fear that large concentrations of power of any sort are an inherent threat to individual freedom. Hamilton shared this fear, but he believed that in the United States political institutions responsive to the people provided an adequate safeguard. Individual liberty, in his view, was much more likely to be threatened if a weak and negligent government allowed public problems to fester than if a publicly responsive government acted vigorously in the public interest.

Ebb and Flow

Throughout the course of American history, the tide of federal activism has ebbed and flowed according to what measures were considered appropriate at different times. Whenever activism has been out of favor, Jeffersonian arguments for limited government have come to the surface, and they have always been advocated by some part of the American people. When national government has assumed a vigorous role, Hamiltonian arguments have been in the ascendant.

George Washington, who had to preside over the Hamilton–Jefferson debate, wrote, "I frankly and solemnly declare that I believe the views of both to be pure and well-meant, and that experience only will decide with respect to the salutariness of the measures which are the subject of this dispute."[5]

Experience has decided. Across the fluctuations in federal activism, the course of American history has displayed a strong Hamiltonian drift. In most periods of American history, government at the national level has played a large role in solving the common problems of our national life, and that role has become increasingly large with the passage of time.

Jefferson, himself, as President reached far beyond Constitutional mandates to purchase the Louisiana Territory, impose protective tariffs, and take other activist measures that he considered essential to the general welfare. In some cases these cost him dearly in terms of personal scruples and public support, but a measure of his greatness was his willingness to bend to the needs of his times.

In the first decades of the nineteenth century, government at all levels rushed to promote the development of commerce in a host of different ways. Public bonds were used to build railways and canals, tariffs and concessions were used to encourage favored industries, government and entrepreneurs became partners in jointly funded and jointly managed enterprises, and public lands in the West—the vast and unsettled "national domain"—were granted to promote education, business, and the orderly development of agriculture.

It was called the American Plan for developing the nation, and its chief advocates were John Quincy Adams, Daniel Webster, and Henry Clay. Americans today should realize that "free enterprise" in the United States on any large scale had its origins in the policies of Hamilton and in the American Plan. It was, and always has been, the creation of government as well as of entrepreneurs.

With the election of Andrew Jackson in 1828, national activism entered a period of decline. Jackson thought that the promotion of business had gone too far, and he fought to dismantle many of the activist policies that he believed served "the money power" at the expense of ordinary citizens.

It was during this period of revolt against national activism that Americans commonly began to refer to their country as a "democracy." Both Hamilton and Jefferson stressed the more "republican" aspects of our Constitution. They believed that government should act in the interests of the public and be accountable at elections, but they thought that too great a sensitivity to public views was destabilizing and unwise. The will of the majority should always prevail, Jefferson said, but "that will, to be rightful must be reasonable."[6] During the Jacksonian period, the idea that public officials should echo popular opinion gained ground. Majority opinion was presumed to be right—whether or not reasonable.

Synthesis

In the decades following Jackson's presidency, Webster, Clay, Polk, and other activists directed federal energies toward opening the West and supporting internal improvements. But the national leader who most powerfully asserted the activist tradition in the nineteenth century was Abraham Lincoln.

An American Plan man by background, Lincoln extended the federal role in education, agricultural improvements, and transportation. To fight the Civil War, he instituted the first income tax, established controls over currency and banking, and levied the first draft—all measures well beyond the confines of any strict construction of the Constitution. And he stretched the powers of the presidency to their limits to issue one of the major instruments of social reform of any period: the Emancipation Proclamation.

Lincoln justified these and other extensions of the federal role as essential measures to combat the greatest danger to the general welfare in his time: secession from the Union. But he repeatedly argued that the battle to preserve the Union was not just a fight for the territorial integrity of the United States. In his first annual message to Congress, the beleaguered president put his case in the following terms:

> This is essentially a people's contest. On the side of the Union it is a struggle for maintaining in the world that form and substance of government whose leading object is to elevate the condition of men—to lift artificial weights from all shoulders; to clear the paths of laudable pursuit for all; to afford all an unfettered start, and a fair chance in the race of life."[7]

In the words of the Gettysburg Address, the larger purpose of the war was to ensure that "government of the people, by the people and for the people shall not perish from this earth."

With this formula Lincoln united the divergent strands of American political life. Like Hamilton and other activists, he believed that the welfare of all parts of the United States and of all of its citizens is deeply interconnected. And he believed that only government at the national level, acting for the whole American public, can protect their common interests and help them achieve their common ideals. This is "government for the people." But like Jackson, Lincoln believed that government at the national level should reflect the views and aspirations of ordinary Americans—that it should be a democratic government of and by the people. The two need not be incompatible. In the American system activist government can be the people's instrument—the arm of democracy. Finally, like Jefferson, Lincoln believed that the basic conditions set down by the Constitution should be strictly observed whenever possible. His demands of the Southern states were only that they maintain the terms of the fundamental compact, not that they abolish slavery or do anything else beyond what the Constitution clearly required.

Lincoln's presidency was a turning point in the evolution of activist government, because he joined the ideas of Jackson and Jefferson to the activist tradition. An activist president could call on the ideas of Jacksonian democracy to support his policies on the grounds that the public was demanding government initiatives to solve national problems. And an activist president could also rest his case on the Constitution by arguing that unless national government dealt with public discontents, the entire Constitutional fabric would be dissolved. All succeeding activist presidents have used this synthesis of activism, democracy, and concern for the essentials of the Constitutional scheme to justify "government for the people" in their times.

Lincoln's successors in the nineteenth century wound down many aspects of the extensive social role he had created. Business interests used Jeffersonian arguments for limited government to justify freedom from public oversight. But continuing government subsidies to business helped fuel economic growth, and the Interstate Commerce Act of 1887 as well as the Sherman Antitrust Act of 1890 started the process of bringing monopolies under control. Post–Civil War politicians also extended the federal role by Constitutional amendments that abolished slavery and by civil rights laws (albeit soon disregarded) that attempted to give former slaves an equal footing in American society. And the same politicians tried to outbid each other in establishing an increasingly extensive system of veterans' pensions. As late as 1912, it was estimated that over two-thirds of the white males in the North sixty-five years of age and older were receiving pensions from the federal government.[8]

Social Activism

All these developments laid the groundwork for the explosive growth of the federal role in the twentieth century: "The New Nationalism" of Theodore Roosevelt, "The New Freedom" of Woodrow Wilson, "The New Deal" of Franklin Roosevelt, and "The Great Society" of Lyndon Johnson.

The growth of federal activism during its first century was primarily devoted to advancing the national welfare by promoting economic growth through assisting and regulating the business sector. During the second century of activism, this function remained, but to it were added federal programs to deal with many more of the tasks that all societies throughout history have had to perform in some way: caring for the aged and the poor, educating the young, advancing the state of knowledge, and protecting the physical environment.

Many of the pioneers of social activism regarded federal responsibility for these functions as simply the other side of the coin from the federal role in promoting industry. As Franklin Roosevelt put it, "Government in the past has helped lay the foundation of business and industry. We must face the fact that in this century we have a rich man's security and a poor man's security and the government owes equal obligation to both."[9]

Roosevelt and his colleagues were strongly impressed by the fact that Jefferson's agrarian civilization was fast vanishing from the United States. The frontier was closed; most Americans worked in factories and lived in cities, rather than on the farm. The New Dealers believed that in the complex and highly mobile civilization that had developed in the late nineteenth and early twentieth centuries, families, voluntary associations, and local governments were less able to perform essential social functions than in the time of Hamilton and Jefferson. The United States had become, in the words of William Allen White, "a wilderness of careless strangers." Even with their best efforts, individuals, families, and communities could no longer cope on their own with some of the most essential problems of life.

The New Dealers also were impressed by the ability of government to mobilize national resources demonstrated during World War I. They believed that the havoc wrought by the Great Depression was a consequence of the underlying interdependence and insecurity of modern life, and that national government could solve many of these problems.

Roosevelt's goal was "to employ the active interest of the Nation as a whole through government in order to ensure a greater security for those who comprise it."[10] Like Hamilton, he believed that free institutions were unlikely to survive unless government proved capable of meeting the most urgent needs of the times. The most urgent need of Roosevelt's era, as he and his colleagues saw it, was to construct new systems of social supports capable of meeting the problems of industrial society. Any government that would turn its back on the suffering caused by those problems could not hope to maintain the support of its own people or the respect of the world.

Like Lincoln, Roosevelt based his program on a philosophy that joined democratic principles to the spirit of activism and the imperatives of leadership. As he explained it in his first Inaugural Address:

> We do not distrust the future of essential democracy. The people of the United States have not failed. In their need they have registered a mandate that they want direct, vigorous action. They have asked for discipline and direction under leadership. They have made me the present instrument of their wishes. In the spirit of the gift, I take it.[11]

The results of this philosophy were a quantum leap forward for the federal social role. The focal point for much of the New Deal's social activism was the Committee on Economic Security. This Cabinet-level group, chaired by Secretary of Labor Frances Perkins, produced one of the most remarkable documents of American political history. Its lucid, fifty-page report is the basic charter of the American welfare state, and it should be required reading for every educated American.[12]

The Report of the Committee on Economic Security of 1935 developed the basic outlines of our Social Security, Unemployment Insurance, Aid to Families with Dependent Children, federal assistance to the disabled and handicapped, and child health programs, and it foreshadowed Medicare, Medicaid, and the long-running debate about full employment policy. Other New Deal initiatives resulted in the Fair Labor Standards Act, the National Labor Relations Act (the Wagner Act), the Securities and Exchange Act, the Agricultural Adjustment Act, and a host of programs to improve housing, land management, and the quality of rural life.

Roosevelt's successors in the activist tradition, Truman, Kennedy, Johnson, and Nixon, all extended the social protections afforded by the national government in new directions: to health care for the aged and indigent, to equal opportunity for minorities, to more adequate nutrition and federal income support for the poor, to housing programs, environmental programs, aid to education, and many other purposes. Once the precedent for social activism was set, the whole array of unmet human needs became part of the federal agenda. And in the era of postwar prosperity, increasing national affluence made it possible to raise the necessary revenues more or less painlessly. In addition, advances in the social sciences and in the organization of government led many to believe that we could tackle problems that had previously seemed unthinkably difficult, such as "curing poverty."

There was a euphoria to much of the activism in the middle decades of the twentieth century. But there was also a hard political reality. New issues came on the agenda because organized groups demanded them. Organized labor and other reform lobbies played an important role. But the growth and directions of activism would have been inconceivable without the civil rights movement and its demands for legal and social justice both for blacks and other oppressed minorities and for the poor in general. In the end, black people in this country were not given their freedom; they demanded and won it.

This activist tradition began to falter and then stall sometime in the 1970s. Both Presidents Carter and Reagan slowed the growth of the social role, and Jeffersonian arguments became more popular. The current reassessment and stalemate in public policy have ensued. In the ebb and flow of activist government throughout our nation's history, the current period has been a troubled stillness of the waters.

Pragmatism

The present stalemate is deeply troubling in large part because it does not reflect the more constructive aspects of our national life. Activism at the national level has been the dominant American tradition. It has been dominant because leaders with various philosophical outlooks, social prejudices, and party affiliations have viewed national government as the most effective and practical solution to some of the great issues of their times. They have been pragmatists.

Hamilton and the American Plan men saw the federal government as the best answer to the problem of stimulating industrial growth; Lincoln saw it as the best answer to the problem of sectionalism; the two Roosevelts saw it as the best answer to the problems of individual security in an industrial age; and Johnson saw it as the best answer to the problems of poverty and racism. The tradition that has united these and other activists has been a willingness to interpret the vague mandate of the Constitution in whatever ways they considered necessary and feasible to address issues affecting the welfare of the nation as a whole.

This is a problem-solving tradition: a tradition of pragmatism, not ideology or interest or deference to the past. The men who contributed most greatly to the growth of the federal role—Hamilton, Lincoln, the two Roosevelts, Johnson, and the rest—were far from being ideologues. They all subscribed to strong, and in some cases fairly complex, theories about politics and society; but the practical lesson they drew from those theories was that no rigid formula could or should dictate the social role of government. Rather, they believed the nature of activism must be adapted to changing circumstances and changing public values. They expected that the social role would evolve over time, and they believed that change is healthy for a democratic nation. As a result, the policies of the New Deal would have been as astonishing to Hamilton as the policies of the Great Society would have been to FDR, and that is doubtless how they would have wanted the course of American history to advance.

Nor has the growth of the social role been driven by subservience to one or a few ''interests''—the business interest, the propertied interest, or any other. Each of these has been the beneficiary of initiatives by activist government at various times, and often several have been beneficiaries at the same time.

Finally, the social role has not grown because of Constitutional mandates that government supply certain services, because some dominant political party carried the activist flag, or because of some structural bias toward activism in our institutions. The American Constitution, in fact, mandates very few government activities. Activist leaders have worn all party labels, and our institutions have allowed periods of retrenchment, as well as growth, in the federal social role.

Engines of Growth

The federal social role has grown because the problems of the nation as a whole have increased with the passage of time. In 1787 the nation did not have the problems of industrialism that the two Roosevelts faced because it did not yet have an industrial system. In 1860 the nation did not have the problems of equal opportunity for blacks because most black people were legally property, not citizens.

National opportunities have also increased. Economic growth over the last two centuries has made it possible for Americans both to enjoy a higher standard of living in their private lives and to spend more for public purposes.

The social role has grown, too, because it has developed its own internal dynamic. Once the federal government was seen as an instrument for national problem solving, both the general public and leaders were more inclined to turn to it. And as government developed more institutional capacities, it was more willing and better able to respond to these demands. Hamilton counted it a great success to have organized a system for gathering even the roughest information about the volume of exports and imports at various American harbors. The founders of the Social Security system counted it a great success to register all the people eligible for the program and establish field offices to administer it. In an era of computers and telecommunications, these administrative accomplishments seem small compared with what the federal government can do.

The growth of the social role also has been driven by an increasing sense of nationhood—of how much we all have in common and of the need to rely on common resources to meet problems and achieve goals that we cannot deal with in any other way. To a degree, the growth of nationhood has been a self-fulfilling prophecy: the federal government's increasing activism on behalf of the nation as a whole has encouraged Americans to think of themselves as one people. But, in part, it has almost surely arisen from a perception of the greater interdependence of society that has developed as Americans have moved off the family farm and into the complex world of urban life, from the improvements in communications that have allowed us to know each other better, and from the common adversities of the Great Depression and the two world wars.

Finally, in those periods when elected officials have turned away from activism, the social role has often continued to grow as a result of decisions by the Supreme Court. John Marshall was Chief Justice when Thomas Jefferson was president. Marshall's decisions asserted that the authority of the federal government to overrule state actions and resolve a wide range of domestic issues was far more extensive than Jefferson believed appropriate. And the Chief Justice made his decisions stick by establishing the right of the Court to "say what the law is."[13] The Supreme Court was also instrumental in sparking the civil rights revolution. Chief Justice Warren's decision in *Brown* v. *Board of Education,* the school desegregation case, occurred during the relatively quiescent Eisenhower years and helped to commit both Eisenhower and subsequent presidents to an activist role in the area of equal rights for minorities.[14]

There has been no consistent pattern to the relationship between the policies of the Court and those of elected leaders; nor has the Court been a consistent supporter of activism. In the late nineteenth and early twentieth centuries judicial decisions presented roadblocks to activist presidents and support for their opponents. In the 1960s and 1970s the Court was even more aggressive than a succession of activist presidents in pursuing the goals of equal opportunity and in extending federal policy to areas such as the right of women to have abortions and the use of capital punishment.

The General Welfare

Why have we developed an extensive federal social role? In principle, the answer is that activist government reflects some of our most basic values: nationhood, democracy, and a concern for the welfare of all our citizens. In practice, Americans over the past two hundred years have found that government at the national level is the most practical and effective means of solving an increasing number of common problems and of achieving common opportunities.

There is, of course, a sense in which this tradition of pragmatic problem solving is no tradition at all. An injunction to do whatever is necessary for the public interest does not provide any precise standards for government action. And if our public life is guided by principles as vague as nationhood, democracy, and the general welfare, it can be accused of being unprincipled as well. In this sense, the American tradition of government has been to have no tradition: to judge each issue on its merits as time goes on. And the American principle of government has been to have no specific fixed principles: to adapt general ideas to the nation's evolving needs. Or, to take a more positive view, our public life is a collection of many traditions and many principles, each surrounding particular problems and initiatives.

But there is more to it than that. Each new federal initiative has been strongly opposed by people who did not want to see government take an active role. The tradition which has prevailed has been the nationalist belief that many problems and opportunities are shared by most Americans and that we should be willing to use federal authority to deal with them. By contrast to the Jeffersonian view, pragmatic activism is not an empty or unprincipled tradition. It is a course for government that Americans have chosen because they believe it makes necessary and concrete contributions to their well-being.

A single instance epitomizes the significance of this tradition. Article I, Section 8 of the Constitution stipulates that Congress may levy taxes for, among other purposes, promoting "the general welfare." In 1791 Jefferson complained that relying on this provision to justify federal action would "reduce the whole instrument to a single phrase, that of instituting a Congress with power to do whatever would be for the good of the United States."[15] In 1937 the Supreme Court upheld the constitutionality of the most comprehensive piece of social legislation ever put forward in the United States, the Social Security Act, on the basis of the "general welfare" clause.[16]

Obviously this did not reduce the Constitution to "a single phrase." American government operates within checks and balances and guarantees of rights—many of them put in place at Jefferson's insistence—and it is answerable to the American electorate. But unless Americans had adopted a broad and pragmatic view of federal power—the view that, within these constraints, Congress should do "whatever would be for the good of the United States"—not only would we never have implemented the Social Security Act, but we also would never have implemented most of the programs that today constitute the federal social role.

3

The American Style
of Activism

F rom May 1831, to February 1832, a twenty-six-year-old French
   magistrate made an extensive tour of the United States. His
ostensible purpose was to prepare a report on the management of
prisons; his reason for accepting the mission was to escape the
troubled political situation in France at the time. When Alexis de
Tocqueville returned home, he wrote a book that many still regard
as the definitive analysis of American politics and culture.
Democracy in America describes what Tocqueville considered to
be the most salient features of our system of government.[1] It does
not describe the activist tradition. Rather, it describes the tradition of limited government advocated by Thomas Jefferson.

Tensions

It is easy to explain Tocqueville's conclusions by saying that
he simply portrayed America as he found it in one of the anti-
nationalist periods of our history. But his ideas also have a larger
significance. Although Jefferson's views have rarely been the
dominant force in American public life, they have at least been
the distinctive American way of looking at politics. Other nations

have activist national governments for many of the same reasons that we do, but there is no other major nation in which the Jeffersonian emphasis on limited government and local institutions, and the Jacksonian emphasis on public opinion, are so strong.

The story of the federal social role is more than the story of Hamiltonian policies trampling Jeffersonian scruples into the dust. Jefferson's perspective on politics and society continues to be a fundamental part of our civic culture. It has always been voiced loudly by some part of the American people, and at certain periods in our history it has been in the ascendant. It is a view that politicians of all persuasions have to accommodate in some way.

This is more than a mere curiosity. While the federal social role has continued to grow in response to new problems and opportunities, the *form* of activist government in the United States has been shaped as much by the tradition of Jefferson as by Hamilton's ideas. Both reflect enduring American values, and together they reflect two enduring tensions in American life:

- the tension between attachment to local institutions and values and attachment to the national community and its values; and
- the tension between individualism and the responsibilities of national citizenship.

Americans have never wanted to make a clear-cut choice between these differing attachments. Our style of politics has been to try to have it both ways.

Why does this matter? It matters because these two tensions and the means by which we resolve them are central to our political culture—to the ideas, habits, and values that structure our public life. They determine how activist government functions in the United States: the types of activities that it undertakes and how it undertakes them. And, as a result, they determine what role it plays in our national life. It is impossible to understand fully what the federal social role is, why we need activist government, and what contribution it makes unless we understand how it functions and why. And it is also impossible to understand, let alone answer, many of the most important questions about the federal social role—what are its dimensions, problems, and likely future directions—without understanding the major elements of the political culture within which it operates and how they affect the directions of public policy.

The First Tension

The tension between local attachments and support for national government is the one more often raised in political debate. There can be no doubt that when politicians advocate the Jeffersonian side of this issue, their arguments have a strong appeal for most Americans. National government, the national interest, the national community are in many ways cold and abstract ideas. For most people, family, church, neighborhood, voluntary groups, their workplace, and local governments are friendlier and more concrete institutions: they are something familiar that people can see and understand every day. They appeal more to sentiment, if not to reason.

To some extent the distinction between friendly local institutions and the more distant and abstract national outlook is simply one of perspective. Like any other large nation, the United States contains a great diversity of institutions and lifestyles. It encompasses scores of ethnic backgrounds, thousands of local governments, hundreds of thousands of businesses, millions of families, and hundreds of millions of individuals, each with separate interests, tastes, and priorities.

But seen from another perspective, all these people and institutions have a great deal in common: we all speak a common language and share a common culture. We all participate in a single national economy, and we have a common interest in how well it performs. We also all have a stake in the welfare of our fellow citizens at every point in the life cycle—in the nation's children who will support us in our old age, in the conditions under which we and others must earn our wages, and in the security of the elderly, who are our parents today and who someday will be us. Common national interests and diversity are just two sides of the same coin. This is true of any large nation, and it is true here.

The major difference between the United States and other nations is that we are both very large and very free. Our size increases our diversity and our freedom allows us to express it. As a result, diversity is more valued here than it is, for example, in the Soviet Union or China, which contain an even greater assortment of cultures, but where repressive governments subdue difference in the name of a rigid ideology of the common interest.

Precisely because the United States contains great social diversity along with strong common interests, the federal social role has always honored both aspects of our national life. Whenever the federal government has extended its authority, it has done so in a way that relied on other institutions to help in meeting national needs. For example, government and the business community have long been partners in promoting the national economy. And as we shall see, when government at the national level came to provide a variety of social supports, it did so in ways that by no means monopolized the field. For example, although the federal government provides various forms of income support to the elderly, we also depend on private pension plans, families, other levels of government, private charities, and individual savings to help support people in their old age. Although the federal government provides aid to education, most of the national investment in schools is made at the state and local level, or by individuals assuming the cost of educating their children and themselves.

In short, in the United States national government is simply one institution among many that perform a variety of essential social functions. Since those functions are vital to the maintenance and well-being of any society, they would doubtless be performed in some way if the federal government restricted its role. The alternative to big government providing old-age pensions, for example, is not turning old people out to starve. It is a sole reliance on corporate benefits, family assistance, local government, and the rest of the existing machinery for supporting the elderly. The alternative to big government regulating business is not unregulated business, but weak and uncoordinated efforts by state and local government to control large concentrations of economic power, such as the nation experienced at the turn of the century.

Capacities of National Government

Because we treat the federal government as only one institution among many for providing social supports, Americans have always had more of a continuing concern than people in most other countries with questions about why we need national government, and when. Those who oppose activist government would argue that, in most cases, there is no very good reason for having it. But all institutions have certain distinctive capacities, and our national experience has shown that the capacities of government at the national level are required to solve a great many of the problems of American life.

The distinctive capacities of the federal government are so obvious that they often escape notice. Its authority is nationwide in scope; its decisions are the supreme law of the land; it is accountable to all the people, not just to one group or section; its actions and deliberations are carried out in public, not in the privacy of a home or the secrecy of a board room; and its avowed purpose is to promote the general welfare, rather than to make a profit or to advance the social ideals of any one group or sect.

Why do we have a compelling need for an institution such as this? The standard academic answer in recent years has been that one of the supposedly friendly local institutions—business—is neither friendly nor local in the United States. American corporations span state, and even national, boundaries. Many are enormous aggregations of social and economic power that have a critical influence over all our lives. They can hire and fire at will. They offer good products and bad. They can provide excellent conditions of work, or abuse their employees. Some are ruinous to the environment or engage in unscrupulous trade practices, and some are model corporate citizens.

For over a century, activists have been arguing that we need a strong national government because American business often has strong incentives to treat us badly. Its primary motive is profit, and there is often more profit to be made by exploiting labor, providing shoddy goods, and disregarding the environment than by engaging in socially responsible behavior. A more generous view of the situation holds that, even with the best will in the world, it is sometimes very hard for American corporations to "do the right thing." Because there are so many of them, one rotten apple can spoil a barrel by adopting abusive cost-cutting measures that give it a competitive edge. Also, because there are so many companies, standards of conduct are inevitably hard to coordinate and uneven in application.

In addition, the mobility of labor from one job to another makes it difficult for any one employer to express a lasting concern for the well-being of particular employees. Finally, because American corporations are so dependent on each other for products, technology, and capital, periodic economic downturns resonate through the entire system and leave particular companies with no choice but to lay off employees and reduce standards or else perish and destroy their role as providers of jobs and services entirely.

Many theories of the federal social role focus on these and other problems of modern business to explain why activist government at the national level is required. Because the federal government is nationwide in scope and can marshal the resources of all the people, it is the only institution that can possibly take on the task of monitoring, regulating, and, for that matter, promoting these large aggregations of power. Individuals, families, voluntary institutions, and local governments are overshadowed by corporate giants. National government has the authority and scope to require that companies "do the right thing." And where competition, labor mobility, and other factors make it inherently difficult for business to attend to the welfare of its employees, national government has the resources to step into the breach: for example, by providing old-age pensions to everyone, organizing unemployment insurance, and offering protections for the poor.

The Madisonian Argument

These conventional arguments for activist government are doubtless sound, as far as they go. In large part the social role has grown out of a love-hate relationship with business and the social conditions modern corporations have helped to create. But there is an older and more far-reaching explanation for why we need an institution with the capacities of the federal government.

While Hamilton and Jefferson were exchanging broadsides, James Madison was belaboring another idea. Madison believed that *all* social institutions tend to be abusive in their various ways. He was particularly concerned with local government. Because of their small scale, local institutions might seem to be "closer to the people," but Madison argued that precisely because of their scale they are easily dominated by a small group of people who often become petty tyrants. National government might seem more remote and threatening, but because of its scope and charter, it contains so many conflicting interests that no one of them can dominate: all have to compromise around some consensus view of the common good.

This idea led Madison to conclude that we must have both national and local political institutions conjoined in a common constitution. "The federal constitution," he wrote, "forms a happy combination in this respect; the great and aggregate interests being referred to the national, the local and particular to the State legislatures."[2]

In more generalized form, Madison's argument can be applied to all social institutions. Families, voluntary organizations, corporations, and local governments are all, in practice, run by one or a few people for parochial reasons. They can, and often do, abuse or neglect their members. National power can be abusive, too, but it has the advantage that problems, from whatever source, can be heard and balanced against conflicting points of view.

The problems posed by the business sector are, then, only a special case for why we have activist government, according to this Madisonian view. The problems of racism, single-parent families, and the limits of local institutions present as strong an argument for federal activism as the problems of unemployment and pollution.

This is not an argument for concentrating all power at the federal level. It is, rather, an argument for the solution Americans have adopted: treating the federal government as one parallel institution among many for solving public problems. No single institution can do all the work of a large and complex society. Moreover, as long as we have parallel institutions, there is less chance that federal power will be abused. Because those institutions have their own self-interests, they will resist undue extensions of federal power, and they will give us some form of "fall back" protection if the federal government fails, or if we decide to withdraw its influence from a particular area of American life.

Moreover, as Madison suggested, there is a natural division of labor in the American political system. A large and diverse nation requires a degree of uniformity in its solutions to public problems, but it also often requires those solutions to be tailored to the special circumstances of differing localities, groups, or businesses. Sound public policy is sensitive to both common national concerns and the differing form those concerns take at the grassroots level.

The Second Tension

The second major tension in American politics—between individualism and a sense of nationhood—is more of a continuing theme for scholars and critics than for politicians, although politicians have made ample use of it from time to time. Virtually every commentator on American culture has described us as an exceptionally individualistic people. Such foreign writers as Tocqueville, Dickens, and Bryce made the observation. Cooper, Melville, Twain, and other American intellectuals have concurred. We like our individual freedom. We don't like being pushed around by other people. We like to think that we can take care of ourselves. The image of the lone cowboy riding off into the sunset is engraved on all of us.

As a result, we have an instinctive aversion to government. The Bill of Rights, the checks and balances in our Constitution, the multiple levels of our federal system, are all designed to limit government's authority over our lives. Membership in a family is inevitable; membership in private associations, businesses, and other institutions is voluntary; but government is an institution that compels us to live up to the obligations of citizenship—to pay our taxes and obey the law—whether we want to or not.

The individualist impulse causes us to look at government measures from the perspective of "What's in it for me?"—with the "me" being a compound of all the multiple interests, affiliations, and loyalties that make up each human being. It is the impulse that brings about tax revolts and often disregards the interests of people who are "not like me."

The other side of the coin, of course, is that we all take pride in being Americans, and the national government both symbolizes and allows us to express our sense of nationhood. Every institution calls forth certain distinctive feelings from its members. We feel family sentiments and ties of loyalty to work and community, but the feeling of nationhood is also part of our experience. We feel it most strongly in times of national adversity or triumph. No one who experienced the Great Depression, World War II, the shock of President Kennedy's death, or the landings on the moon can forget the feeling of national community those times called forth. And we feel it when we contemplate the achievements of the past. They arc *our* history; they belong to each and every one of us.

The feeling of nationhood is different from the sentiments we have toward family, friends, and neighbors. It is the feeling that, despite our differences, we are "all in the same boat" as a people. And the boat is not adrift. The feeling of nationhood is a feeling of power. As citizens of a democratic republic, we can take our common destiny into our own hands. National government provides us with an opportunity to determine our future as a people. In fact, it is the only opportunity we have. On election day, when we write to our congressmen, or when we organize to influence opinion, we are no longer at the mercy of large and impersonal social forces. If we act and feel as one people, national government allows us to topple presidents, corporate giants, local potentates, and others among the great and powerful.

Nationalism also brings with it a different morality. It expands our moral sense to the national community. The morality of democratic nationhood is a willingness to put ourselves in each others' shoes, to have concern for the well-being of people who are "not like us."

This outlook, to the extent that we adopt it, has many different aspects. In part, it is a simple feeling of fraternity. People "not like us" are Americans, too, and we believe that all Americans are entitled to a decent share of the good things of life. Our standard of living as a people is a source of pride. In part, too, we put ourselves in each others shoes because we perceive common interests in the social and economic well-being of all our fellow citizens. If agriculture or the oil industry is depressed, the whole nation suffers. If we discriminate against the poor, minorities, or women, if they become second-class citizens, there is some danger that we could become second-class citizens at some point too.

Finally, being joined by a common government, we have the expectation that people "not like us" will reciprocate any help we may provide by giving us a hand when we need it. When farm income is depressed, city dwellers do not tell the farmers to shift for themselves, in part because the farmers pay taxes to help rebuild our urban infrastructure. What's in it for the city dweller to help the farmer? The expectation that the farmer will help clean up the subways. And this reciprocity, in fact, takes place, however adequate or inadequate urban or agricultural policy may be at any particular point in time.

George Washington put the national idea best in his farewell address to the nation. "The name of AMERICAN," he wrote, "which belongs to you, in your national capacity, must always exalt the just pride of Patriotism, more than any appelation derived from local discriminations."[3] This is not an inherently anti-individualistic idea. It calls upon the individual to realize the larger circumstances of his life, the greater opportunities of citizenship in a democratic republic, where he has a voice in determining not just his own fate but the fate of millions.

And it is not a cold and abstract idea. When the federal government delivers a Social Security check, helps a farmer out of trouble, or lends a young person money for college, the benefits of nationhood come close to home.

A Practical Response

But of course, most of us don't think about government this way most of the time. By and large, participating in our national life is like going to a football game. One day a week Americans arrive in their separate cars from their separate homes, hold tailgate parties with a few friends and associates, then plunge into the cheering mass for a few hours, only to return home in their separate cars to their separate lives.

Politicians have tried every rhetorical device to encourage a more continuous sense of national feeling. One of the more common ploys has been to cast day-to-day public problems in terms of what William James called "the moral equivalent of war."[4] Woodrow Wilson tried it, and Lyndon Johnson tried it most memorably by labeling his domestic program "The War on Poverty." But this rhetorical turn has never been persuasive. Americans are sophisticated enough to know the difference between national emergencies and long-term problems.

The practical response Americans have found to the continuing tension between individualism and nationalism is a remarkably inclusive political style. Every institution must accommodate the interests and desires of its members. Families must accommodate the demands of both parents and children; corporations must accommodate stockholders, workers, and management; local governments must accommodate all sectors of the community. The federal government is the most comprehensive institution we have—it covers the broadest range and the greatest variety of interests and activities. Because of its scope, and because it is accountable to all the people, it has a bias in favor of projects from which almost everyone benefits. These are the types of activities that are the easiest to support politically: a Congress accountable to highly diverse local constituencies can most easily agree on projects that benefit them all. And in a larger sense, projects that benefit almost everyone are the most direct way of demonstrating that we are "all in the same boat."

Provision of nationwide, uniform social services, such as Social Security benefits, is the type of activity that receives the strongest and most consistent support at the federal level. Regulating industries that find it in their self-interest, as well as the national interest, to be regulated also fits into this pattern. Responding to widespread public outrage of the sort that arose over the treatment of blacks is another straightforward case, at least as long as the outrage lasts.

At a more complex level, an inclusive federal policy is often the result of political horse-trading. One interest group will support the demands of another until all are satisfied.

The bias toward inclusiveness is so strong in the United States that it often defies common sense. The federal agenda is cluttered with small, specialized programs that directly benefit only very limited sectors of the American public. For example, Congress has erected a whole phalanx of policies primarily intended to protect the family farm; it has created a special pension program for railroad workers; and it supports the market for middle-income housing in a variety of ways. Moreover, the benefits of major grant programs are often dispersed far more widely than they need to be. Virtually every school district receives funds from the federal program originally intended to help improve the education of disadvantaged children, and until 1987 virtually every municipality received federal revenue sharing funds originally intended to make up for the limited tax resources of central cities. Does every school district have so many disadvantaged children that it needs federal help to assist them, and was every municipality tax-poor? It seems unlikely.

Yet, symbolically, this pluralistic clutter is not as foolish as it might seem. By these various forms of inclusiveness the federal government asserts, to a fault, that it is the government of all the people—that everyone should benefit from its actions and no one's interest should be neglected. And it receives a continuing stream of information and expertise from the many interests that fall under its protection. Whatever may be said in criticism of the army of lobbyists who defend special interest legislation, they ensure that federal officials obtain a level of feedback about the effects of their actions that officials in more closed political systems might well envy.

4

Dimensions
of the Social Role

What have two hundred years of activist government and the American style created? What form of public policy has emerged from the pragmatic traditions of our national life?

When most people think of the social role, the first image that comes to mind is "welfare." Programs for poor people are often regarded as synonymous with social programs, generally. In fact, only about 10–12 percent of total federal spending and 17–22 percent of spending for social purposes is devoted to programs primarily targeted at the poor.[1]

Another image that comes to mind is spiraling government expenditures. In fact, over the last decade, total federal spending has consistently hovered around 24 percent of the gross national product (GNP) and between 55 and 60 percent of the federal budget has been devoted to social programs. In the years immediately following World War II, social spending as a percentage of GNP fell from about 8 percent in 1947 and 9.5 percent in 1950 to just over 6 percent in 1951, but it has grown slowly and steadily since that time, reaching 13 percent in 1975.[2] Social spending has remained at around that percentage of GNP ever since, declining slightly in recent years.

But government spending, by itself, is not an adequate measure of the social role, although it is the measure most often used. In fact, over $300 billion each year in federal revenue forgone due to tax exemptions, exclusions, and deferrals, over $200 billion in loans and loan guarantees—as well as tens of thousands of regulations, judicial decisions, and activities of the Federal Reserve System, the Treasury Department, and other agencies to control economic downturns—probably have as much of an effect on "the general welfare" as all federal spending combined.

Finally, when most people think of the social role, they think of a growing army of federal bureaucrats supported at public expense to administer government programs. In fact, the federal civilian work force has been remarkably stable in size—about 2.8 million employees—for almost twenty years, and as a percentage of the American population it has fallen from about 1.4 percent in 1955 to 1.2 percent in recent decades. About one-third of federal employment is accounted for by two agencies: the Postal Service (over 730,000 employees) and the Veteran's Administration (over 220,000 employees). By contrast, state and local government employment has increased from 8.3 million workers twenty years ago to 14.2 million in 1986.

These and other popular images of the social role indicate that there is widespread misunderstanding of its basic dimensions, both among the general public and among many policymakers and "experts." In the current reassessment of social policy, a great many people have seriously mistaken ideas of exactly what it is they are arguing about.

This is not surprising. Activist government at the national level in the United States has grown gradually over the last two hundred years. The process of growth has been one of layering over old policies with new. New initiatives have not displaced previous federal undertakings; they have added to the scope of the social role. In a modified form, the policies of Hamilton are still with us. To them were added the American Plan ideas, the initiatives of Lincoln, the two Roosevelts, Truman, Johnson, and Nixon. Old policies have sometimes evolved into new forms and adjusted to changing circumstances. There has been some attrition along the way, but not much.

As a result, the present structure of social policy in the United States resembles the design of some improvising architect. It is a jerry-rigged structure that somehow holds together, despite its ungainly size and inelegant proportions. It is so complex that the President's annual budget, which contains a few paragraphs at most about each federal program, ran to 1,127 double-columned pages in 1986 (slightly longer than the year before). The Federal Civil Code, which contains the laws on which those programs and other activities of the national government are based, has now reached more than 150 enormous tomes. The Social Security Act, as amended, is by itself a book of over a thousand pages, and the Federal Register, which lists all new and proposed government initiatives, has averaged well over one hundred pages daily in recent years.

It is no wonder that nobody entirely understands so enormous a system and that most people misunderstand large parts of it. But if the nation is to engage in a constructive debate about the future directions of federal social policy, it is essential that citizens and policymakers understand at least its basic dimensions.

This is an achievable goal. All the building blocks of the social policy structure are not the same size; and for most purposes, the several dozen largest ones matter most.

The ultimate purpose of the social role is to promote the well-being of the American people. Practically speaking, there are three basic tools which the federal government uses to accomplish this goal:

- *Spending*—through programs that provide cash or in-kind benefits to individuals or institutions and through programs that purchase goods and services, such as highways or medical research, which benefit the public at large.
- *Creating incentives*—for individuals and institutions to act in ways that will further the general welfare, through programs of tax preferences, loans, and economic management.
- *Requiring* individuals and institutions to act in ways that will serve the national interest—through laws, regulations, and court decisions.

The federal government uses each of these policy tools in a variety of ways, and it often uses them in combinations to achieve the same purposes. For the most part they are interchangeable tools—any one of them could be used to achieve most public goals.

Spending

The easiest way to understand the scope of federal activism is by looking at how the national government spends its annual budget. Spending is easier to understand than other aspects of social policy because it can be measured and compared in terms that are familiar to everyone.

According to the Office of Management and Budget, the federal government spent about $989 billion in 1986. Because of the way in which the government keeps its books, however, expenditures are usually underestimated, so the round number of $1 trillion is probably closer to the mark. This is a great deal of money—more than the total gross national product in any year before 1970—but it was only about 24 percent of the gross national product in 1986, roughly the same percentage as five years earlier, and up from 19 percent in 1960.

The accompanying chart shows some of the major purposes for which the federal government divided up this $1 trillion pie. The relative size of different pieces gives a rough indication of federal spending priorities.

The domestic portion of the federal budget—the part devoted to programs intended to secure the general welfare here at home—was about $570 billion, or 57 percent of the total budget. The rest went for defense, foreign affairs, and interest on the national debt. Of that domestic budget, almost $250 billion was devoted to the two major programs providing assistance to elderly people: Social Security Retirement and Medicare. This is roughly one-quarter of the total federal budget—a slightly smaller portion than defense— or 44 percent of domestic spending. In terms of sheer magnitude, these two programs, from which almost all elderly Americans benefit, and to which almost all workers contribute, clearly dom-

TOTAL FEDERAL OUTLAYS
by Program and Purpose
Fiscal Year 1986
(in billions $)
Total = $989.8ᵃ

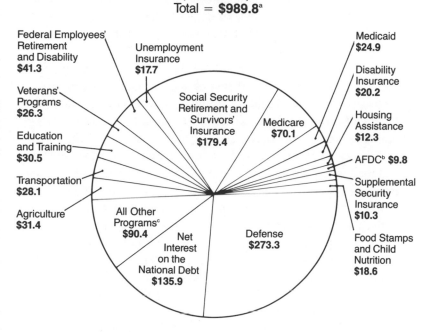

Federal Employees' Retirement and Disability $41.3

Unemployment Insurance $17.7

Veterans' Programs $26.3

Education and Training $30.5

Transportation $28.1

Agriculture $31.4

Social Security Retirement and Survivors' Insurance $179.4

Medicare $70.1

All Other Programsᶜ $90.4

Net Interest on the National Debt $135.9

Defense $273.3

Medicaid $24.9

Disability Insurance $20.2

Housing Assistance $12.3

AFDCᵇ $9.8

Supplemental Security Insurance $10.3

Food Stamps and Child Nutrition $18.6

ᵃAmounts in the diagram do not add to $989.8 because of: 1) rounding error, 2) $33 billion in undistributed offsetting receipts.
ᵇAid to Families with Dependent Children.
ᶜOther Programs include:

General Government	$ 6.1
Administration of Justice	$ 6.6
Commerce Credits	$ 4.4
Energy	$ 4.7
Community & Regional Development	$ 7.2
General Purpose Fiscal Assistance	$ 6.4
General Science, Space and Technology	$ 8.9
Natural Resources and Environment	$13.6
International Affairs	$14.1
Other Income Security	$ 9.1
Other Health	$ 9.3

Source: Executive Office of the President. Office of Management and Budget: *Special Analyses of the Budget of the United States Government, Fiscal Year 1988* (Washington, D.C.: U.S. Government Printing Office, 1987), pp. A-32–A-43.

inate the domestic budget. In fact, if we add to them retirement programs for federal civil and military employees, the Supplemental Security Income program for impoverished elderly people, and the portion of Medicaid and various other programs that the elderly receive, over half of domestic spending is devoted to caring for older citizens, and about one-third of the total federal budget serves this purpose.

Another way to look at the budget is to say that programs for the elderly, defense, and interest on the national debt add up to three-quarters of total federal spending. Everything else that the federal government does—all of those thousands of federal programs—come out of the remaining quarter—about $250 billion.

This way of looking at the budget is important, because defense and foreign affairs are clearly activities from which everyone benefits in a very direct way, and interest on the national debt is an obligation we all share. Retirement programs also benefit us all, both in the sense that we will all become elderly at some point and collect benefits from them, and in the sense that most of us have elderly relations or friends for whom we would feel obliged to provide support in some other way—by helping them out financially or providing more personal care—if there were no public provision for their needs.

In short, three-quarters of the federal budget is devoted to those programs which most clearly fit the requirements of a politics of inclusiveness: almost everyone benefits or is obligated in a very obvious way. In fact, if we add spending on national parks, the administration of justice, highways, and a variety of other programs, the portion of federal spending from which almost everyone clearly benefits is even larger.

Another important feature to note about the federal budget is how little of it is spent on poor people. A large part of the social policy debate in the United States has always been about welfare—programs that give money or services, such as health care, exclusively to the poor. The major programs of this sort are Medicaid, Aid to Families with Dependent Children (AFDC), Supplemental Security Income (SSI), Food Stamps, and low-income housing assistance. Some portion of education and training expenditures and Disability Insurance is also devoted to low-income individuals.

If we total the expenditures on the five major programs and add in a number of smaller ones, the most generous estimate of how much the federal government spends on programs intended primarily for poor people is about $100 billion, or 10 percent of the federal budget. Federal spending on AFDC, which is usually regarded as *the* welfare program, was only $9.7 billion in 1986, or about 1 percent of federal spending. In other words, a large part of the argument about the federal social role has focused on activities that account for less than 10 percent of federal spending and come to significantly less than the interest on the national debt.

It is also important to note that the debate about welfare seldom focuses on the largest federal antipoverty program: Social Security. In 1984 over 12 percent of Social Security recipients, sixty-five years of age or older, were poor, and it is estimated that if Social Security benefits had not been provided, up to 47 percent would have had incomes below the poverty line.[3] Social Security is not *primarily* an antipoverty program, but because it is an inclusive program—both rich and poor benefit—it has been immune from most of the criticisms leveled against other federal activities that help alleviate poverty. In fact, a large portion of its benefits either goes to poor people or serves to lift incomes above the poverty line. When the contribution of Social Security is included, the percentage of federal spending that helps alleviate poverty is about 20 percent rather than 10 percent.

A third important perspective on the federal budget is to look at it in terms of the "welfare state." Americans often say that they have a "welfare state," although they are not very precise about what they mean by this. One possible definition equates the welfare state with the 10 percent of government spending targeted at the poor. A broader definition includes all federal programs that directly transfer cash or in-kind benefits (such as food stamps or medical care) to individuals. By this broader definition, the

American welfare state costs about $480 billion—slightly less than half of total federal spending—or about 85 percent of domestic spending.

The Census Bureau has calculated that in the first quarter of 1984, 47 percent of all households in the United States and about one-third of all individuals received some form of benefit from the welfare state.[4] About three-quarters of welfare state spending was devoted to programs for the elderly. As a nation of individualists, the United States has arranged its social spending so that most of it goes directly to individual beneficiaries, and so that almost everyone benefits at some point.

But the federal social role—the things that the federal government does to promote the general welfare—extends well beyond the welfare state. Even if we look only at the largest federal spending programs, it becomes clear that tens of billions of dollars are spent on constructing highways and mass transit systems, protecting natural resources and the environment, on urban and regional development, on the administration of justice, and on other purposes which benefit all citizens. There is also a host of smaller programs that have an important impact, such as maintaining national parks and supporting cultural institutions.

The other side of the coin is that, in a nation that practices a politics of inclusiveness, a large portion of federal spending is aimed at special groups. The poor have already been mentioned. Veterans, federal employees, farmers, and the disabled also receive special assistance. Smaller programs provide help to American Indians, disabled miners, railroad workers, and others. In terms of spending, the social role comprises a few enormous programs from which everyone benefits and a large number of smaller programs targeted at a wide variety of specialized groups.

If the federal government were a business firm, we would say that it was a highly diversified enterprise, but that its primary lines of business were clear. It is obviously in the business of helping retirees, veterans, and poor people. Also if we add up bits and pieces of spending scattered throughout the budget, we would say that it is heavily in the health care business, to the tune of over $130 billion per year. It is also in the business of education and training, on which it spends about $30 billion; in the housing business, to which over $12 billion in direct expenditures were committed in 1986; and in the business of promoting both military and civilian research and development, at a cost of over $50 billion per year. These are the major purposes of the social role, measured in terms of spending.

Incentives

Federal spending is one measure of the social role, but, taken alone, it greatly underestimates the scope of activist government in the United States. A second major tool the federal government uses to provide for the general welfare is the creation of incentives for individuals and institutions to engage in activities that are deemed to be of public benefit. One major way of providing incentives for favored activities is by offering various tax advantages—exemptions from taxation, reduced tax rates, or deferral of tax payment. Collectively, these incentives are often called tax expenditures.

The federal government has always given tax breaks to help selected industries develop, weather hard times, and compete more effectively in the international marketplace. In the nineteenth century, most federal revenues were raised by tariffs and customs duties, and favored industries were given preferential treatment in the setting of rates. When the present individual income tax was first adopted in 1913, it too contained various exemptions, which at the time were largely justified on the grounds that they reduced taxes for people with limited "ability to pay." In recent years the number of exemptions has multiplied greatly, and the "ability to pay" argument has given way to the argument that all exemptions do or should serve to encourage activities that in some sense promote the common national interest.[5]

By 1986 there were over one hundred categories of special preference with a total value of nearly $400 billion. The system had become too complex and confusing and was too often used to unfair advantage. In 1986 Congress adopted a sweeping overhaul of the Internal Revenue Code that eliminated or reduced many preferences. It will be some years before the effects of this tax reform will be fully known, and no one is sure exactly what the resulting tax system will look like. It is clear that the total value of tax incentives has been reduced—to an amount closer to $300 billion than $400 billion. But it is also clear that, although the tax code was altered in many ways, most of its major incentives remain unchanged, and their size—the amount of tax payment exempted, reduced, or deferred by each preference in any given year—has remained about the same. As a result, it is possible to get a rough idea of how the tax incentive system is likely to work for the foreseeable future by focusing on the preferences that were not greatly affected by the 1986 reform.

Tax expenditures mirror direct federal spending in a great number of ways. Before tax reform about 80 percent of the value of incentives went directly to benefit individuals; the remainder went to corporations. The 1986 reform will direct an even larger proportion to individuals. By far the largest category of incentives encourages private provisions for retirement, just as the largest portion of federal spending is for retirement programs. If we add up the exemptions or deferrals for employer contributions to employee retirement funds, IRAs, KEOGHs and the partial deductibility of Social Security benefits, over one-fourth of tax expenditures benefiting individuals are devoted to this purpose.

By limiting eligibility for IRAs and KEOGHs, tax reform reduced the amount of retirement benefits likely to be exempted in future years. But it was a small reduction, because the value of exemptions for company pension plans and Social Security benefits has been much larger than that for individual savings plans. The former set of preferences totaled more than $62 billion in 1986; the latter totaled only $17 billion. Also, by eliminating other categories of preference, tax reform probably increased the percentage of tax expenditures, measured in dollar value, that will be devoted to retirement benefits in the future.

Among other large categories of individual incentives are employer contributions to employee medical insurance premiums (over $23 billion), interest on home mortgages and other real estate investments (over $33 billion), and deductions for individual consumer credit ($18 billion), which were largely eliminated by the 1986 reform. The earned income tax credit ($1.4 billion), is a smaller but important benefit to low-wage earners, which is intended to offset partially the cost of their Social Security contributions.

This pattern of tax incentives tells pretty much the same story as the pattern of federal spending. Through incentives, as through spending, the federal government helps to support retirement, health care, housing, and business research and development—although tax incentives are used to a greater extent than is spending to encourage the development of housing and to aid the business sector. Tax reform in 1986 somewhat reduced incentives for business, while leaving the emphasis on housing pretty much unchanged. Tax incentives also provide some relief for the poor, which was increased by the 1986 reform. About six million low-income Americans will no longer have to pay federal income taxes because of increases in the personal exemption and standard deduction.

The other important thing to note about tax incentives is that they illustrate the theme that the federal government is only one institution among many providing social services, and that it tries to support other institutions in performing functions parallel to its own. Over 20 percent of individual tax incentives were directed at encouraging employers to provide retirement and health care benefits for their employees. Over $15 billion in exemptions helped to support individual charitable giving. And about $42 billion worth of individual incentives took the form of exempting payments of state and local taxes and interest on state and local bonds. States and localities believe that these incentives, which were restricted by the 1986 reform, make it easier for them to raise revenues and to perform services that sometimes complement and sometimes go beyond the federal social role.

Loans and Other Forms of Credit

The tax system is not the only way in which the federal government subsidizes or creates incentives for activities deemed to be in the public interest. In addition to its other functions, the federal government is heavily involved in the credit business.[6] In 1986 the amount of federal, federally assisted, or government-sponsored credit outstanding was over $1 trillion. This makes the federal government by far the nation's largest banker.

There are more than 350 federal credit programs. Their aim is to make loans available for selected activities on more favorable terms than banks or other financial institutions would otherwise offer. Unlike tax preferences, federal credit programs do *not* closely mirror federal spending priorities. The activities that benefit most heavily from credit policies are housing, agriculture, higher education, foreign military sales, and other export activities. The favorable terms created by the federal government assure that more of the nation's stock of available capital will be invested in these areas than would otherwise be the case. Credit programs increase the amount of housing, farm products, and higher education Americans produce.

Credit programs also increase the national debt. Although not included in most calculations of total federal debt, most are funded by issuing special government or government-backed securities. In effect, this resulted in about $141 billion in federal or federally backed borrowing in 1986 over and above the $236 billion the government had to borrow to finance shortfalls in its spending budget and for other purposes. In total, federal or federally assisted borrowing has added almost $1 trillion to the $1.6 trillion in debt that the government has accumulated in other ways over the years, making total federal and federally sponsored indebtedness over $2.5 trillion. The difference between debt resulting from credit activities and other federal debt is that the former is secured by liens on property or obligations by individuals and institutions to repay, whereas the latter must be repaid by tax dollars.

The federal government has almost always been involved in the credit business in some way. Manipulation of credit was an important part of Hamilton's policy. Present federal activity in the housing and farm credit fields had its origins in the Great Depression, when many banks collapsed and credit markets were generally in disarray. Home mortgage foreclosures were commonplace, and new financing for homes was hard to come by.

Federal credit activity in housing was intended to make mortgage money more affordable and plentiful so that people could hold onto the homes they had and so that new generations could realize the "American dream" of homeownership.

The Depression also brought ruinously low agriculture prices, a shortage of credit for putting in new crops, farm foreclosures, and a withering of funds to build homes or make public improvements in rural areas. Farm credit policies were intended to stabilize commodity prices, provide a source of credit in periods of hardship, and, generally, help to modernize rural life.

Higher education loans originated in the late 1950s as an effort to increase the pool of national talent in science and technology. Their purpose has since been broadened to increasing the stock of talent in all areas of learning.

The government has pursued the goals of all these program areas vigorously. In fact, it has pursued them so vigorously that it has become a dominant force in financing home ownership and agriculture, and it provides about one-third of the funding for higher education in the United States (counting both grants and loans).[7] All three areas of enterprise would doubtless collapse if the federal role were withdrawn and no private sector substitute provided.

Federal programs provide credit support in three different ways: direct loans, loan guarantees, and government-sponsored enterprises. Of these three credit mechanisms, direct loans are the smallest in volume. The government mainly extends credit by creating incentives for private financial institutions rather than by serving as a lender itself. Most direct loans for social purposes are made to farmers. In 1986 the Commodity Credit Corporation extended over $17 billion in price support loans, and the Farmers Home Administration, the Rural Electrification Administration, and other farm lending institutions lent another $9 billion for rural housing, equipment, telephone and power systems, and other ventures to improve the quality of rural life. The government also made about $1.8 billion in loans for low-income public housing. (Most of the balance of its approximately $41 billion in loans supported military and civil exports or other business activities.)

Loan guarantees are a more substantial area of federal credit activity. In 1986 the federal government committed itself to insure over $159 billion in loans by private banks and other credit sources and actually disbursed $89 billion in loans. Over 85 percent of the commitments were for loans on middle-income housing, about $8.9 billion for Guaranteed Student Loans to more than three million college students, and the balance for commodity and export loans. These guarantees are the form in which the ordinary citizen is most likely to meet the federal government as a source of credit.

A student who needs money for college, for example, simply goes to a regular commercial bank, or to an agency that approaches the bank for him, and fills out an application. Among the federal eligibility requirements for the Guaranteed Student Loan Program are carrying at least half a normal academic course load and a demonstration of need. If the requirements are met, the bank makes the loan from its normal credit resources and the federal government insures it against default. In fact, the federal government does even more than this for student loans. It guarantees the bank a rate of interest higher than the student is charged and makes up the difference; it also pays all of the interest while the student is in college and offers to buy the loan from the bank after the student graduates with funds raised by issuing special securities through the Student Loan Marketing Association (Sallie Mae). The banker can't lose.

Loan guarantees for housing work in a similar way, but are less generous. The Federal Housing Administration (FHA) simply acts as an insurance agency for most loans, charges a fee for its services, and provides no outright subsidy. In recent years the FHA has run at a $2–3 billion loss, largely because Congress and the administration have encouraged it to insure innovative but risky loans and low-income housing projects. The Veterans Administration (VA) provides insurance but does not charge a fee and covers loans with lower than usual down payments. The government offers to relieve banks of both VA and FHA loans by buying them with funds raised by issuing securities through the Government National Mortgage Association (Ginnie Mae). This frees up the capital of banks to make new loans.

Similar arrangements exist for insuring commodities and export loans. Obviously, at a rate of over $159 billion per year, the government's insurance coverage has grown very large. By 1986 it was covering about $450 billion in loans. The cost of making up defaults not covered by insurance premiums and subsidizing the interest on student loans exceeded $11 billion—over $1 billion more than the federal government spent on AFDC.

Government-sponsored enterprises are technically private, investor-owned businesses chartered by the federal government to achieve social purposes. They include the Federal National Mortgage Association (Fannie Mae), which issues private bonds and uses the proceeds to buy up mortgages from commercial banks, the Federal Home Loan Mortgage Corporation (Freddie Mac), which performs a similar function for savings and loan institutions, and various other farm and commercial credit corporations. These institutions were chartered to increase the availability of credit for housing and other purposes. By buying up mortgages and other loans from banks, they free the capital of those banks to make further loans of the same type. Securities they issue to finance these purchases, in effect, supplement the resources available to banks for home loans and other purposes. Although this arrangement costs the federal government nothing, there is a general assumption that it will bail out any of the government-sponsored enterprises if they ever get into serious financial difficulty. This belief, together with certain forms of favorable treatment of their securities by the federal government, makes them especially attractive to investors. In 1986 government-sponsored enterprises had a total of about $450 billion in outstanding securities and held loans of about an equal amount.

Regulation

Federal spending and incentives affect many aspects of our lives, but by far the greatest day-to-day effect of the federal social role results from federal regulations.[8] The reach of federal regulatory activity is so extensive it is possible to tell the following story without exaggeration:

The Regulated American

The average American wakes up in the morning in a home that is financed according to rules set by the VA, FHA, or some other government agency. He turns on the light, which is powered by electricity from a public utility that is regulated by the Federal Power Commission and subject to federal environmental regulations. He brushes his teeth in water that meets federal clean water standards and uses toothpaste approved by the Food and Drug Administration. Out of the corner of his eye, he watches the morning news on a television station licensed by the Federal Communications Commission.

His breakfast of bacon and eggs has passed the scrutiny of federal meat and poultry inspectors. The suit he puts on was made by unionized workers whose right to organize is protected by the National Labor Relations Act and who earn at least the federal minimum wage. He drives to work in a car that has seat belts and a catalytic converter, as a result of federal requirements, and he probably breaks the fifty-five-mile-per-hour speed limit, imposed on states by the federal government, while he glides along interstate highways, largely financed by federal funds and designed within federal specifications.

On his way to work, he drops his children off at a school that is desegregated, thanks to federal efforts, and where, if necessary, they will benefit from special education programs mandated by the federal government. When he arrives at his workplace, which is designed to meet federal occupational safety standards, he will be greeted by colleagues against whom he cannot discriminate in hiring, firing, or any other way on the basis of sex, race, age, or ethnic background. Regardless of his line of business, the goods or services his company produces are subject to a host of safety, environmental, and consumer protection regulations.

If today is payday, he will find certain deductions from his check mandated by federal law, among them withholding of income taxes and Social Security contributions. Probably also deducted will be a contribution to his company pension plan, which must meet the requirements of ERISA, the Employee Retirement

Insurance Security Agency, a federal agency that supervises private pensions. If his pay envelope contains a pink slip, he will walk over to the federal-state unemployment office to register for benefits. But if things are going well, he will deposit his check in a federally regulated and insured bank.

Having secured his financial affairs, he may leave on a business trip. Perhaps he takes a bus, which is designed according to federal standards to accommodate the handicapped, to the airport, which is operated under the supervision of the Federal Aviation Administration. His takeoff will be approved by federal air traffic controllers, and most of the details of his flight will be subject to FAA safety regulations.

The story could go on, but we will leave the average American up in the air. Federal regulation is both the most extensive and most poorly understood aspect of the social role, and it is probably misunderstood precisely because it is so extensive. But it is important for Americans to make some sense of the mass of regulations that impinge on their daily lives. There are two keys: understanding the way in which regulation functions within the governmental process, and understanding the different types of regulations that have been developed.

The Regulatory Process

All regulatory activity of the federal government is authorized by law, and almost all federal laws result in some form of regulatory activity. The Sherman and Clayton Anti-Trust acts, the Federal Trade Commission Act, the Securities and Exchange Act, the Civil Rights Act, and the Clean Water Act are some of the best-known laws specifically concerned with regulation.

In the laws it writes, Congress sets out goals and purposes for government activities to promote the general welfare, and in some cases it spells out in considerable detail the means by which those goals are to be achieved. But as the social role has extended into more and more aspects of our increasingly complex pattern of modern life, it has become apparent that Congress could not possibly spell out all the details of how some particular purpose—

such as assuring full disclosure of securities trading or ensuring clean drinking water—should be achieved in a piece of legislation. The legislation would have to be unmanageably long, and members of Congress, who are usually generalists, could not be expected to have the expertise to evaluate all of its details.

In addition, specifics of the situation that calls for government action may change with time, although the basic congressional intent may not. For example, drinking water may have been imperiled primarily by untreated sewage in many areas when the Clean Water Act was passed, but it may increasingly be imperiled by industrial waste. Whatever the source of threat, the congressional intent is the same: to keep the water safe. But to keep up with changes in the source of pollution by legislation would require frequent amendments.

Finally, most government policies ultimately must be applied to individual cases. Someone must decide exactly which industrial plants pollute too much, how dangerous they are, and exactly what should be done about these problems. Out of fairness, these decisions must be made on the basis of rules that are applicable to all cases.

In the nineteenth century, when government social activism was not as extensive as it is now, the application of laws to particular cases was primarily handled by the courts. As social activism became more extensive and entered more areas requiring technical expertise, pioneers of regulation such as Charles Francis Adams, Louis Brandeis, Theodore Roosevelt, and Woodrow Wilson saw that the courts did not always have the ability to handle the problems of applying congressional intent.[9] In addition, judicial procedures were too time-consuming or otherwise ill adapted to meet the need.

As a result, Congress adopted the procedure of delegating to administrative agencies the authority to make and enforce specific regulations that would carry out its laws. Sometimes these agencies are executive departments of the government; in other cases they are "independent" regulatory bodies established by Congress, whose members are appointed by the president. The first of these, the Interstate Commerce Commission, had largely investigatory powers and could only enforce its decisions by going to court. With the passage of the Hepburn Act regulating interstate railways in 1906, the ICC was given enforcement powers of its own, and the modern process of regulation began. It has grown during every period of activist government since then, and today there are literally scores of regulatory agencies.

The Reach of Regulation

Because of the function regulation performs in our political system, it is no wonder that the federal regulatory role is so extensive. Activist government requires a large number of rules, regulations, and decisions to make its policies effective. But regulation is not an undifferentiated mass of activities. Every regulation has its origin in law, and the ordinary citizen's confusion about the process can be clarified by going back to the laws on which it is based.

Broadly speaking, there are two kinds of federal regulations: those that simply implement spending or incentive programs, and those that set up programs of regulation to achieve other purposes. The first sort is easy to understand. It is simply the administrative work required to put any policy decision into effect, and it is generally carried out by executive branch agencies. If, for example, Congress decides that there should be a contributory Social Security system, that certain kinds of people should be required to participate, and that its finances should be so managed as to make it self-supporting, someone has to decide how to register participants in the system, collect payroll taxes, and issue checks, and someone must calculate whether the level of contributions will match the benefits paid in the present and future years. It would be a full-time job for Congress to do these things. In fact, it is the full-time job of several thousand employees of the Social Security Administration in the Department of Health and Human Services.

Legislation establishing programs of regulation is harder to understand. Here the congressional intent is to further the general welfare, not by providing money, services, or financial incentives but by compelling people and organizations to adopt certain modes of behavior deemed to be in the general interest. Roughly speaking, regulatory programs can be divided into two types: those primarily targeted at business practices (most regulatory programs are of this type), and those that serve more general social goals.

The federal regulations directed at businesses, in economists' jargon, are intended to address various forms of "market failure." In an ideal, competitive marketplace, every business would try to produce the best possible products at the lowest possible prices and to treat its customers as well as possible in other ways. Otherwise some other company would grab up its share of the market. In an ideal marketplace, too, each company would provide its employees with competitive wages, benefits, and working conditions, because otherwise they would find jobs somewhere else.

Unfortunately, we do not have ideal, competitive marketplaces that produce these results, so government steps in to protect the general welfare. Federal regulation of business takes many different forms. Among its major purposes are:

- *Keeping markets as competitive as possible*—by preventing monopolies or other concentrations of business power through enforcement of the Sherman and Clayton Anti-Trust laws by the Justice Department, the Federal Trade Commission, and the courts.
- *Regulating the prices, conditions, and quality of services of those industries where some degree of concentration of market power is inevitable*—through, for example, regulating public utilities by the Federal Power Commission, and regulating aspects of telecommunications and interstate transportation by the Federal Communications Commission and the Interstate Commerce Commission.
- *Ensuring that the financial industry, which is fundamental to all other economic activity, is soundly managed and treats its customers fairly*—through requirements for securities registration and dealing administered by the Securities and Exchange Commission and requirements that

banks follow reserve and investment guidelines set by the Federal Reserve Board, the Comptroller of the Currency, and other agencies.

• *Protecting employees*—through the right to organize and bargain collectively supervised by the National Labor Relations Board, through laws prohibiting child labor and setting a minimum wage, through requirements for the management of employee pension plans, supervised by the Employee Retirement Insurance Security Agency (ERISA), and through workplace safety requirements by the Occupational Safety and Health Administration (OSHA).

• *Protecting consumers*—from unsafe food and drugs by laws administered by the Food and Drug Administration, from unsafe transportation through the National Highway Traffic Safety Administration and the Federal Aviation Administration, and from other hazardous products and deceptive advertising through regulations of the Federal Trade Commission.

The other body of regulation, also significant, though smaller, might be called "social" as opposed to narrowly "business" regulation. It affects not only businesses but all levels of government and, to some extent, every one of us in our day-to-day activities.

Two prime examples of social regulations are civil rights and environmental protection laws. The former have their origins in the Civil Rights Act of 1964. Its seven titles outlawed discrimination in voting, education, public accommodations, public facilities, private employment, and, more generally, all programs receiving federal financial assistance. It is administered primarily by the Civil Rights Commission and the Justice and Labor departments, but virtually every federal agency and program has some responsibility for seeing that its goals are met. Subsequent legislation has extended many of the same protections to prevent discrimination on the basis of age, sex, or national origin.

Federal regulations to protect the environment also had their origins in the 1960s. The Environmental Protection Administration administers a large body of legislation intended to ensure clean air, clean water, and protection from toxic wastes. Other agencies protect endangered species and monitor land management practices.

Administrative, business, and social regulation all impose costs—both in the paperwork required to implement them and in terms of altered practices by businesses and others. No one has ever found a good way to calculate the costs, in part because the task is so monumental. Some years ago economist Murray Weidenbaum ventured the estimate of $100 billion, only to be cut to shreds by his professional colleagues.[10] But Weidenbaum made the important point that we pay a large price for a competitive market, fair employment practices, product and environmental safety, equal rights, and the other goals of regulations.

Judicial Policy

Regulations made and enforced by administrative agencies are, of course, not the only means by which the federal government requires individuals and organizations to act in ways that promote the general welfare. Decisions by federal courts, and especially by the Supreme Court, perform the same basic function. Like regulatory agencies, courts interpret and apply laws and often create new law in doing so. Unlike regulatory agencies, federal courts interpret and apply the Constitution, as well as other laws.

Narrowly conceived, the role of the courts is to guard the basic design of our political system and to protect our individual rights to free speech, a free press, due process of law, and other fundamental liberties. These are certainly among the most important functions of the federal social role. They establish the preconditions for our enjoyment of most of the other things we value in American life: a free and open society and a representative democracy.

But there are many ways to interpret what the basic guarantees of our rights and liberties mean when applied to concrete cases. Each generation of judges has interpreted those guarantees in different ways and applied them to different areas of American life. In recent decades, controversy has arisen over court-ordered school busing, standards for equal opportunity in employment and education, decisions upholding a woman's right to have an abortion if she chooses to do so, the rights of persons accused of a crime, and the legality of school prayer.

Most of these subjects were not touched on by federal policy of any sort twenty or thirty years ago. By rendering decisions that affected previous practices by federal, state, and local governments, as well as other institutions, the Supreme Court has extended the social role in major ways. Most of this growth in judicial social policy occurred in the 1960s and 1970s, but in recent years the courts have by and large held firm to the precedents established during those decades.

Economic Management

A final, critically important, dimension of the federal social role lies somewhere on the borderline between regulation and creating incentives. This is the federal role in promoting the stability of our national economy as a whole. Periodic economic downturns—recessions or depressions—have always been a fact of life in industrial and postindustrial nations, and governments have always tried to moderate their adverse effects. In recent decades, economists have believed that the best way to reverse economic downturns is some combination of stimulating consumption, either by more federal spending or tax cuts, and increasing the availability of money, by lower interest rates and other measures. Congress and the president have most of the authority to stimulate consumption, but most of the authority to increase the money supply rests with an independent federal agency, the Federal Reserve Board.

But combating business cycles is not the only way in which the federal government promotes economic stability. It closely monitors, regulates, and insures the banking industry. In 1986, for example, deposits insured by the Federal Deposit Insurance Corporation and other federal agencies exceeded $2 trillion. The government also offers low interest loans or special contracts to large businesses in danger of failing and endangering related firms. And it takes an active role in promoting international trade and protecting American companies against unfair competition from overseas. Finally, many federal regulations intended either to prevent unfair trade practices or to protect consumers help to make companies more secure by setting standards for business conduct to which all competitors must adhere. This often simplifies and cuts the costs of doing business. And when something does go wrong, such as bank failures or the release of toxic fumes from a chemical plant, federal inspection and insurance programs protect both individual companies and sometimes whole industries that might be endangered by a loss of public confidence.

Shifting Dimensions

These are the basic dimensions of the federal social role. Although they have not changed greatly during the last decade of reassessment, there have been some changes. On a five-point scale we have witnessed:

- *Much more* federal spending (in terms of dollar amounts) on Social Security pensions, health care programs, farm programs, and the national debt. The major priorities of federal spending have become increasingly larger parts of the social role.
- *Somewhat more* federal credit activity of almost all sorts.
- *Somewhat less* aid to state and local governments, enforcement of business and social regulations, judicial activism, tax expenditures to benefit individuals, and total spending on the poor.
- *Much less* regulation of the financial, transportation, and communications industries (where federal regulatory authority has been wholly terminated or greatly curtailed by Congress and the courts), tax expenditures to benefit business (due to the 1986 tax reform), and spending on housing, employment, and training programs for the poor.
- *About the same* level of everything else.

In short, two major components of the social role, spending and credit, have grown; tax expenditures to benefit individuals have been reduced somewhat; and regulatory activity has been on the wane. But the major changes have taken place in a few areas only, and, for the most part, they have reinforced biases that have been built into the social role for some time.

Interchangeable Tools

In assessing these changes, and possible future changes, in the federal social role, it is essential to realize that the goals of spending, incentives, and regulation overlap to a considerable degree. More generally, it is essential to realize that almost *any* policy goal—any form of advancing the general welfare—could be achieved by *any* one of these tools.[11] They are interchangeable to a remarkable degree.

For example, if the government's goal is to increase access to higher education by low-income students, it can and does use the spending tool to make cash grants (the Pell Grant Program) and the incentive tool to insure loans (the Guaranteed Student Loan Program). It might also, although it does not, use the regulatory tool in various ways. For example, it might require that all higher education institutions receiving federal assistance (which includes most colleges and universities) devote a certain percentage of their income to scholarships for low-income students, or that all employers include education funds for the children of their workers as part of their standard benefit package. Or the Supreme Court might decide that states that do not provide loans for low-income students to attend state universities are denying those students equal opportunity.

The game of interchanging policy tools can be, and is, played in almost every field. Pollution control is partly achieved by regulations, partly by grants and loans to states and localities, and partly by federal spending for toxic waste cleanups. Individual retirement is provided for by spending on Social Security benefits, regulations protecting corporate pension plans, tax preferences, and loans for low-income housing for the elderly.

A major question that any reassessment of the social role must face is whether we have struck the right balance among the various tools that are or might be used to accomplish the same purpose. The effectiveness and indirect consequences of using different tools vary considerably depending on the goals to which they are applied. But in looking at what the social role should be, the nation should consider not only the usual questions of *whether* it wants to support certain activities that are in the public interest and *how much* it wants to spend on them, but also *how* it wants to promote them—what combinations of tools it wants to use.

5

Myths and Realities

The current reassessment of activist government is seriously
handicapped by misunderstandings about what the full
dimensions of the federal social role are. But it is even more
seriously handicapped by misunderstandings about what effect
major social programs have on American life.

Seven major myths, widely held, stand in the way of any rational
reassessment of the social role.

MYTH 1

The nation cannot afford the federal social role, and it
certainly cannot afford more of it. Federal spending for
social purposes has become so large that it harms the
American economy, and more social spending would have
disastrous effects.

This is the conventional wisdom of most politicians, businessmen, and ordinary citizens. They have watched spending on social
programs grow for decades, both in absolute terms and as a per-

centage of GNP. Common sense leads them to believe that if we take that much money out of the economy for social purposes, the economy must be getting weaker. This view was reinforced when the large growth in social spending during the Johnson and Nixon administrations was followed by back-to-back recessions from 1973 to 1981. Many people assumed that the social role had crossed some magical threshold: we had begun spending ourselves into the poorhouse.

Since that time one of the fundamental assumptions in the debate about activist government—an assumption shared by conservatives and liberals alike—has been that government spending for social purposes cannot increase, at least as a percentage of GNP *No growth* is one of the basic rules of the game in contemporary American politics, and it has been a major factor perpetuating the current policy stalemate.

It appears that the only people who do not believe that spending on the social role has harmed the American economy are the nation's economists. This would seem to be an issue on which they can claim the relevant expertise. But for some reason they aren't telling anyone that the prevailing opinion in their profession squarely contradicts the conventional wisdom. In a recent review of literature on this subject, University of Wisconsin economist Robert Lampman concluded:

> In short, the attitude of most economists toward the relationship between social spending and economic performance can probably best be characterized as permissive agnosticism; there is much that they do not know about the relationship and what they do know leads them to the conclusion that there are no great grounds for concern. They tend to advise policymakers that there are no compelling economic reasons to oppose present or moderately higher levels of social spending.[1]

Why have the economists been so quiet about all of this? Because, as a leader of their profession confided, "There is no point in arguing. Nobody would believe us."

But it is very important that everyone should believe them, or at least hear their views. The essence of their argument is easy to understand. It has three parts.

First, historically there has been no consistent relationship between the rate of growth in social spending and the performance of the American economy. During the postwar period, social spending has risen at a steady, gradual rate for less than 1 percent of GNP per year. By any measure, however, the American economy has fluctuated wildly with periodic booms and busts. How could a level of spending that grows at a fairly steady rate cause economic fluctuations that are irregular and intermittent? It just does not make sense to believe that it could.

The only period when social spending grew at a rate much faster than average was 1968–1972. And this was, of course, followed by a period of "stagflation" in the economy. But did the surge of spending cause the stagflation? Not likely, according to most economists. They point to the fact that in 1973 and again in 1977 oil price increases shocked the economy not only of the United States but of the entire world. There were also several major corporate failures (Lockheed, Chrysler), which cannot by any stretch of imagination be linked to social spending. In addition, to control increases in inflation, the Federal Reserve raised interest rates to historically high levels.

Most economists believe that while social spending may have made some small contribution to economic problems in this period, other forces were the real villains. In short, historically, the belief that social spending harms the economy rests entirely on the experience of a short period of time, and the relationship in that period is dubious at best. Clearly, there was no consistent relationship between the level of social spending and economic performance before then, nor has there been since.

Second, international comparisons throw cold water on the idea that social spending harms the American economy. This is probably a more pertinent consideration for many critics of social spending. They generally argue *not* that spending creates economic fluctuations, but that it reduces the long-term growth rate around which the economy fluctuates from time to time. According to this argument, if we had spent less on social programs over the years, our economy would have grown faster and we would be enjoying a higher standard of living today.

Ultimately, this argument is probably unprovable one way or the other. Yet a strong case can be made against it by examining the experience of other highly developed countries. If we look at the nineteen major industrialized countries (members of the Organization for Economic Cooperation and Development), we find a great deal of variation in both levels of social spending and economic growth, but the two factors seem to have very little relation to each other.

Most solid information about this point measures differences in spending on social welfare: the programs to aid individuals to which the United States devoted about $480 billion in 1986. By world standards we are a low spender. Of the nineteen OECD nations, thirteen devote a higher percentage of their GNP to social welfare than the United States does and five devote a lower percentage.[2] These relative rates of spending have been about the same for more than twenty-five years. For the period 1961–1975, all but one of the nations which spent a larger percentage of GNP on social programs experienced a higher rate of economic growth than we did. And from 1975 to 1981, the economies of half of those countries which spent *more* than we did grew at about the same or a higher rate than ours. In both periods, half the nations that spent *less* on social programs than the United States had a higher level of growth, and half had a lower level. Most notable among those nations spending a smaller percentage of GNP on social programs is Japan, which has sustained a consistently higher growth rate than we have enjoyed. But Greece has also been a low spender. Would anyone like to argue that the United States should cut back on the social role so that we can emulate "the Greek economic miracle?"

These crude international comparisons only illustrate a point that has been documented at length by economist Robert Kuttner and others: if we use the world as an experimental laboratory to test the theory that social spending inhibits economic growth, we find that the theory is not confirmed.[3] There is no reason to believe that the basic laws of economics operate differently in the United States than in other advanced countries. And if we look at the experience of other countries, we find that sometimes high social spending accompanies rapid economic growth, and sometimes it doesn't.

Third, theoretically there is no reason to believe that social spending harms the economy by reducing growth rates, GNP, or our standard of living. In theory, social spending should help to solve at least one major economic problem: periodic downturns or recessions. Social spending should help to stabilize the economy because a large portion of that spending (means-tested programs for the poor and unemployed) either increases or stays the same during recessions. Social spending, thus, helps to moderate the severity of downturns by maintaining the demand for goods and services.

Of course, if a recession is accompanied by high inflation, as it was during the late 1970s, continued growth in social spending that supplements individual incomes may help fuel the rise in prices. In his review of the literature about the effect of social spending, Lampman concludes that, in periods of stagflation, "it is simply not clear whether high levels of social spending help or hurt the nation in achieving the goal of economic stabilization."[4]

How else could social spending theoretically affect the economy? Economist Martin Feldstein once argued that spending on Social Security reduced the amount of national savings, thereby reducing the capital available to create economic growth. But errors were found in Feldstein's calculations, and most economists have rejected this theory.[5]

Clearly, social spending *helps* rather than hurts the economy to the extent that it is devoted to upgrading the skills and experience of our work force (human capital), by investments in education, training, and other areas. A widely respected body of research by economist Edward Dennison and others has shown that next to technological innovation, improvements in human capital are the single most important factor making for economic growth in the United States.[6] The social role clearly includes heavy investment in both human capital and technology, and there is every reason to believe that this investment pays off.

What about taxes? Have we been harming the economy by taxing existing corporations too heavily or reducing incentives for people to establish new companies by high tax rates on their earnings? By no means. Effective corporate tax rates have declined from the 1960s through the mid-1980s, and the marginal tax rate on high-income individuals has also declined in recent years.

The only other way in which social spending might even theoretically harm the economy is by reducing work effort—the willingness of people to apply their human capital to productive efforts. Most economists assume that there is some reduction in work effort as a result of social programs. This is mostly due to early retirement made possible by a combination of Social Security and government-subsidized private pension plans, but it is also partly due to the effects of disability programs, unemployment insurance, and welfare benefits. Economists cannot agree how large an effect these various programs have on work effort. Estimates vary widely. Lampman estimates that the *maximum* effect would be to reduce GNP by 1 percent, which is more than offset by the positive effects of social spending on human capital.[7]

And then there are effects of social spending on the economy that are almost impossible to measure. Economist Moses Abramovitz eloquently described these in his 1981 presidential address to the American Economics Association:

> The pace of growth in a country depends not only on its access to new technology, but on its ability to make and absorb the social adjustments required to exploit new products and processes. . . . The enlargement of the government's economic role, including its support of income minima, health care, social insurance, and the other elements of the welfare state, was therefore—at least up to a point—not just a question of reducing irregularities of outcome and opportunity, though that is how people usually think of it. It was and is—up to a point—a part of the productivity growth process itself.[8]

What is the theoretical verdict? Social spending probably reduces work effort slightly, but this effect on the economy is certainly outweighed by positive effects that result from investing in human capital and technology and in a more just and stable society. As far as economists are concerned, all other effects are either nonexistent or unknown.

The Cause for Misunderstanding

In short, on theoretical, historical, and comparative grounds there is little or no evidence to support the idea that present levels of social spending have harmed the American economy, or that we cannot afford to spend more. *The conventional wisdom is simply wrong.*

And the fundamental reason why it is wrong is easy to see. Social spending does not take money out of the economy and destroy it. Social spending reroutes money. It takes it in the form of taxes and spends some on goods and services like highways, hydroelectric projects, and basic research and development that clearly enhance economic growth. It also spends tax dollars on cash grants to individuals who buy food, transportation, clothing, and other things. Clearly, if we have a high level of social spending we will develop a different kind of economy than we would otherwise have. If there were no social programs and no taxes to support them, today's taxpayers would have more money to buy goods and services, and the mix of goods and services they would buy is certainly different from the mix the nation currently consumes. For example, less of the national income would probably be spent on health, because many people wouldn't be able to afford adequate medical services without assistance from Medicare, Medicaid, and other federal programs.

But that is one reason why we have social programs—to reroute money in ways that serve the general welfare. Social programs change the shape of the economy, but there is no reason to believe that they harm overall prosperity. Because of the federal social role we probably buy and produce more health care and fewer Cadillacs: this does not make the economy less prosperous, just different.

Of course, it is possible to design a social policy that would ruin the American economy—for example, a 100 percent tax on corporate profits or a ban on private savings. But this takes us into the realm of fiction. We do not have this type of social policy and we never will. Certain forms of public spending are also less helpful to the economy than others. For example, many economists believe that military spending is less helpful than social spending because it contributes less to increasing domestic consumption and the overall productive capacity of the economy.

It is important to note, however, that these conclusions about social spending do not endorse federal budget deficits. Most economists agree that the deficits of the mid-1980s are too high and will sooner or later imperil our national well-being. But those deficits were created largely by cutting taxes in 1981 and increasing spending on defense, not by social programs. The way to cure them is to increase taxes to the point where we are paying for the government we have. Handled responsibly, a tax increase should not cause economic harm. All of the evidence supports the notion that the United States can afford present or somewhat higher levels of social spending *and the taxes to support them.*

In short, the level of social spending or taxes by themselves are not detrimental to our economy, but the form of taxing and spending could be, and an imbalance between the two (deficits) certainly is.

The lesson for the current period of reassessment is clear: there is no reason why plans for the future of the federal social role should be constrained by worries about the economic effects of higher levels of social spending. Doubtless there are other reasons why we might want to restrict the social role. We may not want to devote so much of our income to public purposes, or we may not like the way government reroutes it. But policymakers and others who want to cut government spending should not be blindsided by economic myths or hide behind them. Whatever reasons policymakers have to oppose social spending, adverse effects on the economy should not be among them.

MYTH 2

Social programs are ineffective in achieving their goals. By and large, they are a waste of money.

Whole libraries of books and articles have been created that debunk this myth, and yet it still persists. Obviously there is always room for improvement in any social program, and there is always cause for finding fault. But, for the most part, the activities of the federal social role have been enormously successful, and grumblings that they have not been successful enough are tantamount to throwing out the baby with the bathwater. Here we can only touch on the highlights of what political scientist John Schwarz has called "America's hidden success."[9]

The social role has dramatically reduced poverty in the United States. Were it not for federal cash and benefit programs such as Social Security, unemployment assistance, and AFDC, over 18 percent of American families would have fallen below the poverty line in 1985.[10] Those programs reduced the poverty rate for families to 11 percent. In-kind benefits such as food stamps and low-income housing reduced poverty even further. In 1985, the individual poverty rate was 14 percent, down from 22.4 percent in 1959.[11] Social Security alone lowered the poverty rate for elderly people from what would have been 48 percent to about 12 percent in 1985.[12] Over 9 million older people were lifted out of poverty. Moreover, low-income and elderly Americans have far better access to health care than they did a few decades ago. Should we do better? Probably. But there have been enormous gains.

Housing has improved. In 1940, 40 percent of Americans lived in substandard housing. In 1985, due in part to federal investments, the percentage was less than 5 percent.[13] More generally, federal incentives that have channeled a large part of our private spending into housing have made the United States, by many measures, the best-housed nation in the world. We have a larger percentage of single family homes, more square feet of housing per person, and greater amenities in our homes than do the people of any other country.

The level of education has been upgraded by social programs. In 1955, before federal student loans and other aids to higher education were available, about 15 percent of college-age Americans attended institutions of higher education; in 1985 almost 28 percent attended.[14] While factors other than federal assistance have certainly been at work, it is undoubtedly the case that a great many of the 8 million young people who received federal aid in 1985 would not otherwise have been able to continue their studies.[15]

And the benefits have not only occurred at the college level. According to the House Select Committee on Children, Youth, and Aging, preschool programs such as Head Start can save as much as $4.75 for each dollar invested, by reducing the need for special education and welfare later in life and by improving the productivity of workers.[16]

Americans are living longer: the average life expectancy has increased by over four years since 1960, and the rate of infant mortality has been cut almost in half.[17] In part this is the result of improved lifestyles. But federal spending on medical research and greater availability of health care and adequate nutrition made possible by government programs can take much of the credit. For example, it has been estimated that the small WIC program (which provides nutritional supplements to pregnant women, nursing mothers, and their children) has reduced future health care costs by $3.00 for each dollar spent.[18]

Federal programs have obviously been effective in the environmental area too. Scarcely anyone who lives near a large body of water can have failed to see the improvement. Twenty years ago most of our rivers and lakes in or near urban areas were heavily polluted; today many are fishable and swimmable again. And after carefully weighing a large body of conflicting evidence, economist Paul Portney concludes that, "It seems indisputable that the CAA [the Clean Air Act amendments of 1970] has played an important role in improving or preventing further degradation in air quality in the United States."[19]

Progress in civil rights has been probably the greatest accomplishment of the federal social role in the postwar era. There are no more legally segregated schools, restaurants, or other public accommodations in the United States. And while de facto segregation still exists in many areas, the end of legalized separation between the races has brought a far greater measure of equality to education, employment, and other areas of American life.

Many of the areas of progress are gains that we now take for granted. They only seem impressive in historical perspective. There is virtually no more child labor in the United States, incidents of harm from impure food and drugs are rare enough that they create public scandals, progress in medicine and other areas of science, funded in large part by the federal government, has been phenomenal. Fifty years ago retirement was a guarantee of poverty and destitution for many Americans. Today, a combination of Social Security benefits and federally subsidized and regulated private pension plans has made it possible for most retired Americans to maintain a reasonable standard of living.[20]

Are these and other federal programs as effective as they should be? Probably not. Does the nation achieve enormous gains in public welfare for its investment of more than half a trillion dollars? Clearly it does. Activist government has made enormous and very tangible contributions to the well-being of each and every one of us.

MYTH 3

Government social programs for the poor do more harm than good. They entice poor people into taking a free ride on welfare rather than earning their own way.

This is a very old myth. Social policy in most countries during the late nineteenth and early twentieth centuries was haunted by the fear that if benefits for the poor were made too generous, people would stop working and live off the state. Americans have always harbored such concerns. The most memorable statements of this case are to be found in the works of William Graham Sumner, but even reformers who do not share his theories of "social Darwinism" have been wary about the effects of social spending on the poor.[21] This is one reason why welfare benefits in the United States have been kept very low.

How low? The AFDC program, which is one of the major federal programs targeted entirely at the poor, allows each state government to set its own level of benefits, but it requires states to establish a "standard of need" for recipients, against which the adequacy of benefits can be measured. In 1986, as in previous years, only about one-third of the states provided benefits that met their own standards of need, and the median state benefit for a one-parent family of three was a cash grant which, when combined with the value of food stamps, equaled only 73 percent of poverty-level income.

For the most part, fear that the poor would abuse welfare benefits has been an unspoken assumption in the United States during the postwar period. It found a vocal advocate in 1984, when Charles Murray published a book entitled *Losing Ground*.[22] The book's basic conclusions were embraced by most conservatives, including the president of the United States. As a result, the version of this myth about welfare that has come to dominate the current period of reassessment is Murray's version.

Murray's major assertions concern the AFDC program. He claims that increased benefit levels and broader eligibility standards instituted in the 1960s and early 1970s made AFDC so generous that many poor women organized their lives to become eligible for the program. Poor, unmarried women with children make up most of the AFDC caseload, and there is a federally established maximum amount of income they can earn without having their benefits reduced. Murray believes that because of the more generous benefits, many poor women choose not to get married if they become pregnant, not to work after they become eligible, or at least not to earn more income than the program's regulations allow them to earn without a reduction in benefits. Poor men, he argues, cooperate in this conspiracy by not marrying their girlfriends and, presumably, living at least in part on the AFDC income that the women earn. The result, Murray claims, has been a rapid growth in illegitimate births among the poor, in female-headed households, in unemployment, and in long-term welfare dependency. All of this is bad for society, but it is even worse for the people who have taken a free ride on welfare, because they are forgoing their chance to get jobs, form stable families, and otherwise improve their condition.

Murray's thesis makes perfect sense if we adopt a cynical view of human nature. Who wouldn't take a free ride? And many people readily stereotype the poor as lazy and improvident—the perfect customers for a free ride that gets them nowhere.

But if we look at how poor people actually behave, another picture emerges. Everyone who has studied the subject agrees that illegitimacy, female-headed households, and unemployment are higher now than they were when AFDC benefits were made more generous in the Johnson and Nixon years. But illegitimacy rates and the rate at which female-headed households were being formed were rising *before* the improvement in benefits as well. And over the last two decades these rates have been falling for blacks, who, Murray believes, are the group primarily dependent on welfare, while they have been increasing for whites.[23] If welfare is the cause of illegitimacy and female-headed households, how can this be true? Clearly, there are other factors at work.

Also, if higher benefits caused women to have children out of wedlock, we would expect that in states that pay lower benefits there would be less illegitimacy and fewer single-parent families than in states that pay high benefits. State benefit levels vary widely, and this creates an ideal "natural experiment" to test Murray's theory. Mary Jo Bane and David Ellwood of Harvard have researched this question.[24] Their findings show that there is *no* relationship whatsoever between the level of benefits paid by particular states and the rates of illegitimacy among poor women.

Probably the most damning evidence against Murray comes from the results of the Reagan administration's reforms in AFDC. In 1981 the administration substantially reduced the amount that AFDC mothers could earn without losing benefits and thereby made about half a million women ineligible for the program. To become eligible again, all these women had to do was to stop working, and most observers believed that they would. In fact, practically none of them did. They kept working at about the same rate they had worked before. Today many are poorer because of the loss of benefits, but they have not done what Murray's theory about AFDC predicts poor women typically do: work less or not at all in order to gain benefits.

The truth is that the reforms in the Johnson and Nixon years did, in fact, increase the AFDC rolls. That was what they were intended to do: make more single-parent families eligible, although many people believed that the work incentives built into those reforms (and since neglected) would eventually reduce the number of families needing help. Since the time when these newly eligible families entered the program, the number of AFDC recipients has varied little. And most recipients use the program only for a short time—to tide themselves over periods of unemployment or to adjust their lives to the responsibilities of a new child. Clearly large numbers of people have *not* become "dependent" on AFDC, and use of the program has *not* been on the increase.

In short, there is a powerful body of evidence to disprove the idea that AFDC and other programs induce poor women to take a free ride on welfare—evidence that neither Murray nor anyone else has been able to refute.[25] This does not mean that some people do not abuse the system. They probably do. It means that there is no systematic and widespread abuse.

It also does not mean that AFDC has no effect on work effort. The program is intended to have at least one major effect. Both Congress and the administrators of the program have believed until recently that women with very young children should not work—that they are more valuable to society if they devote their time to caring for their families. As a result, there has been very little effort to help those women find employment or to force them to work. Since many poor mothers with young children have few job skills and significant numbers would prefer to stay at home, it is not surprising that many are unemployed.

Obviously, if there were no AFDC program, a large number of poor women would have to find jobs. But the fact that many do not work is not a perverse and unexpected effect of the program. It is the intended result of public policy. In these circumstances, it is remarkable that AFDC has such a small effect on work effort: by most estimates it reduces hours worked by less than 10 percent.

Finally, refuting Murray's theories does not mean that we should be unconcerned about the problems of the welfare population in America or about the problems of the poor, generally. The numbers of illegitimate births and single parents as well as rates of unemployment among the poor *have* increased. About half of AFDC recipients at any point in time *are* heavily dependent on the program, in the sense that they have received benefits for eight years or more—although they make up only a small percentage of the people who passed through the program over that period of years. A large number of Americans *would* be poor today were it not for the benefits that AFDC and other government programs provide. These facts are grounds for serious concern. AFDC is not the cause of the problems afflicting America's poor, but the causes should be found and the problems solved.

It is equally important to realize that AFDC is not the solution to most problems of the poor. The program was never intended to "cure" poverty, in the sense of making its recipients more able or willing to fend for themselves. It has always had one purpose only: to protect the *children* of poor families by supplementing their families' incomes and providing them with more decent homes. The program achieves this goal: 7 million of the 11 million beneficiaries are children. Without AFDC benefits their circumstances would be even more tragic than they are today.

MYTH 4

Social programs primarily benefit one economic class: the poor, or the middle class, or the rich. They redistribute income to people who don't deserve or need it.

Both social critics and ordinary Americans like to talk about the social role in terms of "winners and losers." With all that money moving around, someone must come out on top. But people have different images of who the winners and losers are. The social role is sometimes denounced for redistributing the income of hard-working Americans to the (presumably undeserving) poor. Or it is criticized for being too fat with "middle-class entitlement" programs. Or it is excoriated for allowing the rich to get richer.

Whoever the winners and losers are, it seems that the social role can't do anything right: if it is wrong for the poor *or* the rich *or* the middle class to benefit from its programs, then the only way activist government could be doing the right thing would be for everyone to gain.

And of course, this is what happens. As the preceding chapter described in detail, there is no one in the United States, and no income group, that does not receive substantial benefits directly or indirectly from activist government. The social role comprises spending, incentive, and regulatory programs that are targeted to benefit the poor, the rich, the middle class, and, in many cases, to benefit everyone alike. Because this bias toward inclusiveness is built into our political system, the most meaningful answer to the question of who benefits is "everyone."

But people who are concerned with winners and losers mean something else: they mean that some income groups benefit more and pay less for the social role than others. This is certainly true, but depending on how the benefits and costs are measured, different groups turn up winners and losers.

If we ask simply, what income group pays the most taxes and gets the most benefits, the answer is easy—the middle class. Why? Simply because the United States is a middle-class country. The vast majority of Americans make incomes toward the middle of the income distribution. As a result it should be no surprise that middle-class Americans pay most of the taxes to support the social role: collectively they have most of the income in the United States. Nor should it be surprising that they reap most of the benefits.

A majority of federal social spending goes for the Social Security and Medicare programs, from which everyone benefits, but since most Americans are middle class, "everyone" is mainly middle-class people. A major part of the tax incentives provided by government is related to home ownership and employee benefits, which are mainly enjoyed by the middle class. Most government credit activities support housing, education, and agriculture, and again, the primary beneficiaries are middle-class people.

From this perspective, a large part of the social role exists primarily to protect middle-income Americans from downward economic and social mobility—to ensure that they remain middle class. Social Security, Medicare and government-subsidized pension plans help them to maintain their standard of living when they retire; unemployment insurance keeps their earnings from falling abruptly if they lose their jobs; housing incentives help them to hold on to the middle-class dream of home ownership; educational programs make it easier for their children to go to college and achieve a middle-class lifestyle.

Wealthy people, obviously, do not need these kinds of social supports, and poor people benefit from them much less than do members of the middle class. For example, poor people are unlikely to be protected by private pensions in addition to Social Security; they are less likely to qualify for Unemployment Insurance, to have the down payments for home ownership, or to be able to pay the costs that any family must bear for a college education, irrespective of government grants and loans. From this perspective, much of the social role is an enormous insurance policy for which only middle-class people can, or would want to, pay the premium.

But there is another way of looking at winners and losers according to which the poor and the rich come out winners. This view is based on asking what net effect social programs and the taxes that support them have on the incomes of different economic groups.

With regard to taxing, the answer on which most authorities agree is that the federal tax system has had only a very small effect on the distribution of national income, in the postwar period. Imagine, for example, that we divided the American public into five groups, with the richest 20 percent in the top group and poorest 20 percent in the bottom group and everyone else ranked by incomes in the groups between.[26] We would find that the richest group still had about the same percentage of all national income (about 45 percent) after taxes as it did at the beginning of the period, and the poorest still had about the same percentage (about 8 percent).

If we looked more closely, we would see that the richest of the rich (the top 1 percent) and the poorest of the poor had a slightly lower percentage of national income after taxes, but the effect on both groups was very small indeed—about a 1 to 3 percent reduction in their income shares in any given year. We would see, too, that the rich benefited from the Reagan tax cut of 1981, and taxes for the poor were significantly reduced by the tax reform of 1986. Overall, we would see that, for the vast majority of people, taxes have not had much effect on whether they are winners or losers in the American economic game.

If we look at government spending and taxing together, however, a different picture emerges. Although the poor pay about the same portion of their incomes in taxes as everyone else (and will pay a smaller portion after 1986), this does not amount to very much money, simply because they *are* poor. And they receive over $100 billion in federal benefits, far more than they pay in taxes, as a group. If we look at the middle class, we see that the least affluent middle-income people, the 20 percent with incomes just above the poor, receive about as much in government benefits as they pay in taxes, the next more affluent 20 percent pay a little more than they receive, and the top 20 percent of the middle class receive less than they pay. The rich—the top 20 percent of the income distribution—pay far more than they receive in benefits. So the poor are the winners—they gain more than they pay.

However, looked at another way, isn't it the rich who are the winners? After all, most Americans believe that rich people should pay not only more taxes than poor people but also a higher *percentage* of their incomes in taxes. We believe in a progressive tax system, and the American income tax is at least *nominally* progressive: according to the tax tables, people with higher incomes are supposed to pay at higher rates. Yet, as mentioned, the rich pay only a slightly higher percentage of their incomes in taxes than does everyone else. Although the 1986 reforms may make the American tax system somewhat more progressive, the net effect of taxes that supported the social role in the past has been to benefit the rich by providing them with exemptions and loopholes that allow them to avoid paying at a progressive rate.

In short, there is no single correct answer to the question of who wins and who loses from the social role. There is a sense in which everyone pays and everyone benefits, but there is also a sense in which the middle class mainly pays and benefits. Certainly the rich pay lower proportions of their incomes than a truly progressive tax system would demand. And certainly too the social role distributes about $100 billion to the poor, who pay only a small amount in taxes, although they pay a larger percentage of their incomes than they probably should.

The reason why there is no simple answer is also clear. Americans do not generally think of policies in terms of social or income classes. There are no working-class or upper-class parties in the United States. As a result the social role was not designed to benefit one class or another. It was designed by a politics of inclusiveness to benefit everyone. Most government activity is paid for by and benefits the middle class, the rich don't quite pay their fair share, and everyone subsidizes the poor in some way.

In a middle-class country with a social conscience, this combination is probably the only way everyone could possibly benefit. If income were transferred to the rich, or none was transferred to the poor, our social conscience would be outraged. And if the vast majority of people—the middle class—were not the primary focus of social programs, the programs could not possibly find the necessary political support.

If the United States were Dickensian England, where the political system was run by a few wealthy people who did not feel obliged to share their bounty, the outcome would be different. The poor would subsidize the rich and gain little from the social role. If our country were the Soviet Union after the Revolution, the poor majority would feel no compunction about benefiting at the expense of the rich and the middle class. But because ours is a middle-class nation with an inclusive tradition, everyone benefits from the social role in some way.

MYTH 5

Federal social programs discourage initiatives by other sectors of society. The business and voluntary sectors, families, and state and local governments do less than they might to help solve social problems, because their role has been preempted by federal activism.

It stands to reason that if the federal social role has expanded over the years, other institutions will do less as the federal government comes to do more. Or does it?

Economist Robert Lampman has undertaken the backbreaking task of measuring the rate of growth of "social welfare spending" by all institutions in the United States between 1950 and 1978.[27] By social welfare spending he means "cash benefits for income maintenance and in-kind benefits for health care, education, and a miscellaneous category of food, housing, and other welfare services." He finds that spending on these services by all sources—all levels of government, families, businesses, and voluntary organizations—increased from 17.2 percent of GNP in 1950 to 27.6 percent in 1978, an increase of about 60 percent. Spending by government programs (federal, state, and local) increased at a slightly higher rate: from 11.3 percent of GNP in 1950 to 19.6 percent in 1978, or 73 percent. Spending for corporate social welfare benefits increased faster than spending by government: from .7 percent of GNP in 1950 to 3.4 percent in 1978, or 385 percent. Philanthropic giving remained steady, at about .6 percent of GNP throughout this period. Interfamily giving declined slightly, from 4.7 percent of GNP in 1950 to 4.0 percent in 1978.

It is hard to imagine, from Lampman's numbers, that government spending discouraged corporate provision of social benefits, when corporate benefits increased five times faster than government outlays. In fact, as New York University professor Beth Stevens has shown, federal policy has had an enormous influence on the growth of corporate welfare systems.[28] The federal government has stimulated corporate welfare by providing tax incentives for company health and pension plans, by national policy in the areas of labor relations, and by price and wage constraints that encouraged unions to seek increased compensation in the form of fringe benefits.

Lampman's analysis does not provide a federal / state / local breakdown. But other sources indicate that in recent decades spending by states and localities from their own tax sources has risen more slowly than federal commitments, and there are indications that a few federal programs, such as grants for capital spending on wastewater treatment, have led to a reduction in effort by other levels of government.[29] Nevertheless, spending by states and localities from their own sources has continued to increase,

and there can be no doubt that the major intergovernmental programs initiated by the federal government, such as AFDC, Medicaid, and Unemployment Insurance, have stimulated most states
to invest far more in many areas of public service than they were
investing before. Nor can there be any doubt that in recent years
states and many localities have taken major initiatives in the areas
of education and economic development, often with little help
from Washington. In short, far from discouraging spending by
other levels of government, federal programs have often called
forth greater state and local efforts and federal activism has been
compatible with initiatives by other levels as well.

It is harder to tell whether the growth of activist government
has reduced philanthropic and interfamily giving. They have not
grown significantly as a portion of GNP since 1950, but they also
have not declined. There is some reason to question Lampman's
measures of family assistance, however. Neither he nor anyone
else has found a way to quantify what is probably the most important form of intrafamily giving—time. A large part of the contribution that families make to caring for children, handicapped
people, and the elderly consists of devoting time to providing
fairly simple but very vital forms of support. If children, the
dependent elderly, and the handicapped were cared for entirely in
institutions, rather than at home, a large part of the cost would be
for the time of teachers, nurses, and paraprofessionals. In his
accounting, Lampman does not include any measure of the value
of time that family members devote to caring for each other.

In the period from 1950 to 1978, much of the baby boom generation was born and passed through its formative years. This
must have called for an enormous increase in the time devoted to
caring for children at home. And toward the end of this period,
the number of elderly dependents began to increase in the United
States, creating a growing number of three- and even four-gen-
eration households—homes in which adults in their middle years
are simultaneously responsible for taking care of their children,
their parents and, often, their grandparents. There is, thus, reason
to believe that family contributions measured in nonmonetary terms
have increased since 1950.

But even if Lampman's figures are generally correct, they only tell part of the story, as he would be the first to admit. To evaluate the relationship between the social role and other institutions we need to know not only how levels of activity in the different sectors have changed, but also why they have changed. Most of the social programs measured by Lampman's figures had their origins in the Great Depression. The New Dealers who designed those programs, and other activists since, believed that the nation as a whole had to do far more to combat social distress. They thought that families, charities, and state and local governments had accomplished as much as they could and that only the national government could mobilize the necessary resources to accomplish more. The federal role, as activists have always envisioned it, is to supplement the efforts of families, charities, and other levels of government—to do more on top of the best efforts of these institutions.

The New Dealers and subsequent activists put forth the proposition that much of the growth in social services *should* come primarily at the federal level, rather than from other sources. They argued that Americans should develop a more vigorous response to the need for public goods and to such problems as poverty, illness, and unemployment, not primarily by giving more to charity or by providing greater help to their family members but by paying taxes. And the nation has ratified this idea whenever it has been put to the test in elections and opinion polls. Politicians who have proposed dismantling major aspects of the social role have not fared well, and a solid majority of Americans consistently has endorsed these programs in surveys conducted over the postwar decades.

The result of this national decision to expand social services largely by provision at the federal level is that private effort has been maintained, but the major growth in overall national effort has come from federal programs. This is the national idea of government at work—the people as a whole taking responsibility for major common problems through the federal government, rather than leaving those problems entirely to individuals or groups.

Does this mean that federal activism has discouraged family efforts and charitable giving? To discourage people is to dissuade them from doing something they want to do. If the American people have elected to make increasing use of federal provision of social services, rather than to make increasing use of family or charitable services, it is hard to argue that they have been discouraged. They have simply made a choice. In these circumstances, people who argue that the federal government has discouraged other institutions from contributing to social welfare are, in effect, arguing not about facts but about values. Their argument comes down to the contention that other institutions *should* do more and that the federal government *should* do less, rather than that federal programs have placed a damper on other institutions.

There is little evidence that the federal government has "crowded out" other efforts. Rather, it has sometimes encouraged, sometimes supplemented, and sometimes built on top of them. None of this has been done mysteriously in the dark of the night. It has been done with the approval of the American people.

MYTH 6

Business or the voluntary sector could do a better job than the federal government of providing many public services. Much of the social role could and should be privatized.

"Privatization" is a new term that entered the nation's political vocabulary during the recent period of reassessment to represent a very old idea.[30] It has long been an article of faith for many Americans that business and the voluntary sector are inherently more efficient, more productive, and more responsive to public demands than government. This belief is part of the bias against government that cuts across our political culture.

Advocates of "privatization" draw the conclusion that one way to break the current stalemate in public policy is to turn over more of government's functions to the private sector. This idea has served as a rallying point for conservatives, who reject much of the activist tradition. And it has aroused the interest of many other people who are disappointed by the performance of government in recent years.

In fact, privatization is a political mirage: the closer we examine it, the less substance it has. It does not provide a way out of the current stalemate or even advance the debate very far. After wrestling with the phantom, we are left with the same difficult choices about the social role that we faced before.

The major reason privatization is not a useful idea is that, at the national level of government, there is very little to privatize. With a few exceptions, the federal government does not deliver services to the American people. Rather, it provides cash benefits and vouchers to individuals who buy medical care and food from the private sector; it subsidizes home building by private companies; it contracts with construction firms for public works; and it makes grants to states and localities to deliver a variety of personal social services. Commonly, state and local governments, in turn, contract with voluntary agencies, such as Blue Cross or Catholic Charities. In fact, over half the government-funded social services in the United States are delivered by private nonprofit institutions.

What is left to privatize? There are, of course, the numerous technical and support functions required to keep the federal government running—such as data processing, printing, and building maintenance—that are currently performed by civil servants. Evidence from the experience of state and local governments indicates that contracting out for some of these can reduce costs and improve quality.

Privatization of technical and support functions—"petty privatization"—is certainly worth considering, but it does not raise or resolve any serious questions of public policy. The issues surrounding it are issues of public administration, rather than concerns about the purposes and directions of the social role. If contracting out can improve data processing, housekeeping, and the rest, why not give it a try?

Privatization of this sort raises few difficulties because the only question that has to be answered is whether government employees or private contractors can most effectively reach some fairly straightforward, measurable goal—such as processing a certain number of checks per hour at the lowest possible cost. The goal remains the same whether public or private institutions are employed; the only issue is how best to achieve it.

But there is another version of "privatization" that does raise serious policy concerns. Because the federal government is only one institution among many that support social services, there is always some private sector alternative to anything it does. As a result, we can always imagine some way in which the federal role could be diminished—either by turning over the few services that it does provide to some other institution or by providing them in a way that relies more on the private sector. And this is precisely what some critics of activist government have proposed under the banner of privatization.

For example, the federal government does, in fact, provide health services through the Veterans Administration and the Public Health Service. Why not sell the VA hospitals to health care companies, let the doctors enter private practice, and provide for needy veterans and public health beneficiaries by the Medicaid or Medicare systems? The federal government also owns some large physical assets—Amtrak, public lands, national parks. Why not sell off Amtrak and the public lands (which are mostly leased to private users in any event) and let private concessionaires manage the public parks? The federal government subsidizes public schools and public housing projects through grants to needy areas. Why not give poor people educational or housing vouchers and let them shop around for the best deal?

Most challenging of all is the notion that, in the Social Security retirement and Medicare systems and in many of its credit activities, the federal government implicitly acts as an enormous insurance company. Why not drop Social Security and Medicare programs for rich and middle-income people who can afford to invest their contributions to those systems in private retirement and health care plans? Public welfare programs could be retained to provide for everyone else. And why not let private financial institutions take over the insurance functions of the FHA, VA,

FDIC, and other federal agencies that guarantee credit?

Of course we could do these things, but why *should* we? One standard answer that advocates of privatization give is that privatization of this sort would make for greater efficiency. Because business and the voluntary sector are more efficient in delivering goods and services, the American people would have more of the public services that they want at a higher quality and a more reasonable price if we turned these and other government activities over to the private sector.

The reason for privatizing major government programs is represented to be the same as the reason for petty privatization: the goals of public policy—adequate health care, income security, and so forth—would not change, but the nation would achieve them in a more effective way.

There are two problems with this answer. First, it draws a false comparison between an idealized private sector and the realities of government. If we look more carefully at the performance of public and private institutions, it is hard to support any across-the-board conclusion that the private sector is more efficient. It is true that many private companies are managed extremely well. But in recent years the nation has witnessed the stumbling of corporate giants, such as Lockheed, Chrysler, and Bendix, and the faltering of many private financial institutions—most due in some degree to mismanagement. The nation also has witnessed revelations of fraud, waste, and abuse by major defense contractors. Whatever the shortcomings of government, the private sector often performs very badly as well.

There is also a large body of evidence that directly compares public and private providers of social services. Contrary to popular belief, there is no evidence that for-profit hospitals, on average, provide better or worse service than nonprofit hospitals do for the same price.[31] And, taking account of quality of service as well as price, for-profit daycare centers are apparently not superior to nonprofit or publicly operated facilities.[32] Experiments in the 1970s with contracting out the management of public schools to private companies were terminated because the results were disastrous. And we are now living with one of the forms of private sector provision that privatizers would like to expand: private medical insurance for the elderly. Medicare currently covers only 45 percent of the acute health care costs of senior citizens and almost none of their long-term care costs. A number of companies offer "medigap" policies to pay the rest. How well does the market perform in this case? Not very well. The medigap market sells policies that cover expectable costs but typically fail to cover the major risks to which Medicare beneficiaries remain exposed.[33] And the price of many medigap policies is inflated by excessive overhead.

Many nonprofit, voluntary institutions are also very well managed. But after a four-year survey of nonprofit agencies in the United States, political scientist Lester Salamon concluded that there is widespread "voluntary sector failure"—amateurism, narrowness of vision, and poor administration in a broad range of institutions.[34] Direct comparisons between public and nonprofit providers of services show strengths and weaknesses on both sides.

But there is a yet more difficult problem in comparing public and private sector performance. The conditions under which they work are different. Government programs often operate under funding constraints that would not prevail in the private sector. For example, government computers lag behind state-of-the-art equipment used in the private sector because for many years Congress refused to appropriate funds to upgrade federal data-processing systems. Government programs cannot pick and choose their clients as can private concerns. Public schools are often worse than private schools because they must be nonselective. In education, as in many other areas, the private sector appears to provide better services because it can skim off the easy problems and leave government with the hard cases. Finally, government programs are often tangled with regulations and paperwork, because most people expect greater accountability for the way that public funds are spent than most corporations would demand of their operating units.

In short, one reason why it is wrong to assume that privatizing major government programs would improve them is that the evidence about efficiency is mixed. We cannot take it for granted that business and the voluntary sector would provide better services at a lower cost, and we certainly cannot take this for granted if they had to operate within the same cost and performance constraints that bind government.

The second reason why privatizing major public services raises difficulties is that it is emphatically *not* analogous to petty privatization. If we privatized government printing operations, the goal of government—producing documents to specifications—would remain the same; only the means would change. If we privatized Social Security, the Veterans Administration, or other major services, both the means and the goal of policy would be altered. Privatization of major services would change the nature of those services in very important ways.

For example, most of the major services targeted for privatization are "inefficient" in strictly business terms because they contain subsidies. In Social Security and Medicare wealthier contributers subsidize the poor and active workers subsidize retirees; in credit programs, all taxpayers subsidize certain favored activities; in education and housing grants, subsidies are targeted at certain institutions; in the management of Amtrak and public lands certain users are subsidized. Privatization would create different types of services, not just shift responsibility for the existing ones, precisely because it would do away with subsidies, at least in their present form.

In many cases, eliminating subsidies would create the problem that economists and actuaries call "adverse selection." Private companies providing health care, pensions, or education would have an incentive to discriminate in favor of those people who are least expensive to serve. For example, while Medicare currently covers almost all elderly people and charges them all the same premium, any private sector company that developed an equivalent service would find it most profitable to insure only the healthiest retirees, or to charge very high rates to the least healthy (and probably, on average, the least able to pay). The elderly would still be offered health-care insurance, but the nature of that insurance would be radically different if the system were privatized.

Another way in which privatizing major programs would fundamentally change their nature arises from the fact that those programs are based on promises by the federal government to deliver certain services—to pay Social Security benefits or back up its insurance of financial institutions. People may be skeptical about these promises, but in light of the mixed performance of the American economy in recent years and the failure of many private pension funds and financial institutions, they should also be skeptical about how much they can rely on private sector alternatives. In any event, privatization would change the nature of the guarantee behind what are now public programs—from a guarantee that citizens can enforce through holding public officials accountable at elections to the more elusive guarantees of the free market. And if anyone doubts that the political guarantee works, he should recall the political firestorm that descended on the Reagan administration when it proposed to reduce Social Security benefits in 1982 or tighten eligibility for disability benefits in 1981.

In a larger sense, privatizing major public services would transform them from being undertakings for which the *whole* public has responsibility and which are *open* and *accountable* to all citizens into undertakings for which each individual or *closed, private* companies, not necessarily accountable to the public, have responsibility.

The major issue raised by privatization, then, is not the issue of efficiency. It is whether certain services are important enough to the general welfare that the whole nation should take responsibility for providing them and whether provision should be public, open, and accountable to everyone. People who advocate privatization by and large do not believe that this is the case with regard to Social Security, veterans' benefits, public schools, public housing, and various financial incentives.

But seen in this way, privatization disappears entirely as a separate issue. It becomes a host of different issues about whether government should be in the business of providing various services, not whether somebody else can do the same job better.

Comparing public and private sector alternatives is like comparing apples and oranges. Do we want a universal, publicly accountable old age retirement system that subsidizes the poor, or not? The major consideration in deciding whether we want to maintain the Social Security system is not whether it is more efficient than some private sector alternative. The major consideration is what *type* of retirement protection we want to provide.

There are, then, two major myths about privatization. The first is that the private sector is necessarily more efficient than government in delivering services. On this point the evidence is mixed. The second myth is that turning over responsibility for major public programs to the private sector would result in better services in some other way. The truth is that privatization would result in *different* services. Whether they would be better depends on a host of value judgments that theories of privatization do not help us make.

Yet as the federal social role has evolved over the last two hundred years, Americans have been making those value judgments. By and large they have been made in a pragmatic way: a public problem is identified, and the political system wrestles with the issue of how best to solve it, consistent with national values and practical constraints. In America, unlike some other countries, there has rarely been a general assumption that public solutions—creating new government programs or agencies—are best. As noted, there is a powerful strand in the American character that presumes exactly the opposite. And, as also noted, whenever American *do* adopt public solutions they bend over backwards to include the private sector as a partner with government in providing social services.

What has been the verdict of the nation after two hundred years of pragmatic decision-making on an issue-by-issue basis? The federal social role has gradually grown throughout our history. We have found that an increasing number of functions can be performed best by the public sector. In part, this has been due to the failure of the private sector to perform important functions as well as the American people's belief that they should be performed. That is the reason why many issues were placed on the public agenda to begin with. For example, private sector failure is why we developed Social Security and Medicare, as well as why the government owns Amtrak and extensive public lands. In part, too, the reason for growth in the public sector is simply that in an increasingly complex and interdependent society, Americans have decided that they prefer to have major common services performed by an institution that is open, public, and accountable to the nation as a whole—they simply trust government more when it comes to these vital concerns. Finally, part of the reason is doubtless that, in our complex society, many of the functions the American people want to see performed—such as providing retirement benefits to everyone—require the scope and resources of national government, and many of the values that they wish to see embedded in those functions—such as subsidies to low-income people—can be performed better by government, than by companies that must look to the bottom line.

For whatever reason, Americans have progressively rejected private sector alternatives, in a pragmatic, nonideological way. Advocates of privatization, therefore, can be faulted not only because they contribute little to the public policy debate. To the extent that they are saying anything at all, they are swimming against the tide of American history and advocating an across-the-board ideological preference for private sector provision that is alien to our political culture.

MYTH 7

The Social Security System is bankrupt. The baby boom generation will not be able to depend on it when its members retire.

This is an easy myth to debunk because it is based entirely on unfounded rumor. In 1981 and 1982 there were widespread media reports of a "crisis" in the Social Security pension fund. The reports claimed that Social Security was running out of money and that Congress was deadlocked over how to solve the problem. That was apparently about as far as many Americans read. There were subsequent reports that the system had somehow been fixed, but the rumors of a "crisis" and of a system teetering on the brink of bankruptcy that began in 1981 and 1982 have never been entirely dispelled.

In fact, the early 1980s were just one of many occasions on which the Social Security system has been adjusted to keep up with changing circumstances.[35] These adjustments have been necessary because of the way in which its finances are structured. Social Security is a "pay as you go" plan. Payroll tax contributions by active workers and their employers are used to provide benefits to retirees. In the past, only a small reserve fund has been maintained—usually about enough to pay one year's benefits if anything goes wrong. Social Security is also an indexed pension plan. After years of congressionally mandated increases, a benefit level was established in 1972 and indexed to inflation. Each year in which the inflation rate increases, benefits are automatically raised to make up for the inflation that has occurred since the last increase.

Because it is a "pay as you go" system indexed for inflation, Social Security has always been extremely sensitive to the performance of the American economy. In times of high unemployment and sagging wages, payroll tax contributions fall. In times of high inflation, benefits rise. In normal circumstances these effects come close to offsetting each other: periods of high unemployment usually are accompanied by low inflation, and high inflation usually is accompanied by low levels of unemployment and rising wages.

In the late 1970s and early 1980s the nation experienced a prolonged period of "stagflation": high inflation combined with high unemployment. Stagflation threw the Social Security System off balance. Benefits rose and contributions to support the system fell. By 1982 the reserve was draining away.

Problems of keeping contributions and benefits in balance have arisen before, usually because of congressionally mandated changes in benefits, coverage, or management of the system. Congress has usually been unwilling to deal with these problems on its own, because the solution to them generally involves some change in taxes, benefits, or both. The customary way to handle issues of Social Security financing has been to convene a commission of experts.

And that is what happened in 1983. A commission was established under the chairmanship of economist Alan Greenspan. It would have been fairly easy for the members to deal with the immediate problem. By 1983 stagflation was abating, and a small increase in the payroll tax would have secured the reserve. But the Greenspan Commission was exceptionally farsighted. It went beyond its mandate and looked at the next fifty years.

The commission observed that demographic changes were certain to create future problems for Social Security. Between the mid-1980s and about 2010, the number of workers contributing to the system will increase much faster than the number of retirees. This is because the work force will consist primarily of members of the large baby boom generation, whereas retirees will be members of the relatively small generation born during the Great Depression. Around 2010, however, the numbers will reverse. The baby boomers will begin to retire and the active workers will be their children. But because members of the baby boom generation have not had as many children as their parents did, there will be fewer active workers to support each retiree.

Because of this "demographic twist" the Social Security System was headed for trouble. If it continued to operate as a "pay as you go system" with a small reserve, payroll taxes would not have to be raised in the 1990s, because the numbers of workers will be so large relative to the number of retirees. But if this happened, payroll taxes would have to increase abruptly and to very high levels when the baby boom generation retires.

The Greenspan Commission decided that the nation should begin to prepare for the retirement of the baby boomers before it occurred. As a result of its recommendations and subsequent deliberations by the administration and Congress, several major changes were made in Social Security. Rather than plan for low payroll taxes in the 1990s, the architects of these changes scheduled several tax increases between 1983 and 2010. They also planned to raise additional revenues by extending coverage to government workers and raising the age of eligibility for full benefits gradually so that it would reach sixty-seven by 2003. The result of these measures is that by the time the baby boom generation retires, the system will accumulate an enormous reserve—about $2 trillion.

This reserve will make it possible for the smaller "baby bust" generation that follows to pay for the retirement of the baby boomers without an enormous increase in their contributions.

In effect, the architects of these changes devised a system by which the baby boom generation would finance a large part of its own retirement. Over the next thirty years, at least, Social Security will be less of a "pay as you go" system and more like a funded annuity. The reserve is deposited in government securities. One interesting result is that by 2010 the Social Security system will own a large part of the national debt.[36]

Because of the changes stimulated by the Greenspan Commission, the Social Security retirement system is safe for as far as the eye can see. Only catastrophic economic developments could derail it. Speculation about its future more than thirty to forty years from now involves predictions about the overall state of our economy well into the twenty-first century, which no one can make with any confidence. The baby boomers can rely on Social Security as surely as they can rely on anything in the future and more surely than they can rely on most things. It was redesigned specifically to ensure that their benefits would be secure.

6

In Arrears

"That the American nation is a great nation, in some particulars the greatest the world ever saw, we hold to be true, and are as ready to maintain as anyone can be; but . . . it is lamentably in arrears to its own avowed principles."[1] That was James Fenimore Cooper's verdict on his country in 1838, and it is a fair verdict today.

The preceding chapters may seem to give a clean bill of health to the federal social role. That is not their intention. Rather, their purpose is to debunk false diagnoses of what ails activist government in the United States so that we can come to grips with its real problems.

There can be no doubt that those problems are severe. When the myths and misconceptions that have clouded perceptions of activist government are put aside, a troubled reality comes to light. The social policy landscape is littered with half-measures, neglected issues, inequities, and questionable priorities. The policymaking process seems destined to perpetuate these problems, rather than set them right. Activist government has accomplished a great deal, but its accomplishments are too often incomplete. It addresses many problems, but it addresses too few of them thoroughly enough.

A great many of these concerns boil down to the question of adequacy: whether the social role provides solutions to the common problems of American life that are commensurate both with the nature of those problems and with our national values. While questions of adequacy by no means exhaust the shortcomings of current social policy, they are the issues of most immediate concern to the majority of Americans, and they provide a good pathway to explore other major concerns.

Of course, the adequacy of social programs is a question on which people can and often do differ. But there are some major failings that it is reasonable to suppose would offend the vast majority of Americans. The full litany of these shortcomings is long and dreary. But their nature and severity can be illustrated by a quick look at the two areas of social policy that most people consider best developed and most adequate to meet the nation's needs: health care and pensions.

Health Care

The financial risks of ill health potentially threaten everyone. And there is ample evidence that most Americans would like to guard against these risks by prepaying their health care costs through some form of insurance. A superficial look at the social role suggests that, directly or indirectly, the federal government provides fairly complete protection against the costs of health care through a system of interlocking programs.

Most retirees receive protection from Medicare, a contributory social insurance program. For retirees too poor or otherwise ineligible to participate in Medicare, we have Medicaid—government assistance that is based entirely on financial need. Medicaid benefits also are extended to other large categories of the poor— the blind, disabled, AFDC recipients, and impoverished elderly citizens requiring long-term care. Most active workers receive medical insurance through federally subsidized plans provided by their employers. The federal government also maintains the extensive Veterans Administration health care system, which offers virtually every form of medical service to disabled or elderly former servicemen. And it subsidizes the cost of hospital construction, the training of physicians, and other components of the health care system. Finally, as an employer, the federal government manages health insurance plans for over 1 million civilian employees and provides medical care to 10 million active or retired military personnel and their dependents.

But despite this elaborate system of protection, over 35 million Americans were not covered by health care insurance of any kind in 1986—an increase from 28 million in 1978—and over 17 percent of those under sixty-five were unprotected.[2]

Who are these people? The overwhelming majority—two-thirds to three-fourths—are the working poor—people with low incomes who hold down jobs at the minimum wage or less in the thousands of small businesses that do not offer private health plans, or people who fail to qualify for corporate plans because they are part-time workers.[3] Or they are the dependents of low-wage workers. Often dependents are not covered by private medical plans, or they are only covered if the worker can afford a substantial additional premium. In 1983, 4.1 million dependents of *insured* workers were not covered.[4] Many others are unemployed—people who have temporarily lost corporate health care coverage.

Many of the unemployed and the working poor cannot afford to buy individual health insurance and yet are too well off to qualify for Medicaid—which serves only those who have virtually no income or assets. These are people who are doing "the right thing" by the standards of most Americans—they are working or trying to work, rather than living on charity or welfare. But they fall between the cracks of present systems for providing protection against medical costs.

Other Americans without health coverage span a wide range of the unfortunate in our society: street people, certain groups of the elderly who do not qualify for Medicare or Medicaid, single parents, and children who for a variety of reasons fall outside the detailed eligibility standards for public or private programs. For example, over 100,000 virtually indigent elderly people confined to nursing homes and mental hospitals are currently ineligible for Medicaid because the imputed value of their institutional care increases their assets slightly above the limit for eligibility.

These and other uninsured people are in serious trouble. Modern medical services are fabulously expensive, especially for illnesses of long duration. Without insurance coverage, few people can afford them.

What do 35 million Americans without health care coverage do? Many go without medical services except in dire emergencies, and this leads not only to suffering from acute conditions but also to chronic ill health. Numerous studies have shown that members of most groups not covered by health insurance are far more likely to suffer from chronic conditions than are members of the population as a whole. And, of course, poor health contributes to other social and economic problems. People are less able to hold a job, maintain a household, and carry out family responsibilities if they are chronically ill, and they are more likely to become charges on society.

In the case of serious illness, most people without health insurance sooner or later end up in hospital emergency rooms, where the cost of caring for them becomes a direct public responsibility. Too often these facilities are overcrowded and underfunded, and indigent patients are shifted from hospital to hospital, sometimes with tragic results. Although the cost of uncompensated care by hospitals more than doubled between 1980 and 1985, reaching $7.4 billion, it has been estimated that over one million people are turned away each year because of lack of ability to pay.[5] The unspeakable conditions of medical care in some emergency rooms and individual horror stories of people who have died or been permanently injured after they were turned away because of lack of insurance occasionally make newspaper headlines. But these are part of the day-to-day reality for millions of Americans at the bottom of the health care system. For them the stories and statistics are literally life and death problems.

What of the people who are covered by government or private medical plans? Many of them do not fare very well either. For example, eligibility for Medicaid services is largely determined by state governments. As a result, depending on where they live, poor Americans may or may not receive help. In 1980, 20 percent of poor children in Wyoming received Medicaid benefits, compared with 74 percent in the District of Columbia, and other states covered the full spectrum in between. In 1985, the monthly income that a family of four could not exceed without losing full Medicaid eligibility ranged from 17 percent of the poverty level in Alabama to 91 percent in Alaska.[6] In fact, Medicaid serves largely as a backup system for Medicare. In 1984, only about 25 percent of its payments went to the nonelderly poor.[7]

The quality of service available to Medicaid recipients also varies greatly. State plans differ in the rate of reimbursement to physicians that they allow and the services they cover. Often the reimbursement is below the prevailing level of physicians' fees. As a result, many doctors are reluctant to accept Medicaid patients or to provide them with services that are not covered by state plans. Prosaic as it may sound, podiatry is generally not covered by Medicaid. This matters a great deal for poor, elderly people who cannot walk to the grocery store or carry out other daily living tasks because of what are often fairly simple foot problems.

Medicare, too, offers only limited coverage. It provides almost full payment, minus deductibles, for sixty days of hospitalization and reimbursement for physicians' services to those who pay a supplementary premium. In 1986 Medicare patients paid $492 for the first day of hospitalization and $123 per day from the sixty-first to the ninetieth day of a hospital stay. Moreover, the program does not provide any coverage at all for many health-care costs, such as prescription drugs, and there is no requirement that doctors accept its reimbursement as full payment for their services. In fact, in 1982 about 80 percent of Medicare patients who filed claims were charged some additional amount by their physicians, and Medicare beneficiaries paid $29 billion out of their own pockets for doctor bills in 1984.[8]

If we add up all of these limitations, it becomes clear that Medicare provides only partial protection against the costs of ill health. And because of limits to its coverage, the costs incurred by anyone with a long-term "catastrophic illness," such as cancer, can be ruinous. Even recent proposals to cover catastrophic illness would still require patients to pay as much as $2,000 per year, an amount that would be financially crippling for the large portion of retirees who live below or near to the poverty line.[9]

Also Medicare covers only short stays in nursing homes, and nursing home care is extremely expensive—between $1,500 and $3,000 per month. The number of people using these facilities has increased dramatically in recent years, but the nation has yet to find a satisfactory way to pay for the resulting increase in cost. Medicare pays for only 2 percent of nursing home care, and private insurance pays for only about 1 percent.[10] Chronically ill people who require extended nursing home care must either have substantial personal resources or pauperize themselves by "spending down" their assets to the point where they are indigent enough to be eligible for Medicaid. In recent years, some retirees have become so desperate about this situation that they have divorced their spouses solely to meet the Medicaid income test or set up family trusts to meet paper definitions of poverty.[11]

Family tragedies caused by catastrophic health costs are not something that only happen to someone else. In 1986, the National Center for Health Services Research (NCHSR) reported that one in five American households suffered catastrophic costs—defined as out-of-pocket costs beyond those covered by public or private health systems that exceeded 5 percent of gross income.[12] About one-third of these households had incomes below the poverty line, less than half were headed by people employed all year, and a third were headed by people over sixty-five years of age. Some 3.3 million families had out-of-pocket medical expenses that exceeded 20 percent of their gross income.

And the problem of costs is not limited to those families that experience catastrophic illness. ICF, Inc., a Washington consulting firm that specializes in health care issues, estimated that in 1986 the *average* elderly household will incur medical and related costs of $8,340, about $2,670 of which will come out of the family's own pocket.[13]

The elderly can guard against rising medical costs by purchasing "medigap" insurance policies. And federal law now requires that, if they are retired, their former employers must allow them to continue to participate in corporate plans until they are sixty-nine. But the NCHSR figures, as well as other studies, suggest that employer coverage is often unavailable or too limited and that "medigap" policies are either beyond the means of millions of retirees or inadequate to meet their needs. Also, an increasing number of financially troubled companies have backed out of their commitment to provide health care coverage to former employees.[14]

The same figures suggest that active workers do not always fare well when it comes to health insurance. A 1984 survey of 1,200 companies found that only 42 percent offered plans providing full hospital cost reimbursement, down from 67 percent in 1982. Blue Cross and other commercial policies typically pay only 60 percent of consumers' total health care cost.[15] The coverage provided by many smaller employers is often so inadequate that some policymakers are reluctant to consider extending Medicaid eligibility for fear of competing with them. And while many corporate plans are exemplary, coverage often ends when an employee leaves his job. This means that many of the 7 percent of Americans who are unemployed are not covered by any form of health care insurance. And many corporate plans require a "waiting period" upon reemployment. For these and other reasons, the number of people covered by employer plans has been decreasing. According to one study, about one million fewer people were covered in 1983 than 1982.[16]

What does this collection of problems add up to? Those Americans who work steadily at a good job and retire with a good pension, some personal assets, and possibly a continuation of their employer's health insurance plan are well cared for by the American medical system. But there is an unlucky minority—the 35 million uncovered and the many more inadequately covered by public or private plans—for whom illness is a financial as well as a physical disaster. And their numbers have been increasing steadily in recent years.

The national bill for medical care has been increasing as well. Whereas in 1965 we spent 6 percent of GNP on health services, in 1986 we spent over 11 percent—or over $1 billion per day. Increased availability, new technologies, greater utilization of services, and, to some degree, profiteering by health practitioners have all contributed to the phenomenal growth of national spending on medical care. So has the design of most public and private health care payment systems. Typically they encourage the overuse of expensive hospital and nursing home care by not reimbursing providers for outpatient services or community-based care in many circumstances or by setting reimbursement rates that make institutional care more profitable than the alternatives. Also, until recently, most payment systems gave a blank check to doctors and hospitals by promising to pay for virtually any services at "prevailing" rates. Finally, with the exception of the small and underfunded Public Health Service, public and private health care systems make little investment in preventive medicine and contain few incentives for people to practice simple preventive measures—such as controlling their weight and stopping smoking.

Activist government has accelerated the growth of the nation's health care bill by increasing availability and utilization of services through Medicare, Medicaid, hospital construction grants, and subsidies to private plans, by adopting systems of reimbursement that allow excessive charges and encourage the most costly forms of care, and by providing much of the support for research and development that has led to new medical technologies.

Twenty years ago, when federal involvement in health care began to increase dramatically, only a few people envisioned the explosion in health care costs that has occurred in recent years. Today the federal government, states, and corporations are beginning to take steps to limit the rate of growth in the nation's health care bill, apparently with some effectiveness and with little harm to the quality of care. The fact that it has taken the nation twenty years to get around to confronting the problem of health care costs is, however, a monument to lack of foresight and poor planning in one of the most vital areas of the federal social role. The rising cost of health care obviously diverts national resources from other important priorities. But it has another harmful effect as well: as health care becomes more expensive, larger numbers of the poor and the uninsured are unable to afford it at all or have to settle for second-rate service.

Pensions

Like the nation's health care system, the system for providing retirement income that activist government has constructed or subsidized appears to be quite comprehensive, if we give it only a superficial glance. That system rests on four pillars of protection. To begin with, almost every retiree receives Social Security benefits. In 1985, the average annual benefit for a retiree and spouse was $9,767, somewhat more than the government's rock-bottom standard of poverty level income for an elderly couple, which was $6,503 in that year.[17] Many Americans supplement Social Security with private pension plans that are subsidized, regulated, and insured by the federal government. Many also have private savings for their retirement, some of which take the form of tax-deferred IRA and KEOGH plans. Finally, for the impoverished elderly who are inadequately protected by these means, the federal government provides SSI (Supplemental Security Income)—an income support program based on financial need.

For most Americans, this four-part system works fairly well. Social Security has delivered on its promises in the past and will continue to do so in the future. But what about private pensions? The ERISA legislation of 1974 guaranteed the pension rights of any employee who has been enrolled in a private pension plan for at least ten years (reduced to five years in the tax reform legislation of 1986), thereby correcting a scandalous situation in which workers were sometimes cheated out of their pension by either unethical practices on the part of employers or their bankruptcy.

Nonetheless, in 1984 less than 30 percent of employed Americans had vested rights in private pension plans.[18] Of the 70 percent without such rights, some had not worked for employers with company pension plans long enough to become vested, and the great majority simply worked for employers that did not offer pension benefits at all. Among today's retirees only about 24 percent are drawing private pensions—showing what a major role Social Security plays in the support of the elderly. With the vesting period now reduced to five years, more retirees will have private pensions in the future—possibly as many as 60–70 percent of currently employed Americans, although many of these pensions will be very small. The other 30–40 percent will be unsupported by this pillar in the national retirement system.

Projections of adequacy in private pensions assume that the companies which provide them are still around when retirement time arrives. Since the ERISA legislation, the government has assumed the unfunded pension liabilities of more than one thousand companies.[19] The ERISA system generally accepts these obligations, but this provides no help to those people who have not achieved vested rights at the time of termination. And a large number of the companies that have terminated plans have stayed in business—swelling the number of firms that provide no retirement benefits to their workers.

What about private savings? As many economists have noted with concern, the rate of personal savings in the United States has fallen in recent years. This is in spite of the tax incentives offered by IRA and KEOGH accounts, which apparently often lead people only to transfer savings they would make anyway into tax-exempt instruments. Unless these trends change, the third pillar of the retirement system will become increasingly shaky.

There is always SSI, and sometimes it works extremely well. If you are an individual poor enough to qualify for the program (which generally means that you have virtually no income or assets other than your home) *and* if the state in which you reside generously supplements federal SSI benefits (forty-three states provide some supplement), *and* if you receive a Social Security benefit as well as food stamps, your total income (counting the cash value of the food stamps) will approach 100 percent of the poverty line.[20] But if, due to any of the numerous quirks of any of these programs, you do not receive full, or any, benefits from all of them, your income from SSI alone can be as low as 76 percent of the poverty level.

How well do our national retirement programs work? Almost 14 percent of elderly Americans live in poverty, and more than 20 percent live less than 25 percent above the poverty line. The poverty rate among the elderly is slightly lower than the rate for the total population, but a higher percentage of the elderly are near-poor (20.9 percent as opposed to 18.7 percent for the total population).[21] And who are the poorest among the elderly? They are disproportionately the last people in the world for whom most Americans would like to see the retirement system fail: single (usually widowed) women over the age of seventy-two, 47 percent of whom had incomes under $5,000 in 1985, and 85 percent under $10,000.

Moreover, for most Americans a decent retirement system is not simply one that will keep them out of poverty. Most would like to maintain something approaching their preretirement standard of living in their later years. The four pillars of the American system make this possible for many people—the most recent available data indicate that 57 percent of current retirees have incomes between 60 and 150 percent of what they earned in their last working years.[22] But a distressing 43 percent have considerably lower incomes, and the indications are that for most Americans retirement security rests primarily on one pillar of the system: in 1984, three-fifths of elderly households in the United States relied on Social Security for at least half of their income.[23]

Our national retirement system works quite well for most Americans, but for the aged poor and for the many millions more with unfulfilled expectations, it falls short of adequacy. In addition, the unreliability of many private pensions and reduced rate of private savings do not bode well for the future. Americans realize this. A 1985 survey by Yankelovich, Skelly and White indicates that a significant number of people would like to see Social Security benefits raised.[24]

Other Problems

Virtually every area of American social policy is plagued with inadequacies. Newspaper headlines blare out some of the most telling facts. These examples are from the *New York Times* and the *Washington Post:*

"HUNGER, HOMELESS UP STEEPLY"

"WELFARE BENEFITS VARY AMONG STATES"

"CONDITIONS OF RURAL HUNGER DETAILED"

"MANY QUIT FARMING AS CREDIT CRISIS DIMS HOPES"

"RECOVERY IRRELEVANT TO WORKERS LEFT BEHIND"

"WHITE GRIP ON SOUTHERN SCHOOLS: KEEPING CONTROL"

In the best-housed nation in the world, where the federal government provides hundreds of billions of dollars per year in credit incentives to facilitate home ownership and almost $10 billion per year to low-income housing, over 300,000 people were homeless in 1985, and only about one-fourth of low-income families received subsidized housing assistance.[25] Moreover, members of the baby boom generation were less likely than their parents to be able to afford to buy their own home.

Benefits for major social programs vary widely across the nation. In 1986 an AFDC family of three would have received $120 per month in benefits if they lived in Mississippi and $587 per month if they lived in California (a five-to-one differential); and an unemployed individual would have received $139 per week in the District of Columbia, but only $67 in Arkansas, a two-to-one differential.[26] Both differences are far greater than regional variations in the cost of living, and all of these benefit levels would have left the recipients below the poverty line, even when the value of the food stamps they received is included.

The protection provided by Unemployment Insurance is not only uneven, its duration is also inadequate to tide people over the increasingly long spells of joblessness that many of today's unemployed are experiencing. Although almost all workers are covered by the system, only 34 percent of the out of work population received benefits in 1985. Apparently this was due in large part to the fact that many had exhausted their twenty-six weeks of eligibility without finding a job.[27] And UI obviously provides no help for the largest and fastest growing group of unemployed Americans: young people who have never held any type of permanent job and who are not covered by the system at all.

Some of the most successful government programs for children reach only a fraction of those who would benefit from them. Despite demonstrated success and long-term cost savings, WIC (the nutritional program for pregnant women, infants, and young children), Head Start, and similar programs aimed at getting poor children off to a good start reach less than half of the children who are eligible for their benefits.[28]

Despite large investments in federal food and nutrition programs, many Americans still have inadequate diets. A recent study supported by the Ford Foundation showed that this problem is particularly severe in rural areas, where about 12 percent of the poor consume less than the recommended daily allowance of protein and 30–40 percent have other dietary deficiencies.[29]

After decades of federal subsidies to farmers, the United States experienced a farm credit crisis in the mid-1980s. A combination of market conditions and federal policies left farmers so overextended that roughly 12 percent were close to insolvency in 1986, and 5 percent had given up farming.[30] Billions of dollars in equity were destroyed as land values plunged 50 percent in many farm states, and the farm crisis left in its train the wreckage of banks and other local businesses in rural communities.

Activist government also falls short of adequacy when it comes to social regulation. Although much progress has been made, we are still a long way from achieving the goals of the Clean Air, Clean Water, and other environmental protection acts. The recent emphasis on "regulatory relief" has slowed progress in these areas as well as in transportation and workplace safety.[31] Other social regulations appear to miss their targets. For example, over 5 million Americans worked below the minimum wage in 1986.[32]

Most importantly, progress in achieving the goals of the Civil Rights Act has slowed in recent years. Thirty years after *Brown* v. *Board of Education,* large numbers of our schools and neighborhoods are still segregated, de facto, and no viable policy to overcome this problem has emerged. Despite efforts at affirmative action by government, business, and others, blacks still earn 10–20 percent less than whites, when adjustments are made for all factors other than race. Blacks also experience considerably higher unemployment rates, reap fewer income benefits, and are far more likely to be poor than whites.[33] Judging from the results, policies aimed at eradicating the effects of race on an individual's life chances have been only partially successful.

Finally, government economic regulation and macroeconomic management have met with mixed success in recent decades. The nation suffered from ten years of recession, despite the efforts of federal economic managers, until it was finally shocked into recovery by a government intervention. But the recent recovery has been accompanied by continuing high unemployment rates, soaring foreign trade deficits, and low rates of productivity growth—all disturbing auguries for the future. Furthermore, the recent trend toward economic deregulation has brought corporate failures in the banking and airline industries as well as profiteering in energy and other extractive industries. These short-term effects of deregulation may or may not be the signs of a healthy reorganization that will benefit the nation's economy in the long run.

In short, despite all of its achievements, the federal social role too often provides only partial and inadequate solutions to the national problems it confronts. Of course, no institution is perfect, but it is reasonable to suppose that most Americans would be deeply disturbed by the shortcomings just described. In a democracy there is no good reason why government of and by the people should not achieve its full potential to be government *for* the people as well. But describing the shortcomings of public policy is not enough to call forth solutions. It is necessary to go a step further and discover why those shortcomings occur.

7

National Purpose
and the American Style

W hy is it that national government in the United States always seems to make noble beginnings but never seems to finish the job of solving public problems? The simple answer is that the federal government has been unwilling or unable to assert national priorities as vigorously as the common interests of the American people require. And the fundamental reason for this is not that public leaders have been careless, stupid, or malign. The fundamental reason is to be found in certain distinctive features of our activist tradition.

Problems of the American Style

Treating government as only one institution among many and a politics of inclusiveness—the American style of activism—have been highly effective approaches to managing our public life. They have helped successive generations to build a stronger and more cohesive nation. But we have also paid a high price for these advantages, because the essence of the American style is to accommodate local or particularistic concerns and individualist values by incorporating elements of both into virtually every element of national policy. As a result, the same political style that has served us well since the earliest days of our republic has also placed severe constraints on the scope and effectiveness of the federal social role.

It is almost impossible for the United States fully to achieve any of the purposes that national policy proclaims if the federal government must defer to the forces of diversity in every measure it adopts. Unless and until government at the national level can find ways to assert the common interest more forcefully, the federal social role will continue to be in arrears.

Each of the elements of the American style limits activist government in a different way. In combination they have an even more profound effect.

Institutional Diversity

As mentioned, a fundamental canon of American social policy is that national purposes not only can but *must* be achieved in large part by institutions other than the federal government. The problem with this approach is that in a large and diverse nation particular businesses, states, communities, and other institutions inevitably have differing views about how they can or should respond to federal initiatives. The result is an uneven and often inadequate approach to common problems. Some businesses provide good pension and health care protection; others do not. Some have exemplary records in the areas of civil rights; others are lax. Some make good use of federal incentives to bolster productivity and employment; others abuse the system. Some states and localities provide generous welfare services and leverage federal funds into large gains for their communities; others fall short on both counts.

As a result, many people fall between the stools of federal programs and the provisions made by the private sector or other levels of government. The federal government may contribute its share to meeting public needs, but other institutions may not always do their part. For example, an individual may receive Social Security benefits but not a private pension, or he may receive SSI benefits, but he may live in a state that does not supplement those payments. People also may suffer because the federal government has chosen not to address some facet of a problem at all, on the assumption that it is the responsibility of the private sector. For example, no federal program provides health care protection for able-bodied workers, except government employees—although the federal tax system offers incentives for corporate health care plans to companies that choose to establish them. A major reason why 35 million Americans are not covered by health insurance is that they are able-bodied workers who do not qualify for either a public or a private plan.

Another major effect of relying on a diversity of institutions is that people in similar circumstances are treated differently. AFDC families and people who are unemployed receive vastly different benefit levels depending on where they live. People with the same wage level and occupation receive different corporate benefits depending on where they work.

The federal government could solve these and other problems of inadequacy and inequity by mandating strict standards for the performance of other institutions. But it rarely does. For example, companies are not required to provide corporate health and pension benefits, and states are not required to participate in federal welfare programs—these are voluntary undertakings. And although the federal government sets standards for institutions that assume such responsibilities, those standards almost always provide a great deal of leeway for companies, states, or localities to develop their own plans. Of course, compliance with national policies in areas such as race relations and environmental protection is mandatory, but the regulations that implement those policies can generally be applied in many different forms.

There is simply no way in which a system of policy that relies on the efforts of subnational institutions and allows them a large measure of discretion can produce an overall national response to public problems that is either uniform or adequate. Unless the federal government is willing to assume a monopoly in some areas of public service or to prescribe more stringent standards for the behavior of other institutions, many national purposes will be only partly achieved, and many Americans will continue to suffer from financial and physical hardship.

Inclusiveness

The second element of the American style—a politics of inclusiveness—makes it difficult in other ways to mount an adequate national response to public problems. If a key to the American political process is accommodating most of the plausible demands that are placed on the federal government, two results are likely: we will devote most of our public resources to a small group of favored programs; but beyond these, public efforts will be spread very wide and very thin.

The politics of inclusiveness helps to bind the nation together by giving everyone a stake in what the federal government does. But in recent decades it has shortchanged almost everyone by creating a more extensive range of public commitments than the American political process can manage or than the American people are prepared to support.

The programs favored by an inclusive political style are, as mentioned, those from which almost everyone benefits, at least potentially. Social Security, Medicare, and Unemployment Insurance enjoy extremely strong political support, and they consume the lion's share of the federal domestic budget. These comprehensive programs are usually immune from attempts to reduce federal spending, even in difficult times. In fact, the general inclination of politicians is to try to increase their benefit levels and coverage. And Americans appear to be willing to pay the price: while there has been vehement opposition to most increases in federal, state, and local taxes over the last few decades, Social Security taxes have roughly doubled since the late 1960s with little or no public outcry.

In contrast, support for less favored programs—those which address needs that are more narrowly defined—ebbs and flows depending on political currents and economic circumstances. But although support for those programs may be unstable, it almost never vanishes entirely, and the number of programs has steadily increased over the years. The politics of inclusiveness has both strong expansionary and strong conservative tendencies. This is what spreads the public effort wide and thin.

An inclusive style means that all groups or interests can present their case to the federal government. Sooner or later through the process of political bargaining, many will find a way to pair up with enough other groups to ensure that their needs are defined as part of the common national interest. And the social role will expand to accommodate them, as it has throughout our history.

But the same process that leads to expansion also leads to perpetuation. Once programs are in place, the groups most strongly affected by them can use the process of bargaining to ensure that they stay there. As political scientist Theodore Lowi has pointed out, in the American system every interest group in effect has a veto over what programs are adopted or abolished, because so many groups are required to form a political coalition strong enough to achieve any purpose.[1] This may exaggerate the conservative tendencies of the American style, but it is certainly true that enormous deference is paid to programs in place, and there is great reluctance to take away benefits that even symbolically assist any sector of American society.

The way in which this conservative tendency operates in practice is illustrated in an anecdote by former Reagan OMB Director, David Stockman, about his efforts to reduce the federal deficit for the 1986 fiscal year:

> By May it was time for the Senate to start voting on its package to reduce the deficit by $55 billion in 1986, and by rising amounts in the out-years. One by one the Republican politicians came with their final demands as to what *couldn't* be cut if we were to have their vote. And we needed every single vote among the fifty-three Republicans because no Democrat would play this lousy game of having to tiptoe around the President in public.
>
> As the long, final day of the Republican budget round-tabling passed into the middle of the night . . . I finally saw, as the politicians circled the table one last time, the awesome staying power of the Second Republic.[2]

One senator offered his vote on the condition that there would be no cut in impact aid to localities. Another offered his vote on the condition that antipoverty programs be maintained. Others insisted on maintaining farm subsidies, Urban Development Action Grants, rural housing programs, student aid, and other programs—all for perfectly good reasons—all in fact for the reasons that originally caused the programs to be adopted—until Stockman found that he had little or nothing left to cut.

With so many programs firmly placed on the federal agenda, it is virtually impossible for public officials to exercise appropriate supervision over a great many of them. Inadequacies are often inadvertent. There is simply not enough time to investigate any but the most glaring mistakes of public programs, to improve their design or to fill gaps in the protections they provide. Too often in the hectic world of national government, only the squeaky wheel gets the grease.

In addition, such a large public agenda is very costly. Because of the Jeffersonian strain in our national character, there is more resistance to taxes in the United States—and it is more effective—than in most other countries. In fact, there has been only one general peacetime tax increase in this century: pushed through by the Hoover administration in 1932. Because Americans dislike paying taxes, politicians try to keep the cost of a constantly expanding public agenda down by doing a little bit of everything rather than by doing a really adequate job in very many areas. Regardless of their purpose, most programs—from national parks to child nutrition—are funded far below the levels required fully to achieve their goals. The outstanding exceptions, of course, are social insurance programs that benefit almost everyone. As mentioned, tax increases to support them meet with little or no political opposition.

An inclusive political style also results in a fragmented system of public finance. The same political forces that lock the federal government into a wide range of commitments have also created dedicated taxes and trust funds to support Social Security, Medicare, Disability and Unemployment Insurance, highway construction, and various other purposes.

Once in place, dedicated taxes are as hard to repeal as the programs they support, and the federal government's ability to shift resources to meet high priority problems is greatly restricted. It is by no means clear, for example, that the Highway Trust Fund provides the right amount of money for highway construction. Perhaps more is needed, perhaps less. The Trust Fund simply provides the amount that the various fuel taxes which support it happen to generate. As a result, the federal government denies itself the ability to make a rational choice about what level of resources should be devoted to highways, or about how important highway construction is compared to other national priorities.

The Consequences of Individualism

Another way to see the limits placed on activist government by the American style is not to focus on the tensions in our national life but to concentrate instead on one of the most powerful elements in those tensions: our national belief in individualism. That belief takes many different forms, but the form in which it has the most powerful influence on social policy is the conviction that everyone can and should be self-supporting through work. Individualism in this sense permeates all aspects of the federal social role. Its most significant effect, however, is to help create and reinforce a structure of public policy that rewards people who are successful in the world of work. But the same structure of policy also limits the rewards that public programs offer to successful workers, and it systematically disadvantages the poor.

Because of the importance attached to work, much of the federal social role is devoted to solving problems related to employment. But different people have different types of employment-related problems. The federal social role is designed to give primary attention to the problems of what might be called the "average American"—that perennial hero of our national drama, who used to be called the "common man" or the "working man." Specifically, the average American is someone who works at a steady job and earns a good income during most of his life. He also puts aside individual savings and contributes to private pension, health care, and life insurance plans. In short, he exemplifies the individualist values of self-help, providence, and thrift.

Most of us are average Americans—normal, middle-class people. And it is not surprising that in a democracy with an inclusive political style, public policy is designed primarily with our problems in mind. This is not mere supposition. The charter document of the American welfare state, *The Report of the Committee on Income Security of 1935,* clearly defined the intended beneficiaries of federal social programs as self-supporting average Americans, and it identified the work-related problems that they are most likely to encounter: loss of income due to temporary unemployment, disability, and old age.[3]

Much of the growth of the federal social role since 1935 has consisted of developing increasingly strong measures to provide average Americans with protections against these problems: Social Security, Medicare, Unemployment and Disability Insurance. The social role also rewards providence and thrift by subsidizing private health and pension plans and by giving tax preferences to certain forms of individual savings. Obviously the risks of losing income due to old age are greater than the risks of unemployment and disability for average Americans—almost everyone eventually stops working in their later years, but comparatively few middle-class people are unemployed or disabled for long periods of time. As a result, most of the protections against loss of income provided by the social role, and over half of federal domestic spending, are devoted to programs for the elderly.

The effect of individualism on American public policy is even more profound. The major programs of the federal social role are designed not only to assist average Americans with employment-related problems; they are also designed to provide that assistance in a way that is consistent with individualist values. This is part of the reason for the extraordinarily strong political support they enjoy. These programs are popular not only because almost everyone, at least potentially, benefits from them, but also because everyone pays for them during their working years.

Medicare, Social Security retirement, Unemployment and Disability Insurance are all programs to which active workers contribute in the anticipation that they will receive benefits in times of hardship. All are based on the model of private insurance. Individuals have the impression that their benefits are a matter of earned right, like the common law property right they have to claim benefits from private insurance companies or, for that matter, to receive any service for which they have paid.

The architects of these programs designed them as contributory systems in part because they believed that this sense of earned right would build lasting political support. They were right. Contributory systems work political magic. People believe they are simply receiving the fruits of their own labors rather than a public handout. For a nation of individualists this is important. People who have paid into a contributory system strongly resist any attempts to cut it back. They want to protect *their* right to *their* money.

Opinion polls indicate that most people realize that this interpretation of social insurance programs is incorrect in many ways.[4] Unlike a private insurance company, the federal government requires everyone to participate in its programs and it sets the level of contributions—no one may contribute more or less than federal regulations prescribe. And unlike a private insurance company, the federal government does not invest individual contributions and pay benefits from the earnings. Rather, the contributions of each generation of active workers are used to pay the benefits of retirees. Finally, benefits from social insurance are *not* earned rights, in the eyes of the law at least: you cannot sue to receive them in court as you could sue a private insurance company. Congress has a perfect right to terminate or reduce benefits for these programs, as it does for any others, any time it deems appropriate.

Yet because almost everyone contributes to social insurance programs, there is enormous political pressure for government to treat them as if they provided earned rights—to maintain the programs and protect their benefit levels regardless of cost. A nation of individualists demands that the largest and most ambitious of federal programs be managed as if they were simply slightly peculiar ways for people to exercise the individualist virtues of self-support.

But there is a paradox in this system of rewarding individual effort. If people are regularly employed at good wages, why do they need the federal government to help them provide for old age, unemployment, or disability? Why can't they provide for themselves through private savings and insurance of various sorts? This question reveals one of the great divides in thinking about social policy: the long-standing argument between advocates of comprehensive programs and advocates of programs based on need.

The argument for comprehensive programs usually places great emphasis on the fact that the hazards of old age, unemployment, and disability are hard for individuals to estimate. As a result, more of us can know exactly how much we should save or invest in private insurance plans to protect us against hardship. Research on patterns of savings and insurance indicates that while some people are improvident, a great many people build up more savings and insurance than they need to protect themselves toward the end of their lives. Advocates of comprehensive programs argue that it makes sense to adopt a common solution to a common problem: to pool everyone's risks and guarantee benefits that will make a substantial contribution toward meeting everyone's needs, regardless of what good or ill fortune they may encounter.

Champions of programs based on need argue that the same problems of uncertainty could be solved by allowing individuals to make their own provisions for future risks and providing benefits only to people who miscalculate or suffer bad luck.[5] In a sense, the difference between their ideas and the comprehensive approach is a disagreement between two different views of how the federal social role should incorporate the values of individualism—by developing programs that help people to help themselves, or by requiring people who can provide for their own needs to do so and extending public assistance only to people whose individual efforts are inadequate.

In a nation that practices a politics of inclusiveness—where all reasonable views are accommodated to some degree—it is not surprising that the social role incorporates elements of both these differing views of individualism. We have comprehensive programs for the average American and needs-based programs for people who are inadequately served by social insurance.

It should not be surprising that average Americans are served by comprehensive social insurance programs. Most people are more confident that they will receive benefits they believe they have paid for than benefits that government decides they need. And they trust the federal government to deliver on its promises to support social insurance programs—because they can influence it with their votes—more than they trust private benefit plans or investment schemes.

Individualism and the Poor

The multi-tier structure of federal programs designed to guard against financial insecurity, therefore, reflects several different views of individualism. It rewards average Americans who exemplify the individualist values of self-support, although the protections it offers them are far from complete. But it also systematically disadvantages the poor in at least two ways.

Part of the problem has to do with benefit levels. For example, although Social Security retirement benefits are progressive—in the sense that low wage earners receive proportionately more compared to their contributions than do high wage earners—the minimal level of benefits is very low, indeed. As a result, while Social Security has raised millions of elderly people from poverty, millions still live below or only slightly above the poverty line. Minimal Social Security benefits do not provide a decent standard of living for most poor people, nor do minimal Unemployment Insurance payments; and Medicare alone does not meet the health care costs of the elderly.

Yet minimal benefits are all that most people who are poor because they work for low wages receive. Moreover, the unemployed poor, intermittent employees, and low wage-earners are rarely covered by private benefit plans. And they can rarely afford to set aside private savings. In short, they cannot supplement the benefits they receive from comprehensive programs by the means available to most average Americans. Employment—holding a steady job at a good wage—is the key that opens the door to most of our major social programs, and it is a key that most poor people lack.

But there is another even more important reason why comprehensive programs do not serve the needs of poor people very well. As mentioned, the two largest programs—Social Security retirement and Medicare—are designed to provide protection against loss of income at the time when average Americans are most likely to suffer from financial distress: in their retirement years. People who are poor because they cannot find steady employment or any work at all need protection in the prime of life.

We have no comprehensive programs for prime-age workers, except Unemployment Insurance, for which many of the poor fail to qualify. We address their problems mainly by needs-based programs: AFDC, Medicaid, SSI, Food Stamps, and public housing. All of those, except AFDC, also help to supplement the incomes of the impoverished elderly.

But the same individualist values that reinforce comprehensive programs also undermine the adequacy of needs-based protections. In the words of former Health, Education and Welfare Secretary Wilbur Cohen, "Programs for poor people are poor programs."

Federal spending on needs-based welfare programs is far below the level required to provide a decent standard of living by any reasonable definition. In addition, inflation has eroded the value of welfare benefits since the 1970s, and eligibility standards have been tightened. And anyone who applies for benefits from these programs must run the gauntlet of countless arcane and intrusive regulations, and this apparently deters many people from filing claims. Finally, states are allowed considerable discretion in administering welfare benefits, and some states set eligibility and payment standards that are shamefully tightfisted.

This is the dark side of the American belief in individualism. We realize that some people cannot live up to the individualist ideal because of bad luck, bad judgment, or various other reasons. But we are suspicious of anyone who claims that he cannot take care of himself. We suspect that he may be loafing or that if the benefits of welfare programs were more adequate he would be tempted to "take a free ride." There is very little evidence to support these suspicions, but they have been voiced repeatedly by public officials throughout our history, and opinion polls indicate that a large percentage of Americans believe welfare programs are fraught with "fraud, waste, and abuse."

In short, there is enormous resistance in the United States to providing public income supports to able-bodied adults, unless those benefits are the "earned rights" of social insurance programs. This reluctance is reflected in the miserly provisions of needs-based programs. It is also reflected by the fact that a large percentage of the poor—able-bodied adults under sixty-five who are not the parents of dependent children—are not eligible for any federal welfare programs except Food Stamps, the small Earned Income Tax Credit, and in a fraction of cases, public housing. Somehow we cannot accept the idea that, despite their best efforts, many of these people are simply unable to make a decent living.

Poor people in the United States are, thus, disadvantaged in three ways: by being poor to begin with; by benefiting less from the major contributory programs; and by having to rely on the least adequate provisions of the federal social role.

As a result, there is an element of paradox—or, to be less generous, hypocrisy—in the American creed of individualism. It helps to legitimize programs that help people who can achieve security through their own efforts to become even more secure, but it also stigmatizes programs for people who cannot help themselves. And these two effects are related: if the needs of the majority of Americans—average, middle-class people—are well cared for, there is less of a political constituency for dealing with the problems of the poor. Politicians are inclined to devote their energies to refining middle-class social insurance plans rather than programs for the poor.

From a moral standpoint there is nothing inherently wrong with average Americans using government as a means to enhance their own security. But the federal social role can never truly be government for *all* the people unless it also provides adequate security for people whose problems are not "average." They are citizens, too.

Privilege

Considering the American political style from the perspective of its two major components, and from the perspective of our national attachment to individualism, reveals many of the ways in which that style limits activist government. But there is another perspective on the limits to activism that places less emphasis on the long-term patterns of our political life and more emphasis on the institutions and individuals that create those patterns. Both perspectives are valid, and each reveals a different aspect of the same political landscape.

Among the reasons why the United States relies so heavily on institutional diversity and why we have such an inclusive political style is that certain institutions and the individuals who control them occupy a privileged position within our political system. Chief among the privileged institutions are business and nonfederal levels of government. Because the United States has a capitalist economy and a multiple-layered structure of government, they are among the major centers of power within our society. For both practical and political reasons it is very difficult for national government not to give special attention to their needs and views. While our political style accommodates all institutions to some extent, the interests of business and of state and local governments are accommodated far better than most.

Public policy in the United States has generally been deferential to business interests, in large part because American business is "the goose that lays the golden eggs" of economic prosperity. In fact, political scientist Charles E. Lindblom argues that, in normal circumstances, business can effectively exercise a veto that overrides all other interests in the process of political bargaining.[6] If the business community claims that certain policies will cause economic disruption, public officials generally back off, unless the claim is clearly without substance. There is a sense in which this is reasonable: predicting the economic effects of government actions is a very imprecise science, and most policymakers would rather be safe than sorry.

But businessmen do not have a monopoly on crystal balls. Like other Americans they speak up for their interests, and for the national interest as they see it, but there is no reason to believe that they are always right. An undue deference to business opinion—a deference that even many thoughtful businessmen question—is a persistent danger of the American political style. So is the possibility that a few unscrupulous businessmen can threaten to abandon certain areas of the economy unless government renders their activities more profitable by subsidies, regulatory relief or other measures.

The days have certainly passed when a Wall Street tycoon could strong-arm a president of the United States by offering to "send my man to talk to your man"—the Secretary of the Treasury— "to work things out." But most politicians think more than twice when red flags go up in the business community. They don't want to be the ones who caused the next recession or corporate failure.

As Lindblom points out, politicians not only treat business with kid gloves, they also have progressively expanded the system of subsidies and protective regulations first put in place by Hamilton. In essence, much of federal regulatory, credit, trade, and other economic policy serves to guarantee profits, and many federal tax expenditures are designed to make it easier in financial terms for business to "do the right thing."

The financial industry, which was the primary target of Hamilton's policies, is particularly well protected. Federal insurance and special interventions virtually guarantee a bailout for major banks that fail; federal credit activities and fiscal management create financial markets and often assure profits; federal regulators attempt to police the industry and create stable conditions for both firms and customers.

In most circumstances, there is nothing sinister about these protections for the financial industry and other business interests. If large banks or brokerage houses fail, panic conditions can send the whole economy tumbling after them. Or, to take another example, if the timber industry suffers from overproduction, congressmen and senators from timber-producing states will appeal for subsidies to keep the industry going, in order to maintain local employment, local economies, and the national timber reserve.

This offends some economists who believe that unproductive industries should be allowed to fail, but it may be a more certain way to maintain overall national employment and prosperity, in the short term at least, than more theoretically pure alternatives.

In a larger sense, helping industries whether they are distressed or not is an element in the politics of nationhood. It creates a direct and visible link between the interests of businessmen and their employees and the overall national interest.

State and local governments also occupy a privileged position. National government is "one institution among many" in part because local attachments are strong. The Jeffersonian assumption that governments "closer to the people" are better able to determine their needs, at least when it comes to the details of designing and delivering public services, is realized in practice by a system of federalism that leaves some of the most important functions of government—such as education, public protection, and local economic development—to states and localities and that endows them with the responsibility for delivering many federally initiated projects—most welfare programs, for example.

Because all problems are in some sense national problems, states and communities often turn to Washington for financial and other forms of assistance with their local responsibilities. And they generally find a very receptive audience. Just as overall economic prosperity depends on the health of the business community, overall effectiveness of public services depends on the health of state and local governments.

For much the same reason that they are unwilling to see a major industry imperiled, national officials are unwilling to see state and local education, transportation, or public safety programs jeopardized. National officials are also receptive to appeals from state and local governments because these levels of government are, in effect, represented in Congress. Senators are elected on a state-wide basis, and congressmen are elected from geographically defined boundaries that generally have some distinctive public service needs—for example, reliance on particular industries or needs for certain forms of public works, such as water projects or highways. Members of Congress are personally sympathetic to the needs of their districts from firsthand experience; they also are politically required to provide for those needs.

As a result, concern for the overall national sufficiency of public services combined with personal and political commitments lead to the investment of tens of billions of dollars in federal programs for state and local community development, local infrastructure, education, personal social services, and other programs designed to meet localized problems.

Programs for businesses and for states and localities doubtless meet legitimate national needs, but they suffer from the same expansionary tendencies that affect the rest of the federal social role. Once one distressed industry is assisted, others demand and usually get assistance. Once school aid goes to one district, the tendency is to extend it to all districts. The federal government has a hard time making decisions about which among its privileged institutions are most in need, and it tends to resolve doubts in favor of extending help to most claimants. This is the politics of inclusiveness carried to the extreme. It broadens the federal agenda enormously and doubtless accommodates a great number of marginal cases. But politically it makes a great deal of sense.

It is far from clear, however, that it makes sense from the standpoint of the nation's overall economic well-being. Subsidies to unproductive industries freeze capital in areas of the economy that have limited growth potential and divert it from more promising areas.

Also, companies are encouraged to compete by "gaming the federal system"—overinvesting in activities that receive preferential tax or regulatory treatment and distorting their operations to show paper tax losses. Too often they "compete through their lawyers"—seeking regulatory changes that will benefit one firm at the expense of others. And too often fortunes are gained or lost, not through productive investment, but through speculation in government created or supported markets—the market for government-backed securities and large parts of the commodities markets.

The privilege accorded state and local governments also creates distortions. Too often their energies and resources are directed to certain types of projects largely because federal funds are available. And too often they compete with each other for industrial investment by using tax-exempt state and local bonding authority to lower costs for the industries they are trying to attract. This form of competition may be rational for the winning localities, but it is not rational from the overall national perspective: the industries would locate somewhere in any event, and the net result of subsidies from tax-exempt bonds is to allow states and localities to decide which industries national taxpayers as a whole will subsidize.

But the influence of business and of other levels of government is not limited to programs that are primarily intended to serve their institutional interests. They also use their privileged positions to restrict the federal government's options in many other areas of policy. For example, the reason why our Medicare and Medicaid systems provide far from complete coverage and why state and local governments are partners in managing welfare programs is not just that Americans have a principled attachment to individualism and institutional diversity in the provision of public services. In both cases, the present structure of policy resulted from major political struggles over who would control important aspects of the services in question.

In 1965 the health care lobby fought to retain control of prices and conditions of care by advocating a far less comprehensive system of national health insurance than many federal policymakers favored.[7] And in the New Deal era, as well as in subsequent years, representatives of Southern agricultural interests fought to retain state discretion over the level of national welfare benefits, because they feared that overly generous provisions would drive up the costs of low-skilled labor.[8] In these and many other cases, advocates of greater federal control over social programs and more adequate benefits were forced to compromise, and the present system of incomplete protection and decentralized control has been the result.

No discussion of privilege could be complete, however, without stating what may seem to be an obvious point: in addition to the privilege conferred on business, states, and localities, activist government in the United States also confers privilege on those who administer it. Major federal agencies and leaders of the legislative branch all have their individual agendas, just as states, localities, and businesses do. The federal social role is often limited by the goals and priorities of agencies and politicians who, for one reason or another, are in a position of strength. For example, numerous studies have shown how events conspired to allow the Social Security Board to restrict the growth of means-tested programs in order to protect the expansion of more comprehensive social insurance.[9] And a large body of literature shows that the internal dynamics of the federal government, as well as the configuration of national politics and national problems at any given time, constrain the agenda that federal policymakers are prepared to consider.[10] Those who are responsible for managing a system that relies on institutional diversity are no less privileged than those who benefit from it.

Hard Cases for Policy

All of the foregoing biases of the American style severely handicap activist government in the United States. They make it extremely difficult to develop federal programs that adequately address major national priorities. Because of them, government at the national level often does not assert a strong enough sense of national purpose, and the federal social role is left in arrears. But there are some problems that run afoul of so many of these difficulties that they belong in a class by themselves. These are the hard cases for American social policy—the problems that the American style is especially ill adapted to address. Notable among these are the problems of minorities, of working women, and of children. They ring all the wrong bells in the American political process.

A disproportionate number of members of minority groups are poor (31 percent of blacks and 29 percent of Hispanics, compared with 14 percent of the population as a whole in 1985). Like other poor people, they have difficulty taking advantage of social programs that are designed primarily for average Americans. But over and above these problems, minorities suffer from a history of discrimination, which the federal government attempts to address with various forms of affirmative action programs. Unfortunately, affirmative action infringes on some of the most time-honored prerogatives of business and other levels of government.

For example, programs intended to enhance the employment opportunities of minorities in one way or another ask companies to change their previous hiring, promotion, and training practices. Because these aspects of employee relations are traditionally among the most important prerogatives of business, most affirmative action plans have a large voluntary component. Policymakers believe there are limits to how much responsibility they can or should ask business to accept for solving social problems. As a result, while many companies have made exemplary strides in improving the opportunities of minorities, others have lagged behind—partly because they have been unwilling to incur the cost and disruption entailed and, in some cases, because of pressures from customers and employees who may be prejudiced against minorities or fearful of what they see as "reverse discrimination."

Other elements of affirmative action have been programs to encourage integration of schools, neighborhoods, and other local institutions. Again, progress has been made, but the extent of continuing de facto segregation indicates that the federal government has limited ability or will to impose its goals on states and localities or on private institutions. In fact, in recent years many past gains in this area have been maintained by the unwillingness of companies and other levels of government to back out of past commitments, despite efforts by the Reagan administration to force them to do so.

In short, the problems of minorities cut across the grain of the American style. Income security policies to address those problems are limited by our individualist values, and affirmative action policies are limited by our attachment to institutional diversity and discretion.

The problems of working women also cut across the grain. Working women are not necessarily poor, but they are far more likely than men to be poorly paid, to be part-time workers, or to have intermittent attachments to the workforce. As a result, they often fail to reap the full benefits of major income security programs for the same reason that many poor people do. Also, because many women have children and most want to continue working while those children are still young, they place special demands on employers—for maternity and child care leave, which are costly to the employers and have met with limited acceptance. Nor have women been successful in getting government to mandate that employers foot the bill for these benefits or in gaining government funding to support them.

Children are obviously a hard case because one aspect of our individualist values is the presumption that their welfare is primarily the responsibility of their parents. Public authorities become involved only in cases of child neglect or abuse and through the educational system. All of these are traditionally state and local responsibilities. When the federal government addresses the problems of children it is perceived to be invading the prerogatives of both families and of other levels of government, and it has been reluctant to do either.

Obviously, children do not form a vocal lobby for federal attention, and those who lobby on their behalf have difficulty gaining public support, because, as one children's advocate put it, "Everyone is concerned about programs for the elderly, because everyone grows old, but too few people are concerned about children's programs, because nobody grows young." As it is, the federal government provides some assistance to children through programs for elementary and secondary education, Aid to Families with Dependent Children (which benefits 9 million children), Medicaid, and a few small preschool, health, and nutrition programs. The total cost is about the same amount that the national government spends on highways and mass transit.

Immigrants and American Indians are other groups whose problems social policy in the United States is ill adapted to address. The fact that we have made substantial commitments to minorities, women, children, and these other groups is testimony to our sense of common citizenship. The fact that the American style of activism limits those commitments is testimony to the limits of our sense of nationhood.

8

Prospects
for Reform

G laring inadequacies, institutional privilege, neglect of the disadvantaged, a range of activity that is simultaneously too broad and too shallow—these are the problems on which the current reassessment of the federal social role should be focusing.

Without a doubt, the federal government has the authority to provide, or require that other institutions provide, more adequate and uniform protections for the general welfare, to restrict national commitments to manageable proportions, to improve the conditions of groups that presently are neglected, and to scrutinize more carefully the demands of business and other levels of government. But the American style of balancing the forces of nationhood and diversity stands in the way of a more effective expression of the common interest.

Put in concrete terms, the results of this hesitant approach to activism would doubtless outrage the average citizen:

> Why should two people in identical circumstances, except for the fact that they live in different states, receive grossly unequal benefits from the same federal welfare program?

Why should two elderly people—one rich and one poor—
receive different standards of medical care, offered by
two different federal programs?

Why should anyone in this rich nation go without adequate
food, shelter, or health care?

Why should the adequacy of retirement income depend on
the luck of the draw in a person's working life?

Why should the federal government guarantee the profits of
profitable businesses and subsidize large parts of the
economy?

Why should it support state and local programs when states
and localities have the taxing power to support those
programs themselves?

Almost everyone is disturbed by these shortcomings of the federal social role, but one reason why the public policy debate has ground to a stalemate is that no one has been able to devise a way to overcome them. Most of the ideas that have been advanced in recent years fall into two categories: proposals for institutional reform and calls for new directions in the development of social policy.

Institutional Change

Throughout American history, many thoughtful people have believed that the effectiveness of national government could be greatly enhanced by changes in our political institutions. Indeed, the Constitution of 1787 was adopted because the institutional arrangements of our first constitution, the Articles of Confederation, were not strong enough to solve urgent problems of the nation as a whole. In this century, scores of public and private commissions—such as the two Hoover Commissions, the Brownlow Commission, and the Kestnbaum Commission—have proposed major institutional change.[1]

From a certain perspective, this approach to overcoming problems created by the American style makes a great deal of sense. If we evaluated the federal government in the same way that we might evaluate a business, we would have to conclude that it is poorly managed in several important respects. To begin with, it has a hard time setting priorities. Too little effort is made to sort through the enormous accumulation of federal activities to determine which ones should have first call on the attention of policymakers and on taxpayers' dollars. In addition, the federal government devotes too little attention to refining policies that are already in place—improving its various "products" after they have been tested in a field and filling gaps that become apparent only when the system of policy is viewed as a whole.

But the greatest weakness of the federal government from a managerial standpoint is that it does a poor job of planning for the future. Too often it fails to anticipate problems or to take preventive measures. For example, the difficulties of medical cost inflation were identified soon after the passage of Medicare and Medicaid in 1965, but it took the nation twenty years to get around to doing something about them. The inadequacy of income supports for the disabled, the disadvantaged, and the elderly in an industrial society was commonplace knowledge at the turn of the century, but it took us until 1935 to pass the Social Security Act. The farm crisis and the federal deficit problems of the 1980s were all foreseen by people responsible for agricultural and fiscal policy, respectively, but nothing was done until these difficulties reached headline proportions.

The conventional wisdom among both politicians and political scientists is that it generally takes some sort of crisis to force the many interests in an inclusive and decentralized political system to support major policy changes. The Great Depression, the civil rights revolution, and today's problems with deficits, agriculture, and economic performance all had to occur before the nation could gear itself up to tackle problems that were well recognized years or decades earlier.

This crisis-management style of government tends to produce "solutions" that are far more costly than they need to be and often too late to be fully effective. The nation pays an enormous price for it both in financial terms and in human suffering. Yet one of the maxims of a pragmatic approach to activism appears to be, "If it ain't broke, don't fix it."

The United States actually tried national planning once. In the waning days of the Great Depression, President Roosevelt commissioned the National Resources Planning Board to devise a more orderly and comprehensive system of social policy. The board developed first-rate material, but its proposals were disregarded for a variety of reasons: national attention was directed to the war effort, business leaders averse to a more extensive federal role gained control of many executive branch agencies, Southern conservatives held the balance of power in Congress, postwar conditions proved to be better than expected, and the federal government had not developed institutions that could quickly implement the board's recommendations.[2] The National Resources Planning Board was abolished in 1943.

If the federal government were better at planning, establishing priorities, and refining policies, it would doubtless be able to assert the national interest more effectively. In part, as noted, its failures reflect the basic conflicts in our political life. But institutional reformers are right that those failures are reinforced by the structure of the federal government and the political organizations that attend it.

The federal constitution mandates a system of checks and balances that make it exceptionally difficult for any branch of government to implement comprehensive plans or establish priorities. What the president proposes, Congress may oppose, or vice versa, and what the Supreme Court decrees, other branches may circumvent. In addition, both Congress and the Executive are divided into numerous centers of power—committees and agencies—each of which is primarily concerned with a particular area of policy. Agency heads and committee chairmen control the expertise needed to pull together the divergent strands of policy, but they often are reluctant to take a strong enough interest in issues outside their purview or to countenance plans that would reduce their prerogatives.

But policy specialists in Congress and the Executive are not reluctant to work with other people who share their interests. Political scientists long ago identified the problem of "iron triangles''—alliances of congressional committees, bureaucrats, and interest groups dedicated to protecting and enhancing certain government programs. Former HEW Secretary Joseph Califano describes these alliances in the following terms:

> Congress has more than three hundred committees, subcommittees and select committees which are sedulously attended by narrow-interest groups that have weight with individual committee members— whose political campaigns depend on private financing—far beyond their voting power in the electorate as a whole. Because of this, Congress is eager to establish for each interest its own executive bureau or independent board. This structure complicates the ability of the executive branch and of the cities and states to deliver services with the efficiency that the taxpayer deserves and this age of limited resources demands.[3]

Of course, iron triangles have their positive side. They provide public officials with information, expertise, and political support that are essential to the operation of a complex modern government. For example, it is very difficult for members of Congress to develop major legislative initiatives without help either from executive branch agencies or from outside groups. The volume of legislation is so great that personal and committee staffs as well as the various specialized arms of Congress—such as the Congressional Budget Office and the General Accounting Office— are often overwhelmed. In practice, lobbyists, agency staff, or experts at think tanks and universities conduct a great deal of the analysis and other developmental work needed to frame many of the bills that are introduced, simply because there is no one else to do the job.

But, despite their benefits, there can be no doubt that iron triangles balkanize and rigidify federal decision making. Too often they place major roadblocks in the way of innovation and accountability to the nation at large, and too often they lead to lowest common denominator solutions to public problems. Finally, they make it extremely difficult for everyone involved in the political process to weigh different priorities against each other and to propose measures that will best meet overall national needs.

Because of the many shortcomings in the federal government's management style, institutional reformers in the postwar period have devoted much of their energy to searching for some mechanism that could present the nation with a comprehensive program of policy. In the domestic sphere this means trying to find institutions that could present clear and consistent views of what the overall structure of the federal social role should be. If we could develop political institutions that would perform this function, they would have to address questions of adequacy, priorities, and future needs.

For a time would-be reformers focused on the presidency.[4] The growth of the Executive Office of the President—particularly the development of the Office of Management and Budget and the Council of Economic Advisors—was regarded as a hopeful sign that the executive branch had developed a coordinating and planning mechanism. But while the Executive Office has greatly improved the quality of presidential decision making, the hopes of reformers have been realized only in part. Agencies and iron triangles still retain much of their power; the Executive Office has itself become a large and divided bureaucracy; and most presidents want to practice their personal version of the politics of inclusiveness by striking political bargains, regardless of whether they add up to a coherent program.

The search for some institution that could develop a national program also has focused on our political parties. Their platforms might become rival national plans. But American political parties are handicapped by many of the same centrifugal forces that restrict federal policy more generally. National parties draw their strength from innumerable local political organizations, interest groups, and other dispersed sources of influence, expertise, and funding. As a result, their platforms are generally a hodgepodge of proposals that attempt to please as many of their constituent groups as possible.

There have been times in American history when national parties presented programs that set forth definite courses of action to address at least some of the major areas of public concern. These have usually been periods when local politicians found it to their advantage to attach themselves to strong national leaders—for example, during the Jacksonian era or the New Deal—or when party leaders could control political resources. In recent decades, however, the demise of old-fashioned political "machines," the increased cost of campaigning, and more direct access to the mass media have encouraged most politicians to develop their own platforms and sources of support independent of party leadership.

National parties still perform important functions in our political system: as rallying points for opposed teams at election time and as ways of organizing legislative bodies and forming administrations. And there can be no doubt that many politicians feel a genuine sense of party loyalty, although it is often hard to define precisely what the boundaries of that loyalty are. But because of the diversity of views that must be gathered under the umbrellas of national parties, they have not been good vehicles for articulating clear and consistent national plans.

More recently, reformers have placed their hopes in the Executive and congressional budget processes. Developing a comprehensive federal budget forces at least some attention to priorities, tradeoffs, and glaring omissions. Both the Executive and congressional budget procedures have been strengthened in recent years, but politicians and bureaucrats have found innumerable ways to circumvent them. The easiest way is simply not to agree on a budget at all. Over the last decade, Congress often has been unable to pass a final budget resolution. Rather than review national needs and priorities, it has simply extended past appropriations for existing programs with minor amendments. Another tactic is to develop overly rosy estimates of costs and revenues—a practice both the Executive and Congress commonly have adopted.

Distressed by these and other evasions of tough choices, Congress passed the Gramm-Rudman-Hollings budget act in 1985, setting overall spending limits, a process to estimate whether they were met, and an automatic formula for cutting back expenditures to the required levels. Members of Congress immediately expressed regret at this degree of discipline, failed to reach agreement by the timetables specified in the act, and were relieved to have the procedures they had adopted declared unconstitutional.

The federal government clearly needs some mechanism for

planning and establishing priorities—some way to put forward one or more national programs that the public can debate. The development of the Executive Office and reforms in the budget process have brought progress in this direction. They have prevented a large and expanding public agenda from becoming completely unmanageable.

We should certainly bend every effort to find other ways to improve the manner in which the federal government operates. For example, policy planning units have been highly successful at other levels of government, and most federal departments have established such units—with varying degrees of effectiveness. The time may come when the nation is ready to make use of an institution such as the National Resources Planning Board that covers the entire field of domestic policy.

Longer terms for members of the House of Representatives and restrictions on the skyrocketing cost of campaign spending would undoubtedly improve the American political process. And proposals to streamline economic decision making, such as those advanced by former Congressional Budget Office Director Alice Rivlin, certainly merit serious attention. Among other measures, Rivlin suggests combining the Treasury Department, the Council of Economic Advisers, and the Office of Management and Budget in one Cabinet department, creating closer links between that department and the Federal Reserve, adopting a two-year budget cycle, and combining congressional appropriation and authorization processes.[5]

But while institutional reform is commendable, our experience to date suggests that trying to remedy the shortcomings of the social role by improving the structure of government is likely to meet with only limited success. In those periods of our history when Americans have felt the need for more effective institutional arrangements to accomplish major national purposes— fighting wars or overcoming depressions, for example—they have found the means to create new structures for government. Ad hoc planning groups such as the Committee on Economic Security and the Urban Affairs Council of the Nixon administration are good examples of improvised institutional change that had telling effect. But absent some pressing national concern, institutional

reform of and by itself does not seem to be a very promising route
to a more effective social role.

Policy

Most of the current debate about how to improve the federal
social role focuses on ideas for new policy directions, rather than
on proposals for institutional reform. Both liberals and conservatives are concerned about the shortcomings of domestic policy,
but their proposals for change differ greatly.

While there is no such animal as a "typical" liberal or conservative, there are certainly two opposed tendencies in contemporary American politics that would lead the nation down very
different paths. These tendencies are not rigid ideologies or even
"schools of thought." As a result, many public leaders may find
it hard to recognize their views in any concise description of the
liberal–conservative divide. Yet to understand the debate over
reform of the federal social role, it is important to outline at least
the major dimensions of these two tendencies in our public life,
even if such an outline inevitably runs the risk of oversimplifica-
tion or even caricature.

With all due apology, it seems fair to say that the traditional
liberal approach to reform of the federal social role centers on the
idea that all Americans are entitled to certain common benefits of
citizenship. A decent income and access to the essentials of life
should not depend on the accidents of employment, family, economic gyrations, or luck. Economic security should not depend
so heavily on the public and corporate social supports that come
only through having a good job with good benefits. Less fortunate
people may have different problems than the average American
has, but they deserve the same level of public protection. Treating
them as second-class citizens is inconsistent with democratic values and implicitly dangerous for all of us, because if we allow
government to neglect the needs of any of our fellow citizens, the
day may come when, due to bad luck or bad judgment, we are
the ones who are left out.

As a result, the federal social role should not contain multiple tiers or multiple criteria for receiving public benefits. We should settle on one criterion: either everyone should benefit from social programs (in the same way that average Americans receive Social Security payments), or public benefits should be distributed strictly according to need.

In practice, liberals devote themselves to the more pragmatic task of gradually nudging the social role toward common standards of provision. Their proposals are directed toward filling gaps in the present system: extending medical and retirement benefits to groups presently unserved, improving services for the poor and other marginal groups, targeting public works and subsidies to areas in greatest need, and tightening up on both social and economic regulations.

The conservative approach adopts a different ideal. Why shouldn't everyone be able to buy his or her own economic security? Conservatives believe that if the trillion-dollar burden of federal activism were lifted from the shoulders of the American economy, there would be such a surge of economic growth and consumption that many of our present public supports would be unnecessary. "A rising tide would lift all boats." We would all be able to take care of ourselves.

In practice, conservatives are also gradualists; they chip away at the social role wherever it is most vulnerable, which is generally around programs for the disadvantaged. But given their objective, they identify Social Security and other comprehensive programs as the ultimate fortress to be stormed, simply because those programs make up so large a portion of social spending.

There is a great deal to be said on behalf of both the liberal and conservative approaches to reform. But both are unrealistic in a number of ways, and it is partly the failure of either to command very widespread support that has led to the current stalemate in public policy.

Liberal ideals may be morally commendable, but both those ideals and the incrementalist policies that reflect them too often neglect the need to set federal priorities. If we introduced all of the refinements that liberals would like, the federal agenda would become even more enormous and cumbersome than it already is.

Liberals do an excellent job of pointing out unmet public needs, but they are generally reluctant to choose which of these are— and are not—central enough to the common welfare to merit inclusion on the federal agenda. And they are reluctant to choose which items on that agenda should have the strongest claim on public resources.

Pursuit of the conservative agenda is also likely to fail. It ignores the fundamental fact that finally dawned on David Stockman: "Despite their often fuzzy rhetoric and twisted rationalizations, congressmen and senators ultimately deliver what their constituents demand. . . . Consequently, the spending policies of Washington do reflect the heterogeneous and parochial demands that arise from the diverse, activated fragments of the electorate scattered across the land."[6]

The American style is too strong to allow the conservative agenda to proceed very far. The politics of inclusiveness dictate a far more extensive social role than conservatives believe the nation should support. Most particularly, if the ultimate success of their agenda depends on reducing comprehensive social insurance programs, it is doomed to failure. Every element in the American style conspires to endow programs from which nearly everyone benefits with the highest level of political support.

A more fundamental problem is that both the liberal and conservative agendas are essentially backward looking. They take as their point of departure the present structure of the federal social role. To oversimplify, liberals would like more of the types of programs that are at the heart of present-day social policy, and conservatives would like fewer. The debate that ensues has the stale quality of an inside game: a hashing over of old arguments about old proposals that have been won and lost many times in the past. It is no wonder that neither side of the debate, nor the debate itself, has sparked much public enthusiasm.

Progress

As long as the public policy debate is limited to the present range of ideas, the prospects for reform of the federal social role are bleak. Activist government in the United States is an exceptionally conservative institution. It is politically conservative by virtue of its bias toward sharing power with other institutions and accommodating most demands. It is socially conservative by virtue of its bias toward the average American and its emphasis on earned rights. It is economically conservative by its safe definition of government's role in the economy: when in doubt, do no harm. The result is a large, untidy, inadequate, and extremely durable structure of policy that is unlikely to be shaken by any of the current proposals for reform.

Yet reform occurs. It occurred in the early days of our republic, in the Civil War era, during the New Deal, and in the Great Society period, as well as during other periods of American history. How? The fact of the matter is that significant changes in American social policy have rarely come from a gradual refining of institutions and agendas. They have usually come when strong leadership responded to serious threats to the common welfare—the perils of launching a new nation, the crisis of sectionalism, the Great Depression, the trauma of a society suddenly confronted with its own history of social neglect. The Great Society era demonstrated that large changes can also result from great national opportunities—the perception of policymakers in the 1960s that national affluence had created a fiscal dividend which could be used to expand the scope of activism.

In conditions of crisis or outstanding national opportunity, leaders have had to step back and take a fresh look at the needs and priorities of the American people and assert a strong new vision of what the public interest requires.

Enhanced awareness that we are all in the same boat and a clearly articulated sense of national purpose are the keys to progress. With these in hand, activists have been able to turn crisis management to larger purposes. They have brushed aside existing barriers in response to new challenges. What seemed impossible one day has seemed only a secondary issue the next. In some cases dramatic new initiatives have been taken, for example, in the area of civil rights in the 1960s. In other cases, a heightened awareness of common concerns has allowed long-maturing ideas to become realities, for example, in the implementation of Medicare during a time of national crisis. The important point is that major change becomes possible primarily when circumstances compel the American people and their leaders to think boldly about the general welfare.

But even when the forces of change have been strong, activists have rarely tried to swim against the tide of the American style. They have developed new policies that use the biases and untidy features of our public life to support better solutions to common problems. Then the imperatives for activism—common problems and a clear view of the public interest—make the American style the servant rather than the master of public policy. Institutional diversity and the politics of inclusiveness become means for binding the nation together, rather than tearing it apart.

All of this is possible. It has been done. In contemporary terms, this formula for change means that progress is only possible if the nation is prepared to engage in a true reassessment of the federal social role—a debate that starts from where we are now in late twentieth-century America and asks what national needs most urgently require attention, today and in the years to come.

If we step back from the current debate, at least some of those needs are clear. In the hope that increased awareness will call forth a timely response, the next chapters describe the major challenges that currently face American society, what type of public response they demand, and how that response can be tailored to the requirements of the American style.

9

Driving Forces I:
Economic Change

The United States has experienced enormous social and economic change over the last few decades. Much of this change undoubtedly has been for the good. Most of us are living longer, healthier, and in many ways more fulfilling lives than our parents or grandparents were able to live. But the same changes that have made these improvements possible have also created strains in our national life that profoundly affect each and every one of us.

A great number of problems have emerged from this era of change, but four problems, in particular, most severely affect all Americans today:

- threats to employment,
- threats to families and children,
- an increasingly hopeless underclass,
- the aging of our society.

Stated in general terms, these conditions are not new. At least some Americans have always experienced threats to employment; family structures have always been changing and child-rearing has always been fraught with difficulties. There have always been people at the bottom of the social and economic heap; and, with some intermissions, our society has been aging for at least two hundred years.

But recent decades of social and economic change have altered the nature of these problems, in some cases by magnifying their effects and in other cases by transforming them into new and more troublesome forms. If the present directions of change persist—as there is every reason to believe they will—the four major problems that threaten us today are unlikely to become better and, in many cases, are bound to become worse.

In their present form, those problems are of enormous importance, because they severely affect the well-being of each and every one of us. Clearly, they call for solutions from the federal government. They arise from social and economic conditions that are nationwide and, increasingly, worldwide in scope. There is no way that individuals, families, companies, or states can mount an adequate response on their own.

Yet existing federal policies are not adequate to the challenge, and over the last decade government at the national level has not reached out to find new solutions. While the forces of social and economic change have greatly magnified the major problems that face us today, the federal government has been locked in political stalemate and the basic structure of activist government has remained essentially the same as it was in past decades.

This inadequate response to some of our most urgent common concerns should not and will not be acceptable to the American people much longer. Because threats to employment, threats to families, problems of the underclass, and societal aging seriously affect us all and call for common national solutions, they are the driving forces that will determine the directions the federal social role must take in the years to come.

In their origins and effects, these problems are intricately interconnected. Each causes difficulties in its own right, and collectively they create even greater concerns. This chapter describes the forms that threats to employment have taken in recent years; the following chapter discusses the other driving forces and their cumulative impact on the nation.

Economic Turmoil

To understand the nature and severity of present threats to employment, it is necessary, first, to understand the economic conditions that have helped to create them. The last two decades have been a turbulent and troubled period for the American economy. The nation suffered through ten years of slow economic growth and was finally shocked into recovery by government intervention. But that recovery has been marred by uneven growth in GNP, extremely low gains in productivity, mounting public and private debt, an alarming number of failures in the financial industry, and rates of unemployment that stabilized around 7 percent. The process of recovery has also brought a rash of corporate reorganizations that redirected vast amounts of capital, in some cases with dubious benefit to the economy as a whole. And it was helped along by a decline in world oil prices, which may not last for long.

In addition, over the past two decades American firms have experienced stiff competition from foreign companies, both at home and overseas. And our economy has been handicapped by high interest rates and an overvalued dollar that have drawn a flood of foreign investment to the United States and created record deficits in our balance of payments with the rest of the world. Some American companies have also become more competitive with each other as a result of deregulation in the airline, financial, and communications industries. This has created both problems and benefits for the public and the economy.

Observers have claimed that increased foreign competition and changing opportunities for investment have led to a decline in both the output and the market share of the manufacturing sector of our economy. Although most of those claims appear to be unfounded, several major manufacturing industries—including steel, textiles, and automobiles—are clearly suffering from chronic problems.[1] And there is at least one respect in which the once preeminent manufacturing companies have come to play a less important role: the number of workers they employ declined by about 2 million between 1979 and 1985.[2] Manufacturing, which has been our largest source of employment since the early years of the twentieth century, now provides fewer jobs than wholesale and retail trade or business and personal services.

American agriculture has also experienced a bewildering combination of ups and downs in recent years. The productivity of America's farms has soared, creating record harvests. But at the same time, world markets for agricultural products have become highly competitive. Falling prices, together with bumper crops and abrupt shifts in federal policy, have left many farmers and farm credit institutions overextended. The overall results of these changes have been mounting agricultural surpluses, a record number of farm foreclosures, and the loss of almost one million jobs in the agricultural sector since 1979.[3] Because large and more capital-intensive farms appear to be surviving these economic strains better than smaller, labor-intensive farms, it is likely that agricultural employment will continue to fall.

The major job growth has been in what analysts often call the "service sector"—an amalgam of all industries other than manufacturing, construction, mining, and agriculture. This sector currently provides 70 percent of employment in the United States and has been responsible for creating over 90 percent of the new jobs in recent decades.[4]

The Average American

How do these complicated patterns of ups and downs affect the average American for whom the federal social role was designed? They have threatened him in two major ways: by increasing the risk that he will face financial hardship and by reducing the effectiveness of public and private protections against it.

Recall that, in economic terms, the average American is someone who holds a good job at a steady wage, receives adequate private pension and health care benefits, and has enough discretionary income to put aside some personal savings. Far fewer of us meet this definition of the average American today than did so twenty years ago. We are more likely than we were to suffer from periodic unemployment and to face limited prospects for improving our position in the world of work. As a result, we are less likely to be well protected by the combination of public and private economic supports designed for average Americans.

Threats to employment as well as to success and security on the job menace some Americans more than others, but ultimately few of us can tell how perilous our situation is. Although many factors contribute to this increasing incidence of risk, three are of particular importance: the demand for higher levels of skill in the workplace; pressures to reduce labor costs; and the geographical mobility of jobs. Because all three of these factors arise from long-term economic trends that cut across all sectors of our economy and society, public policy will have to wrestle with them and the problems they create for the indefinite future.

There is nothing novel about this diagnosis of employment problems.[5] All the experts say the same thing, but nobody says it loudly enough. It is as if the experts fear that the nation is not prepared to face the full implications of employment issues. Yet beyond these gloomy generalities lie some truly frightening specifics and some clear implications for the federal social role.

Unemployment

The increasing risk of unemployment is the most obvious effect of the economic changes of the past few decades. Unemployment rates exceeded 10 percent during the last recession and remained at over 7 percent during the mid-1980s—an all-time high for a period of economic recovery. But gross unemployment rates mask even greater problems. To begin with, those rates have been higher at the peak of each succeeding economic recovery for the last several decades. It appears that even when the nation's economy is working well, it is less able to absorb the available workforce. In addition, official government employment figures do not count "discouraged workers"—people who have been so unsuccessful in their search for jobs that they have stopped looking. By most estimates they would add at least one percentage point to the unemployment figures, and their numbers have been growing in recent years.

Finally, in some cities, states, and regions of the country where troubled industries or failing farms make up a large part of the local economy, unemployment rates have been at least 50 percent higher than for the nation as a whole, even during the period of recovery. In these pockets of depression, workers laid off during the late 1970s and early 1980s have never come back. Their jobs—often high-paying union jobs or work on family farms—have disappeared, and many have been unable to find other work for prolonged periods of time.

How many displaced workers are there? The Bureau of Labor Statistics (BLS) estimates that over 5 million Americans who had been employed for over three years lost their jobs between 1979 and 1983 as a result of plant closings or slack work, or because their positions were abolished.[6] The BLS also estimates that over half of these people were unemployed for twenty-six weeks or longer. According to other sources, as many as 11 million have been displaced over the last five years, and there are over 5 million "permanently unemployed" people in the United States—a number roughly equal to the population of Missouri.[7]

Although most authorities doubt that so many people are, in fact, "permanently" out of work, there can be no doubt that millions suffered the shock of sudden and prolonged unemployment as they saw their jobs vanish in the last recession. And a large portion of those who found work again ended up in jobs that pay considerably less than their previous employment. Moreover, many of these people had worked in troubled basic industries, where job opportunities have continued to decline. We are likely to have more displaced workers in the future.

The other large category of the long-term unemployed are teenagers and young adults trying to enter the labor force. Although there is a shortage of young workers for certain sorts of jobs in some parts of the country, nationwide the unemployment picture is distressing. Among men sixteen to twenty-four years of age, the unemployment rate was about 14 percent in 1985, and among women it was about 13 percent.[8] But the aggregate numbers are deceptive. The unemployment rate for teen-agers was far higher than the rate for young adults twenty to twenty-four years of age. Of course, the vast majority of teenagers are enrolled in school and looking for or holding part-time jobs to supplement their personal or family resources. But most of the approximately 3 million teen-agers not in school are looking for full-time work—which presumably means that they must live on their earnings. The unemployment rate for this group is over 20 percent for whites and over 40 percent for blacks.

There are about 725,000 unemployed teen-agers looking for full-time work. It is on this group of troubled young people, and on the twenty to twenty-four year olds—for whom the unemployment rate was 25 percent for blacks and 9 percent for whites in 1986—that concerns about youth unemployment should focus.[9] Tragically, unemployment rates for these age groups not only are high, but they have also been steadily rising in recent decades. The rates are over twice as high for whites and three times as high for blacks as they were in the 1960s.

Together, young people struggling to enter the workforce and displaced workers form the hard core of unemployment in the United States. They account for about half of total unemployment, and they are far more likely than most Americans to suffer the hardships of being out of work for prolonged periods of time.

Unfortunately, it is easy to dismiss their problems as special cases that have little to do with the rest of us. Indeed, if young people and displaced workers were not included in the unemployment figures, the overall national rate of joblessness would fall to something like the usual recovery level, and most of the remaining unemployed would be people who are out of work for relatively short periods of time. By performing some mental gymnastics, it is possible to paint a fairly rosy picture of employment prospects in our economy: aside from the special cases of youth and displaced workers, American business accomplished the remarkable feat of absorbing the influx of most of the 76 million members of the baby boom generation into the workforce over the last two decades.

Skills

But it is wrong to ignore the hard-core unemployed, because their experiences are almost certainly straws in the wind for many more Americans. A large proportion of these people lack the skills needed to gain and hold jobs in today's economy. Many of the displaced workers formerly held low-skilled blue collar jobs, and many unemployed young people have only the most rudimentary manual and intellectual skills. The simple fact is that there is less of a market for low-skilled workers today than there was ten or twenty years ago. Most jobs today call for higher levels of education and training, and greater flexibility than the blue collar jobs of the past. And an even larger number of the jobs of the future will call for still higher levels of expertise.

Most new jobs are in the service sector. The popular image that service sector work is typically low-paid and low-skilled— janitorial work or serving in fast food restaurants—is decidedly wrong. In fact, because the service sector accounts for 70 percent of total employment, the work it provides is extremely diverse: ranging from jobs for lawyers and bankers to jobs for nurse's aides and keypunch operators. On average, wages are as high as those in manufacturing, and the fastest growing areas of the service sector are jobs for nurses, accountants, and other specialists. These jobs pay well, but they require high levels of specialized training.

The problem for the hard-core unemployed, therefore, is not that there is a shortage of good jobs. There are plenty of opportunities in the service sector. The problem is that displaced workers and young people often lack the skills needed to seize those opportunities. If they do find service sector employment, it is likely to be in the less well-paying areas—precisely in jobs such as fast food service and janitorial work.

The experiences of the hard-core unemployed of today are an omen for the rest of us; the demand for increasingly high levels of skill in the workplace that handicaps them will limit the opportunities of millions of other Americans in the years to come. As the structure of our economy continues to change, many more blue collar workers either will see their jobs vanish or will face limited prospects for advancement. The foundry worker who once expected to rise through the blue collar hierarchy will find that, beyond a certain point, operating new and complex machinery requires education and training that he lacks.

But it is not only blue collar workers who face limited prospects. All employees of a firm are threatened when it shifts operations to take advantage of the opportunities of a service economy. The experiences of a firm headquartered in the Washington, D.C., area are a microcosm of what is happening to the economy as a whole. In the early 1980s the firm concentrated its operations on uranium mining. A few years later it shifted into machine tools and oil exploration. Finding the opportunities limited in that field, it changed operations again to concentrate on maintenance of jet engines.[10] Obviously, with each of these changes, the firm required a different set of skills in its employees, all the way from the hands-on worker to top management. Almost certainly many people lost jobs in this firm, as they have in the economy as a whole, simply because new lines of business called for skills they did not have.

Large numbers of service sector workers also face uncertain prospects because good jobs are becoming increasingly specialized. An accountant or a nurse today must have far more sophisticated skills to deal with new information or medical technology, respectively, than their counterparts were expected to have some years ago. As a result, a growing number of people run the risk of being left behind in their jobs.

Employees who are middle-aged or older often face especially serious problems. Firms that employ them are likely to promote younger workers with more up-to-date training and lower salary demands. Companies are also increasingly prone to get rid of their older workers by one means or another. And if older workers lose their jobs, they stand a far higher chance than any other group in the workforce of being unemployed for long periods of time—no one else wants a worker whose skills are outmoded.

Finally, many people get trapped by their own specialization. The days of the generalist are over—even in the professional world.

A pediatric nurse may find it difficult to switch to surgical nursing if the demand for workers in her field diminishes. She may have to settle for a less lucrative job at general practice nursing.

A newspaper anecdote captures the employment problems that many highly skilled professionals face today:

> "One thing we are seeing is that middle managers are having a difficult time finding new jobs," said James C. Shaffer, a principal in the Washington office of Towers, Perrin Forster & Crosby, a firm which helps place some of these executives. "A group of people who have been with a company for a long period, who have been with one industry for a long time and who are technically proficient . . . when they walk out the door and start looking for other organizations they would be comfortable with, they are finding the doors closed. The search firms have an overabundance of these people looking for jobs."[11]

In short, for many people in both blue collar and white collar occupations, the demand for increasingly high levels of specialized skills means that employment security, and certainly prospects for advancement, diminish as they grow older. Some companies invest heavily in training and retraining their present employees, and this can help reduce the threats posed by changing skill requirements. But most research indicates that companies tend to invest less in training than would be optimal for society as a whole.[12] This is both because highly skilled workers are more mobile and may not stay with the firm that trains them and because there is a sufficient pool of younger workers who start out with a higher level of skills.

At the extreme, one measure of the mismatch between the skills of American workers and the jobs available is provided by recent estimates that up to 20 percent of Americans read at or below the fifth-grade level.[13] There is virtually no well-paying service sector job that someone who cannot read, write, and compute at more than an elementary level is capable of holding. Moreover, it is unrealistic to expect industry to train people in these basic skills or to provide a great deal of the more specialized education that is essential to gaining and holding a job in today's labor market.

Labor Costs

At the same time that workers are faced with the demand for increasingly high levels of skills, the forces of economic change have placed strong pressures on many firms to reduce the cost of labor. Increasing competition in all industries, both at home and overseas, and the slow growth of productivity have forced firms to seek savings wherever they can. Many economists and businessmen believe that American labor is overpriced. Certainly the average wage level in the United States is higher than in most other countries with whose products we must compete. Whether this means that American labor is "too expensive" in some objective sense or not, many companies have attempted to improve their positions by taking measures that reduce the number and average wage level of their employees.

Sometimes these measures are fairly direct: layoffs or reductions in wages or benefits for both present and former employees. Sometimes they are indirect: the result of other measures taken to improve productivity and competitiveness, such as changing lines of business, production processes, management practices, or sites of operation.

Attempts to hold down labor costs have been most visible in the troubled industries mentioned earlier. Steel and automobile firms made headlines by negotiating lower wages, decreased fringe benefits, and planned layoffs with their unions. They and other troubled firms have also introduced new labor-saving processes and developed two-tier employment policies, whereby some younger workers are hired on less favorable terms than their more experienced colleagues.

But it is not only troubled firms that have sought to reduce labor costs. Leading-edge firms such as Eastman Kodak and Time, Inc., have also laid off thousands of workers to keep costs down. The airline industry presents a good case in point. It is by no means in decline. In the fierce competitive struggle since deregulation in 1978, the number of airlines has increased from thirty-six to one hundred, the number of passengers carried each year has increased by 83 percent, and the number of miles flown has increased 32 percent. But the number of employees has dropped by 30,000, and wages have remained stagnant or declined slightly in real dollar terms.[14] More traffic handled by fewer people at stable wages means increased productivity and profit for the airline industry, but it also means fewer jobs in the industry and less income for its employees.

Many firms have adopted policies that not only reduce labor costs but also give them greater flexibility in expanding or contracting their workforce to meet the problems and opportunities of a fast-changing economy. Companies have begun hiring more part-time workers who have no tenure rights, often receive wages below the level of their full-time counterparts, and rarely qualify for full corporate benefits, or for any benefits at all. Nearly one-fourth of the people who gained employment between 1980, and 1985, are working part-time.[15] And there has been a growing trend toward hiring contract workers—people employed full time for limited durations who receive none of the protections of regular employees. The percentage of the American workforce employed on a part-time or contract basis increased from 11 percent to at least 27 percent between 1965 and 1985. About 30 million people are now working part-time or on contract.[16]

Obviously some people find part-time or contract work attractive. Parents of young children may prefer to work part-time; and contract work includes some highly desirable occupations, such as business consulting and specialized computer programming. But the Bureau of Labor Statistics indicates that about 30 percent of the over 19 million part-time employees, or about 5.6 million people, would prefer to work full time on a regular job.[17] If their numbers had been added to the number of people who could not find jobs at all, the unemployment rate would have been over 11 percent in late 1986.[18]

Wages and benefits have also been kept down by the growth of the small business sector. Firms with fewer than one hundred employees are the fastest growing source of jobs in the United States. They employed about 44 million people in 1984, and they have created more than half of all new jobs in recent years.[19] Typically small firms pay lower wages and provide fewer benefits than big companies. Generally they are not unionized and offer less job security. Many exist largely to provide bigger companies with specialized business services. As a result, there is a sense in which large companies are keeping down labor costs by contracting out to smaller companies jobs that they might otherwise create in their own firms. In some cases, the same effect is achieved by spinning off operations. For example, Greyhound was able to lay off 3,000 employees by transferring the management of its bus terminals to independent operators. Tactics such as this are often considered efficient business practice because, not surprisingly, large companies can often buy the same services from small outside contractors less expensively than they can produce them in-house.

Another way of keeping labor costs down is to move operations outside the United States—often to Mexico, the Caribbean, Korea, or Singapore, where there are large pools of efficient low-wage workers. There is also a continuing dependence on low-wage labor in the United States. Over 5.5 million Americans work for less than the minimum wage. Many are teen-agers holding part-time jobs. Over 2 million, however, are adults who work full time but still fall below the poverty line.[20]

Stepping back from all of these developments, we appear to be witnessing a gradual change in the nature of the employment contract in the United States. Once the dominant model was a contract of indefinite duration, in which the employee provided labor and the employer provided an assured income together with fringe benefits, and, in many cases, opportunities for advancement. The employee was in a great many ways "part of the company." Today, the dominant model for an increasing number of workers is one in which they provide specialized labor for a set fee over limited periods of time, with few expectations of benefits or advancement. The employee is more like a contractor or consultant—someone "outside the firm."

These changes obviously have their advantages. They create more of a free market in labor and help companies adjust wages to economic fluctuations. But changes in the employment contract also have their detriments. Among these, from the standpoint of many employees, are less job security and the growing ability of employers to keep the cost of labor down.

Stagnant Income

A combination of attempts to keep down labor costs, together with the effects of slow overall economic growth in the 1970s, have resulted in stagnant real income for many Americans. While estimates vary, it is generally agreed that average family income for households headed by members of the baby boom generation either declined or increased only slightly between 1979 and 1983.[21] And the number of low-income jobs increased over that period of time, while the number of middle-income jobs declined. Between 1979 and 1984, 44 percent of the new jobs created in the United States, paid wages that were at or below the minimum wage for those working full time, compared with 20 percent of the new jobs created between 1973 and 1979.[22]

These trends mean that a great many members of the baby boom generation have not been able to increase their earnings as they move from the early years of employment to the period of life when most people expect that they will be able to buy homes, form families and enjoy a more affluent lifestyle in other ways. And while real income will probably begin to increase again for as long as economic recovery continues, attempts to hold down labor costs will in all likelihood guarantee that most workers can expect a slower growth in wages and less generous health and pension plans than they enjoyed in the past.

Many authorities would quibble with this projection. They would argue that as the baby boom generation passes into maturity, employers will find a shortage of workers in the much smaller succeeding generation and will bid up wages, benefits, and training programs in a competition to gain part of a limited labor supply. But this is not the only possible scenario. Employers have other options. The growing number of immigrants may make up for any shortage of low-skilled labor, more work can be shifted overseas, and baby boom workers can be retained for longer. Also, more efficient management and production processes can be adopted, and employers may choose to use the resulting productivity gains to cut prices in order to remain competitive, rather than to reward workers with higher wages. Many companies may well turn to these options.

In fact, they may have no choice: if other countries operating with roughly similar technology can produce goods and services at lower labor costs than those that prevail in the United States, American companies literally will not be able to stay in business if they allow labor costs to rise very rapidly. Moreover, judging from the experience of both troubled and leading-edge firms, many American companies can, in fact, manage to operate successfully with far fewer and less well-paid employees. As a result, the baby bust generation may well find an economic environment in which employers not only can but must offer jobs on terms that are not much more favorable than the terms offered today. To be more precise, they may find their real wages increasing at a rate far slower than the wages of their parents and grandparents increased in the 1950s, 1960s, and early 1970s.

Another optimistic thought is that prosperous high-technology industries will be an increasing source of jobs and higher wages. But although high-technology firms have grown rapidly, they still account for only a small percentage of employment, they tend not to be labor-intensive, and many of the jobs they provide are low-paid assembly work. In any case, their growth rate has slowed in recent years due to saturated markets and increased international competition. The high-technology solution to employment problems may come someday, but that day appears to be a long way off.

Job Mobility

The efforts of companies to increase their competitive positions by corporate restructuring, improved management, better technology, and other means has another important effect on the employment prospects of average Americans. Although many workers whose jobs become redundant still have useful skills, the opportunity to use those skills is often in a new location. A lathe operator whose job is eliminated by new computerized equipment may still be employable in another plant owned by his company or another company that has not installed the new equipment. But the jobs may be in another town, often in another region of the country. Likewise, an accountant whose company discontinues the product line he has been monitoring may find opportunities if he is willing to move. Many companies are abandoning old plants or office space in decaying inner cities for new, more efficient operations in the suburbs or the Sunbelt. Often they give at least some of their employees the option of moving with them.

Unfortunately, large numbers of workers find themselves geographically stranded. If job opportunities exist at other firms in other parts of the country, they have no way of knowing about them. And even if they do have the chance to move, they are often tied down by financial, family, or transportation problems. A worker in the central city may find it hard to sell his home for a price that allows him to afford housing in a new location. A move can be extremely costly to him in terms of lost equity. Or a worker whose wife is employed may have to decide whether he can run the risk of living on one income if her opportunities are uncertain in a new location. Urban experts have shown that, for low-wage workers, the problem can be as simple as lack of cheap and effective forms of transportation from their homes in the inner city, where jobs are vanishing, to the growing number of jobs in the suburbs.

As a result of these and other problems, many people do not move to follow employment opportunities. They remain stranded in dying factory towns, inner city neighborhoods, even in prosperous areas where there is little demand for their specialty. Or they may move at considerable personal cost. Either way the worker faced with problems of job mobility loses. And the economy loses, too. Just as there are economically blighted regions in the United States, there are also regions of labor shortage. A truly efficient economy would swiftly match workers with jobs, wherever they are. But because of limited information and other impediments, American workers often are not able to follow the migration of opportunity. The United States has always had problems with labor mobility—as when the major source of jobs shifted from the agricultural to the industrial sector around the turn of the century—and it still has serious problems today.

A Fragile Economy

Increased chances of unemployment, reduced prospects for workers who cannot keep up with the requirement for higher levels of education and training, downward pressures on wages, job migration, and the fact that more of the available opportunities are for part-time and contract work—all of these and other recent trends add up to severe hardships for millions of Americans and greater insecurity for many millions more. And the hardships and uncertainty that many people experience in good times are likely to become far worse in times of economic downturn.

In a recession, displaced workers and unskilled young people will face even bleaker prospects than they do today. Many older workers and others whose skills are outmoded will swell the ranks of the long-term unemployed. Some firms will eliminate the jobs of part-time and contract workers, to whom they have little obligation. Others may choose to retain these low-cost employees and lay off a larger number of regular workers. Wages will be forced down further, and more work will leave the United States. In some cases, small companies that depend on contractual relations with larger firms will flounder. In other cases, large companies will rely more heavily on "contracting out" and reduce their own workforce.

This is not mere speculation. All of these misfortunes occurred during the last recession, and they are likely to occur again the next time the American economy takes a downward plunge. A strong wind knocks down the weak trees. And there can be no doubt that workers with low skill levels or outmoded skills, employees of companies that cannot or will not maintain wage rates, people who hold jobs that are marginal at best, and those whose tasks can be performed by lower cost labor are more at risk of losing out in hard times than are people in better circumstances. However difficult their positions may be today, a growing number of workers face a high risk of encountering even more severe problems if the economy turns sour.

The United States has always suffered recessions and depressions, and there is every reason to believe that it will continue to suffer these misfortunes in the future. Despite all its sophistication, national economic management was unable to prevent or easily reverse the downturn of the 1970s, and few economists believe that it can prevent future problems. Certainly the recovery of the mid-1980s has been shaky from the beginning. The question is not whether the economic pendulum will swing, but when. And when it does, a larger percentage of the workforce is at high risk of facing severe consequences than in the 1970s.

Uncertainty

How many people are seriously at risk? Because we live in turbulent economic times and are likely to continue to do so, there is no good way to answer that question. And this uncertainty is a large part of the problem workers face today. Because the American economy is changing so rapidly and in so many ways, few of us can be confident that our positions are secure.

We may live in a region of the country that enjoys economic prosperity today, but in a few years we may find ourselves in the midst of economic decline. A map of the United States showing the areas with unemployment rates 30 percent or more above the national average in 1975 would look very different from a similar map drawn a decade later. The 1975 map would identify the West Coast and New England as the places where jobs were hard to find and prospects were bleak even for many people who were employed. The 1985 map would show that these areas (except the timber-producing states) are booming, whereas the central part of the country—the manufacturing, farming, and oil-producing states—is in the grip of a prolonged recession. Which of us can predict whether the complex and fast-moving process of economic change will bring good or bad luck to our neighborhood?

Even apparently "sure bets" on the future of the economy often result in disappointment. In 1984, anyone would have staked a month's pay on the continuing prosperity of Texas, Oklahoma, Louisiana, and other states that have a lock on our domestic oil supply. In 1986 those states were suffering from massive unemployment due to falling world oil prices. Silicon Valley seemed to be the promised land for many Americans in the 1970s. But more recently the growth of jobs in the semiconductor industry has slowed, and many firms have been forced to lay off workers. Before airline deregulation, almost anyone would have thought that a job in commercial aviation offered endless possibilities. But each new corporate merger of airlines and other industries in recent years has been accompanied by cutbacks of personnel, reduced wages, and diminished benefits. Finally, it is often forgotten that the United States once had a consumer electronics industry. During the excitement over the growth of television and the introduction of transistor radios in the 1950s and 1960s, any rational person would have believed that there were enormous opportunities in working for American companies that produced those suddenly indispensable devices. Today almost all television, radio, and stereo sets are manufactured overseas—a whole industry has been wiped out.

Looking to the future, how many of us can say that our jobs would be secure if world oil prices increased again or if the shaky structure of Third World debt collapsed and sent our banking industry into a tailspin?

Most of us are not seriously harmed by the forces of economic change. Either they do not impinge on us directly or we manage to adjust to them with little trouble. But the cost of unemployment, reduced wages, lost benefits, and uprooted lifestyles for those who are adversely affected is very great indeed. And the problem is that few of us can predict with much certainty whether we will be among the unlucky group who will have to pay high costs of this sort. In this sense, we are all at risk.

If we add up the people who experience unemployment for some period during any given year, the discouraged workers, the people who are working part time involuntarily, and contract workers, the total number of Americans who have lost or are at severe risk of losing wages, benefits, or both in any recent year

188 GOVERNMENT FOR THE PEOPLE

approaches 25 percent of our workforce. If we then add the people working in the small business sector, whose jobs are particularly vulnerable to economic downturns, and the people for whom employers might substitute part-time, contract, or "out-source" labor, the number is even larger.

Experts have been wondering why Americans continued to rank employment as their first or second domestic policy concern in public opinion polls during the economic recovery of the mid-1980s. If all of us experience serious employment-related risks due to a turbulent economy, and up to 25 percent of us experience acute risk, the high level of public concern is understandable. After all, even in the depths of the Great Depression *unemployment* reached only 25 percent. If *at-risk employment* is almost that high today, we have a serious domestic problem on our hands that urgently requires attention.

Safeguards

Because the forces of economic change place so many of us at risk, public and private supports against financial hardship are increasingly important to everyone. But unfortunately, the same forces that have undermined employment security have also undermined the adequacy of those supports.

Private support systems are tied to employment. As a result, the increasing number of people who have difficulty entering the labor force, who have lost their jobs, or whose employment has become less secure are also unlikely to be protected by corporate health, pension, or other benefit plans. Obviously, young people struggling to enter the workforce do not fall under any form of corporate protection, and most displaced workers have lost company health care coverage and are too young to receive retirement benefits, if they qualify for them. In the words of one displaced worker, they are often "too old to work and too young to retire." Part-time, intermittent, contract, and many small business employees generally receive few if any corporate benefits.

High rates of unemployment, even if much of that unemployment is short term, mean that increasing numbers of people are changing jobs. This makes them less likely to attain vested rights in pension plans and more likely to suffer from periods between jobs when they have no health care coverage. Finally, people who are experiencing stagnant real income are not likely to be able to put away private savings to tide them over periods of hardship.

For people who are steadily employed at a good wage in large or medium-sized firms, the chances of receiving at least sound pension coverage has increased in recent decades. As a result of the ERISA legislation, the percentage of workers covered by private pensions has actually grown. But the portion of the workforce *not* steadily employed at a good wage or employed by small firms has grown as well, and most of these people have little chance of receiving adequate private protection. If the trend toward less security of employment continues—and there is every reason to believe that it will—the percentage of total workers covered by private plans will eventually fall. As it is, a large and growing number of people are either unemployed or employed on terms that make them unlikely to be protected by private benefits.

For this growing number of workers, the sole protections available are the programs of the federal social role. And they are not alone in having to place heavy reliance on federal programs. Others who find themselves in this situation are workers whose pension and health care coverage has been cut back along with their wages, whose companies provide only minimal benefits, or who have lost all or part of their protections under private plans due to corporate restructuring or just plain bad management.

These and other workers with employment problems are almost certain to be disappointed by the protections that the federal social role provides. Unless they are supplemented by private sector benefits and personal savings, these protections do not, and were not intended to, provide adequate solutions to the problems of economic insecurity. For example, few retirees without private pensions or savings can live comfortably on Social Security alone. And people who are unemployed for long periods of time exhaust their unemployment insurance benefits. Because of Medicare's cost-sharing features, few retirees can avail themselves of full medical services unless they have adequate income from public and private programs. And many of the people who are unprotected by private health plans—the working poor, part-time employees, people working in small firms that do not offer health insurance—are not eligible for Medicaid. By themselves, the programs of the federal social role do not fill the gaps in private income security protection. And as more of us fall into those gaps, more of us are left with little or no effective protection from any source.

In addition, an increasing number of people face problems that the current federal social role is not designed to address at all. There are few if any public programs directed at the problems of changing skill requirements, falling real wages, or structural unemployment. The major way in which the federal government addresses these and a great many other employment problems is to try to maintain a general climate of economic prosperity. The hope is that this will make it easier for workers and employees to sort out problems between themselves. But in both good times and bad, it appears that national economic management, at least as it has been practiced, is not an adequate solution.

The other major tool that the federal government brings to bear on employment problems is support for education. Aid to higher education clearly makes an enormous difference in the lives of millions of young people. Unfortunately, federal programs that support elementary and secondary education have never been funded at a very high level, and the limited funds have been widely dispersed. As a result, these programs make only a limited, albeit important, contribution to preparing young people for the workforce.

The federal government also provides a number of small programs targeted directly at employment problems. The Jobs Training Partnership Act (JTPA), the Work Incentive Program (WIN), and the job placement activities of the United States Employment Service are all in their ways trying to do the right thing: to identify people with serious employment problems and provide assistance tailored to their needs. JTPA, which sponsors training and placement programs for the disadvantaged, is the best supported of all these programs, but even its $1.7 billion in funding allows it to reach only a small portion of the population in need.

In short, aside from macroeconomic management and aid to higher education, the federal government mounts only a thin line of defense against the types of employment problems that have become increasingly important in recent years. The federal social role was designed to protect average Americans: people steadily employed with good wages and adequate private benefits. It was, thus, designed to protect people who are already well protected by other means. The growing number of people who do not fit the traditional definition of the average American are not well protected by public and private benefits, and they are unlikely to find help from either public or private sources in facing the threats that arise from economic change.

Transitions

One common theme links all the effects of economic change on ordinary citizens over the last two decades: the need for almost all Americans to make an increasing number of transitions in their worklife and the difficulty they have in doing so. Transitions have always been an important part of the world of employment: transitions from school to work, from one job to another, from unemployment back into the workforce, and from work to retirement. Today all of these transitions pose severe difficulties for a great many people. A growing number of young people are having trouble entering the workforce. High unemployment rates and the growth of part-time and contract work indicate that people are changing jobs more often, and the large number of displaced and discouraged workers indicates that many people who lose their jobs have a hard time making the transition back to work. Workers left behind when their jobs move to another area find it difficult to make geographical transitions. And the fact that people are forced into early retirement or into dead-end jobs at the end of their careers indicates that transitions out of the workforce are not smooth. All of these facts and the evidence that large numbers of people rely too heavily on public health and pension systems in their retirement years indicate that the overall support our nation provides for transitions—a combination of public and private arrangements—is often far from adequate.

On top of these difficulties, recent decades of economic change have created new transitional problems. An increasing number of workers find that they must upgrade their skills, change specialties, or find new fields altogether if they expect to retain employment of good quality and advance up the income ladder.

In many respects, the need for workers to make all sorts of transitions is a sign of a flexible and dynamic economy. But the fact that so many people have difficulty making these changes is a sign that the United States has not developed mechanisms to minimize the social costs of change.

The federal social role was designed in part to help with transitions—particularly the transition from unemployment to work and from work to retirement. But for many people the adequacy of its protections in these areas is being eroded by the pace of change. And the social role scarcely addresses at all many of the most serious transitional problems that have developed in recent years.

There is a great deal that all of us can do as individuals to avoid those problems: we can be more prudent in managing our careers by upgrading our skills, staying aware of economic changes that may affect us and remaining ready to switch jobs when trouble threatens or greater opportunities become available. That is, we can protect ourselves against the problems of transition by trying to plan the changes in our lives, rather than having them forced on us.

But many of the difficult transitions that face us are ultimately the result of nationwide or international economic forces, the decisions of corporate managers and complex local economic forces that most of us cannot anticipate and over which we have little control. As a result, many people have turned to corporations or to state and local governments for help. For example, unions have demanded that companies invest more in retraining and finding new jobs for displaced workers and that they give advance notice of plant closings and other adverse personnel actions. Many states have tried to upgrade their educational systems, to assist young people in joining the labor force, and to create public jobs and training programs for the unemployed.

But, to date, corporate efforts and the efforts of states and localities have only scratched the surface of transitional problems, and there are limits to how much they can be expected to accomplish. Neither individual companies nor states and localities can control events outside the scope of their authority—the many interrelated decisions made on a nationwide or worldwide scale that can spell economic trouble for a particular locality or firm. Both companies and states or localities face a cruel irony: the times in which they are most heavily affected by employment problems are precisely the times in which they are least likely to have the resources to deal with those problem. Bad economic times mean limited income for companies and limited tax revenues for state and local governments.

Clearly the only way the United States can hope to combat its employment problems is to mobilize the resources of the federal government. Almost a quarter of our workforce is either unemployed or holding marginal jobs, and most of the rest of us face uncertain prospects in one way or another. If these problems are not a serious threat to our common national welfare, it is hard to imagine what would be. Solving them requires such measures as promoting overall economic growth, dealing with the special problems of depressed areas, and enforcing responsible business practices. It also requires finding better ways to help ordinary citizens make an increasing number of transitions in their work lives. Because in good times or bad, with or without responsible business leadership, the problems of transition are certain to be with us for the indefinite future.

Only the federal government has the resources and nationwide authority required to take on these tasks. To do so it must update policies designed to solve the employment problems faced by average Americans of the past and direct its energies to the problems of average Americans today.

IO

Driving Forces II: Social Change

D isturbing as its effects may be, economic change is only one of the driving forces transforming American life. Changing personal lifestyles, the development of an increasingly isolated underclass, and the aging of American society also pose serious threats to our national well being. And if we consider these trends along with the effects of economic change, certain common themes emerge that indicate at least some of the directions the federal social role must take in the years to come.

Driving Force: Threats to Families and Children

The men and women who inaugurated the present system of social activism in the United States—the New Dealers of the 1930s—saw the average American for whom they designed public programs as more than just an employee. Like most people, they placed great value on the intimate relations of family, neighborhood, and voluntary groupings as sources of personal and economic support. Public policy in the United States has always assumed that these institutions would solve most of the ordinary problems of life and that those problems need not be the concern of government. The Report of the Committee on Economic Security, as well as other documents of that time and since, indicate that the federal social role has been designed according to a fairly clear and consistent view of what the average American's lifestyle is like.

Described in these terms, the average American is a member of a family very much like that depicted in the television situation comedies of the 1950s and 1960s: the family has two parents and several children; the husband works and the wife devotes herself to child-rearing and housekeeping; they own their own home and the children attend public schools; the family enjoys a rising standard of living and support from friends, neighbors, and collateral relatives; the marriage between husband and wife is stable and likely to continue "till death do us part."

We all know this family. It is the American ideal. It was probably a reasonably accurate description of middle-class family life in the 1930s, 1940s, and 1950s.

But this average American family has almost ceased to exist. By the most generous estimate only about 10 percent of American households now fit this description. Multiple changes account for the virtual extinction of the middle-class ideal. The most dramatic has been the entry of women into the paid workforce. Today 54 percent of all women and 60 percent of married women with children work outside the home.[1] This rapid expansion of female participation in the workforce began when women who took up jobs to boost production during World War II sought to remain employed after the war ended. Many failed in this aspiration, but some succeeded. For a combination of personal and financial reasons, they and their daughters have changed the norm: whereas once most married women expected to stay at home, today most expect to continue in paid employment. The growing strength of this expectation is indicated by the fact that the percentage of married women with children under three years of age who work rose from about 26 percent in 1970 to over 50 percent in 1985.[2]

The average American family also does not stay together "till death do us part." Divorce rates have risen over the postwar period, until today half of all marriages end in divorce and two-thirds of second marriages are unsuccessful. Also births to unmarried women rose from 5.3 percent of all births in 1960 to 19.4 percent in 1982.[3] As a result of divorce and illegitimacy, well over half of American children can expect to spend some time in a household headed by only one parent.

And there are both fewer children and more households. Americans of all backgrounds have increasingly tended to have smaller families. The total fertility rate—a projection of lifetime births per woman based on actual birthrates of a given year—has declined from 3.8 in 1957 to 1.8 today. And women have tended to marry and have children later in life. This means that there are more childless couples (about 19 percent in 1984, compared with 15 percent in 1960), and it is one reason for the growth in the number of single person households (from about 7 million in 1960 to almost 20 million in 1984).[4]

Those families that do stay together have had to lower their material expectations. Slow growth in real income, combined with inflated housing costs, meant that only about 60 percent of American families could afford to own their own homes in 1986.[5] If wives had not worked in the paid labor force, the percentage would have been much smaller.

But Americans are not satisfied with standing still economically. They have always regarded a rising standard of living as part of their national birthright. Many have turned to borrowing. As a percentage of disposable personal income, consumer debt rose from 20 percent in 1970 to over 22 percent in 1985, and the nation's personal savings rate fell from 7.1 percent of disposable personal income in 1980 to less than 3.8 percent in 1986.[6] This escalation in personal debt, combined with dramatic increases in government and corporate borrowing, has created what can fairly be characterized as an "indebted society."

What about the average American's connections to neighborhood and community? Clearly these have become more tenuous. Public schools have gained a reputation for poor educational quality and discipline. Enrollment in religiously affiliated or other private schools has increased: in 1977 10 percent of American children attended such schools; by 1984 almost 13 percent, a total of

5.7 million children did so.[7] In large urban areas—where most of us live—parents increasingly are opting out of one of the most venerable institutions of community life: the public school.

A great many people have little chance to form lasting attachments to neighborhoods or communities. The average American today changes residences once every five years. There is less chance than before of forming lasting bonds with neighbors and community groups. Moreover, with most women working in the paid labor force, a traditional pool of community volunteers, housewives, has become increasingly small.

Extended families still provide supports, but their logistics have changed. More people now live some distance from their elderly parents than was the case several decades ago. And, wherever they live, a combination of improved income supports for retirees, plus changing social norms, means that most elderly people live in their own homes, rather than with their children. This is apparently a satisfactory arrangement for all concerned, but it does not necessarily reduce the demands on working-age adults. Families, and particularly women, still provide most of the help that the increasing number of frail elderly need in their daily lives, although that support may be provided across town or across the nation.

What do all these changes have to do with public policy? Some are simply the problems of economic change wearing a different face. A disproportionate number of the women in the paid workforce (21 percent) are part-time or intermittent employees—sometimes by choice, but often because lack of training or sex discrimination in hiring leaves them no other option.[8] This generally means they enjoy less employment security, fewer employee and public benefits, and lower wages than their male counterparts receive. The millions of women in this situation (over 10 million) are poorly protected by the federal social role.

These employment problems would be less troublesome in economic, if not equity, terms if traditional family patterns were still the norm. But if most families depend on a second earner to maintain even a constant standard of real income, let alone to get ahead, the insecurity of employment for many women is a threat to the economic security of large numbers of people. Moreover, if women face over a 50 percent chance of being divorced, the threat is even greater. Studies have repeatedly documented that divorce results in a significant loss of income for women, particularly if, as is usually the case, the divorced couple have children. To put the same point differently, during that period when children are living with one custodial parent, usually their mother, the family income that supports them is likely to decline significantly, and that income often depends largely on insecure employment.

A Pyramid of Problems

This combination of lifestyle and economic changes places large numbers of ordinary American families at risk of severe economic hardship. But this is not the only form of stress. Families with two earners and slowly growing real income must also face up to the problem of how to care for their children. Usually the solution is some form of daycare during preschool years. Because government and employer daycare facilities are not nearly abundant enough to meet the demand, many parents have to resort to informal arrangements with neighbors or enroll their children in private daycare facilities at heavy expense—often more than $100 a week. Further financial difficulties arise if they elect to send their children to private schools, where the tuition can exceed the cost of education at a good university several decades ago.

If we add up these child care problems, it becomes apparent that a significant portion of America's young people are being reared primarily not by their parents but by private institutions the parents can ill afford. Government at any level provides little help. The federal government offers some assistance in the form of dependent exemptions for children and a small child care tax credit, but these are helpful only to the upper one-third of taxpayers who itemize their taxes and who probably need them least. The government also provides somewhat more than $1 billion in funding for daycare services to the poor—an amount that barely scratches the surface of the national need. State and local governments provide public schools, but these do not address the problems of caring for very young children or supervision after school hours. No one knows exactly how many "latchkey" children there are in America—young people who have no adult supervision after school because their parents are at work—but different studies have estimated their numbers to be as few as 2 million and as many as 7 million.[9] And both public and private reports over the last two decades have repeatedly documented the concern of parents about poor quality of education, lax discipline, the use of drugs and alcohol, and other problems associated with many public schools.

These problems with child care have not yet moved into the center of political debate. This may be, in part, because a combination of smaller families, delayed child-bearing, and the growing number of elderly people in our society has produced a situation in which only 36 percent of households contain children under age 18.[10] But that is still a large number of Americans, and all of us have a stake in the future generations that will eventually run our public and private institutions and, we hope, support us in our old age.

Moreover, the precarious state of employment of many workers, together with heavy debt loads and diminished community or other social supports, puts many families in a vulnerable position financially. Periods of economic downturn can erase part-time or marginal jobs and the incomes that come with them, and families can be left with few assets, many commitments, and nobody to turn to for help. Lest this sound extreme, by the bottom of the recession of the 1970s, when unemployment rates exceeded 11 percent, average family income by most estimates suffered a *decline* in real dollar terms.[11]

The long-term prospects for average American families are also distressing. Whether or not the family remains intact, intermittent or part-time employment of women results in less public or private protection during their retirement years. Because women tend to outlive men by about seven years, and often lose their deceased husband's retirement benefits, many of today's children when they become adults will have to provide financial support to their widowed mothers.

Common Concerns

Some of the changes that have transformed our family lives have leveled off, at least temporarily. The rates of increase in female entry into the labor force, childlessness, illegitimacy, and divorce have slowed, and family income has begun to grow at a slightly faster pace. But personal debt, flight from the public schools, and the demand for child care have continued to increase.

Many of these problems are not addressed at all or are addressed inadequately by public programs. Without public, family, or community supports, people are turning to private institutions—daycare centers and home help services—often at a price they cannot afford and with unsatisfactory results. Clearly the trouble and expense they go to in seeking those alternatives, as well as the enormous investment they make in self-help literature and courses, indicate the considerable effort they are making to gain control of their lives. But in too many cases the means to achieve responsible, secure lives are unavailable or unsatisfactory.

It is easy to dismiss these problems as the responsibility of the people who experience them or to preach a return to traditional lifestyles. But most of us experience problems of this sort to some degree. We have chosen to live the way we do for a great variety of reasons. Railing against those choices once they are made is futile. Lifestyles have changed in ways that may well prove to be permanent—because people on the whole prefer their new ways of life to older alternatives. The question for public policy is whether common responses can be mounted to address the widely shared problems that arise from these patterns of change.

Driving Force: The Underclass

The social and economic changes that now affect average Americans are even more drastic for people at the bottom of the social and economic heap. Poor families are most likely to depend on income from the types of blue collar jobs that are vanishing from the American economy, to lack the education that will allow them to make economic transitions, to suffer all the difficulties of two-earner households, and to be unable to compensate for these difficulties by purchasing help from private institutions. And, as noted in previous chapters, poor families have always been served by public programs that are less adequate than those that support average Americans. As their problems become worse, the inadequacies of those programs have more serious effects.

At the extreme, the problems of the poor in this era of change are dramatized by the development of what has come to be called the American "underclass." This phenomenon has become so well publicized that it is now part of our standard picture of American society.[12]

As usually described, the "underclass" comprises people whose families have lived in poverty for several generations. Adults are either unemployed or work only intermittently. They have low educational attainments—many are school dropouts and a large portion are functionally illiterate. They live in wretched conditions in the slums of major cities or poverty-stricken rural areas. Crime, drug addiction, inadequate nutrition, and other social problems are rife. Rates of illegitimacy are high—most children are reared in households headed by females and never know their fathers.

Most members of the underclass have little or no hope of improving their condition. Mired in a culture of poverty, they see little chance of getting a good education or good jobs that will lead to a better life. And their attitudes, together with their circumstances, pretty well ensure that they will be poor for the rest of their lives. They lack the skills, direction, and opportunities to make progress. For members of the underclass, poverty is an inherited disease passed on from generation to generation each time an illegitimate child is born into an environment where opportunities and hope of any sort are hard to come by.

Although the media have made much of discovering the American underclass in recent years, people such as those just described have been the subject of periodic public concern for some time. They were the subject of Michael Harrington's *The Other America* in 1962, Senator Moynihan described them in his now famous report on black families in 1965, they were characterized as a separate "society" in the Kerner commission's report on civil disorders in 1968, and they were a major target of the War on Poverty programs in the Johnson years.[13]

Deterioration

The underclass, therefore, is not new. What is new is that their conditions appear to be getting worse, and they are increasingly segregated along racial lines. Although a majority of poor Americans are white, the people at the rock-bottom of American society—the underclass—are predominantly black and Hispanic, at least in urban areas.

These nonaverage Americans are apparently losing most of their few social supports. In 1985, the poverty rate for black households headed by females was over 50 percent (compared with about 27 percent for white female-headed households), and about 40 percent of black youth aged sixteen to nineteen were unemployed (compared with about 15 percent of whites).[14] Because of the large percentage of blacks and Hispanics living in poverty, these figures are generally taken to describe conditions among the underclass generally. In fact, they probably underestimate the severity of the problem. Local officials report that rates of illegitimacy, unemployment, school dropout, crime, and drug abuse in poor, inner-city neighborhoods among members of all races are far higher—verging on 80 percent or more for some of these social pathologies. Most of the ordinary patterns of American life have ceased to function in these areas.

Twenty or thirty years ago, all these rates of social decay—illegitimacy, unemployment, and so forth—were half what they are today, or even lower. In the decades since America first discovered the underclass, the condition of its members has become worse by all the usual indicators. Children born into desperate urban environments have far less of a chance of living in a stable home, getting a good education, finding a job, and making a good income. In areas where the problems of social decay are most concentrated, they have very little chance at all.

What about the size of the underclass? Absent a very precise definition, it is hard to measure how many Americans find themselves in these conditions or whether their numbers have grown. The usual ways of estimating their numbers are in terms of AFDC case loads and unemployment statistics. We know that about 3.5 million parents and 9 million children receive AFDC assistance, and that about half of the parents are in the midst of unemployment spells that will last for eight years or longer. By this estimate the underclass is about 6 million women and children—a number that has not increased in recent years. Another way of estimating the size of the underclass is to count the number of people living below the poverty line in low-income urban areas. By this measure only 2.3 million Americans fall into the category; by other estimates the number is close to 3.5 million.[15]

Regardless of how large the underclass is, authorities agree that millions of our citizens find themselves in desperate circumstances, with prospects increasingly bleak. Moreover, a whole new generation has been born since the media discovered and then rediscovered these people at the bottom of society—yet another generation that has never known life without hardship and is further removed from that time when at least some of the poor in depressed areas had a realistic hope of betterment.

Causes

What has created the American underclass? There are many theories, and all of them probably contain an element of truth.[16] The growth of the underclass has been explained by such diverse causes as the disappearance of low-skilled jobs and the movement of businesses out of inner-city neighborhoods. Another factor cited is that improved race relations have enabled middle-class blacks to escape the ghetto for more comfortable suburban lifestyles, leaving behind individuals and families that experience the greatest distress. It has also been explained by changing sexual mores, lack of public investment in inner city schools and other public facilities, and a variety of other factors.

Sociologist William Julius Wilson has recently stitched many of these factors together in a convincing and well-documented theory of why illegitimacy rates and single-parent households have increased so dramatically in recent years.[17] Wilson argues that young women living in poverty face a shortage of "marriageable men." Like most people these women would like to form stable family units, but because most of the available men are unemployed or otherwise unreliable, they are reluctant to marry. But they are as sexually active as other women their age, and many would like to have children. As a result, if and when they become pregnant, they choose to go it alone rather than be burdened by a dependent husband.

Wilson's theory captures most of the elements of underclass culture described by others: limited prospects for both men and women, desperate choices, a continuous cycle of poverty.

His theory also captures what, in relative terms, can be considered good news about the underclass. People at the bottom have aspirations and values that are much more like those of ordinary Americans than stereotypes often allow. By all indications most poor people want to be self-supporting by work. Not only do they say this to researchers, but public programs which have given AFDC mothers the opportunity to gain steady employment have not been lacking for participants.

Also, according to Wilson's studies, people at the bottom of society want to form stable families. They want to reduce crime, of which they are the primary victims, and they want better housing, education, and opportunities. In an environment where all of these things are far beyond their grasp, their efforts to attain them are often feeble. But members of the underclass are not people from Mars: they are people suffering an extreme form of the economic and social displacements afflicting almost everyone in today's society. Starting at a disadvantage, they are less able to adapt to these changes, but they want to be average Americans, just like "everyone else."

Common Concerns

How does the plight of the underclass bear on public policy? Obviously the fact that so many of its members are so seriously disadvantaged is a standing indictment of an affluent, democratic society. If a sense of nationhood means anything, it means putting ourselves in the shoes of the worst-off among us and devising public responses to their problems, as well our own.

Moreover, we all have a selfish interest in helping to solve the problems of the underclass. They cost us money—much of the $100 billion in programs for the poor at the federal level and even more in matching funds and local services by other levels of government. They threaten our safety: most crime in America is committed by impoverished, unemployed young males. They create a dangerous polarization in our society: because the underclass in urban areas is primarily black and Hispanic, its deepening problems reinforce racial prejudices. Explosive situations such as the riots of the 1960s or the school busing confrontations of the 1970s could again tear communities apart.

We also have a selfish interest in the fate of the underclass because their distress costs us human potential. High fertility rates among the poor since the 1960s and low fertility rates among more affluent groups during the same period, mean that a large portion of the future workers on whom the continuing prosperity of American society will depend will necessarily be drawn from the underclass. It is hard to imagine how this can be done when business needs skilled, experienced workers and today's underclass youth are typically illiterate, unskilled, and without the opportunities to gain work experience. Unless we can do something to enhance their abilities and opportunities, American industry will soon find itself short of the qualified workers it needs.

Finally, lack of jobs, particularly good jobs, insecurity of employment, fragmented families, and educational failure are all problems that average Americans share. So we all have a stake in finding better solutions, for the underclass and for ourselves.

Clearly public policy has not adequately addressed these problems for any of us, let alone for the underclass. Many of the War on Poverty programs misfired, or they were underfunded and abandoned. National programs for the underclass today consist primarily of AFDC, Medicaid for AFDC eligibles, Food Stamps, and a fast disappearing commitment to public housing. All are programs intended to prop up the incomes of poor people, although they reach only a fraction of the very poor. Tragically, we invest very little in trying to get to the root causes of poverty: unemployment, poor education, and a debilitating environment. Until these are addressed, more generations will be locked into poverty, and we will all suffer national loss and shame.

Driving Force: Population Aging

The rapid aging of the American population is a phenomenon that will continue until at least the middle of the next century and will have a profound effect on every individual and every institution—indeed, it is already doing so. Population aging is not to be confused with individual aging. Individuals age inexorably from the moment of birth until the moment of death. Populations, however, can get younger or older, depending on changes in the proportions of people in different age groups. The principal facts that affect the "age" of a population are changes in the fertility rate, changes in the infant mortality rate, and changes in life expectancy at older ages.

Two different developments account for the speed with which our population is aging; a rapid increase in both the number and proportion of elderly people, and a rapid decline in the proportion of children.[18] In regard to the first of these developments, we arc seeing the effects now of a high fertility rate and substantial decreases in infant and child mortality in the early decades of this century, as well as improvements in health care that are enabling older people to live longer. Thus, life expectancy has increased by twenty-eight years, from forty-seven to seventy-five, since the year 1900, and just since 1950 the number of people sixty-five or older has more than doubled—from 12 million to 29 million.[19] Within the same time span, those eighty-five or older have quadrupled in number to a total of 2.7 million today—a figure that is expected to increase to about 9 million by 2030 and around 16 million by the middle of the next century.[20]

Another way to measure population aging is by advances or declines in the median age. In 1800 this was about sixteen, today it is almost thirty-two, and by 2030, using the "middle series" of the U.S. Census Bureau, it will be forty-one.[21] A third indicator is the proportion of a population sixty-five or older, this being the conventional definition of "elderly." In 1920 this proportion was less than 5 percent of the population, in 1950 it was over 8 percent, in 1986 about 12 percent, and by 2030 it will be over 21 percent. By that time, therefore, every fifth, and perhaps as much as every fourth, American will be elderly, if sixty-five-plus continues to define that term.[22]

A final measure of the aging of a population is the proportion of children it contains over time. As we have seen, almost half the U.S. population was under the age of fifteen in 1800. By 1900 this figure had dropped to 34 percent, and by 1940 to 25 percent. The proportion rose, of course, during the baby boom but then resumed its long-term decline and is now down to 22 percent.[23] All predictions are for a further drop. Children will become an ever scarcer commodity in our society.

The populations of many other nations in the world are also aging, especially those that are highly developed and industrialized. The aging of our population, however, is distinctive, because the postwar baby boom here lasted considerably longer and was proportionately much larger than similar phenomena in other countries. During the nineteen years from 1946 to 1964, we added 76 million children to our population, a group of Americans now aged twenty-three to fourty-one that constitutes close to a third of our total population and is the equivalent in size of the nation's entire population in 1900. At the height of the baby boom, in 1957, the total fertility rate climbed to an extraordinary 3.8 level— that is, nearly four children per woman. After 1964, however, the rate dropped precipitously, and by 1976 was down to 1.7, a decline that has produced the "baby dearth" or "baby bust" generation—a group that presently includes all of our young people, from newborn infants to young adults in their early twenties.[24] The severity of this demographic twist of boom followed by bust has created a population structure in the United States that will be out of kilter until at least the middle of the next century.

Because the American population has been aging for some time, both the New Deal architects of social activism and the Great Society reformers took account of this trend in formulating their social insurance plans. Calculations to adjust for an increasing number of elderly people and fewer children were built into the Social Security retirement system and Medicare from the beginning. But those adjustments were not adequate: no one anticipated that population aging and the costs associated with supporting an aging population would increase so dramatically at the same time.

Health Care

Chief among these burgeoning costs are Social Security retirement benefits and the rapid growth of health care expenditures for the elderly, caused both by the general inflation of health care costs and by the increasing numbers of old people. Because the Social Security retirement system is in fairly good shape, it is the growing cost of health care that is most problematical. Out of total annual health care expenditures today of more than $400 billion (about 11 percent of GNP) at least $120 billion, or about 30 percent, is spent on the elderly.[25] Conservative estimates suggest that by the end of the century the costs of health care for the elderly will more than triple. Included in this increase will be an anticipated near tripling of total hospital patient days for them, raising their share from about a third to over one-half. By early in the next century the nation could easily be spending 22 percent of GNP on health at present rates of increase, with something approaching half of it for the elderly.[26]

Much of the increased cost of health care for the elderly will, of course, fall on federal, state, and local government, with the lion's share at the federal level. Federal expenditure on Medicare benefits alone, which currently totals over $70 billion, is predicted by conservative estimates to rise by the year 1990 to $116 billion.[27]

In short, one of the major causes of the much discussed problem of rising health-care spending in the United States is clearly population aging. And as our population becomes more "top heavy" with the aging of the baby boomers, we will inevitably have to devote more of our national wealth to the health needs of the elderly.

How much more we will have to spend, however, is a matter of dispute, and it is somewhat within our control. Present doomsday projections of health care spending in the coming decades assume not only a growing number of older people but also a continued increase in the cost of caring for each of them. Inflation of health care costs in the United States has averaged about 2 percent more than general inflation since the 1960s, with greater increases in recent years. And spending on long-term care—the largely nonmedical housing and personal services provided to frail elderly people by nursing homes and other institutions—has increased even more rapidly. The best measures we have of growth in the cost of long-term care are that national spending on nursing homes soared from about $500 million in 1970 to $32 billion in 1984, and that spending on long-term care by Medicaid rose from $3.4 billion in 1973 to $19 billion in 1985.[28]

It is by no means foreordained that the present rates of increase in either overall health care costs or long-term care must continue into the future. Other nations, such as Canada and Britain, have managed to keep health care inflation at or near the general inflation level. And it stands to reason that savings in long-term care can be realized by less reliance on institutions—such as nursing homes—and more reliance on home-based care systems, such as visiting nurses, homemakers, and meals-on-wheels.

The United States is only beginning to take measures to curb health care cost inflation, by restricting reimbursements for Medicare. Thus far, we have done little to attack the long-term care problem. In fact, most private health insurance plans as well as Medicaid help to make that problem worse, by reimbursing providers *only* for institutional care. Absent a very abundant source of funding, *public* home-based care systems exist in only primitive form in most of the United States. On the other hand, *private* home-based care—the personal services provided to elderly relatives by increasingly hard-pressed working-age people—is the major source of support for the frail elderly.[29]

Clearly, the United States is headed for severe problems if we do not begin preparing now for the increased cost of providing health care to an aging society. If spending continues to increase at the present rate, it will be extremely difficult to find the resources needed to meet other national priorities. A country that accepts a future in which 22 percent of GNP would be devoted to health is dangerously constricting its options. It is foolish to believe that the American people will let the situation get that far out of control. But to avoid the shock of either abruptly increased taxes or drastically reduced services at some time in the future, we must begin now to build a responsible health care system.

That system must ensure that the necessary funds are available to provide care for the increasing number of elderly. But in developing it, we must also shop for the best deal possible in terms of cost and quality of service. This means that we must curb medical cost inflation and create more efficient and humane forms of long-term care. In even the best of circumstances, the nation will have to pay a larger bill for health care in an aging society than it does today, but we can and must make sure that the bill is no higher than it has to be.

The Workforce

The other major problem presented by population aging is the future composition of our national workforce. In its simplest form, this problem boils down to a single question: Will workers of the baby bust generation (today's children) be able to support the much larger baby boom age group in their retirement years without a significant reduction in the nation's standard of living? Two time periods are of interest in answering this question.[30] In the period between now and about 2010, when the first baby boomers reach retirement, the size of the workforce relative to the overall population should continue to increase, as it has in past decades, although at a slower rate. The cost of supporting retirees will be spread over more workers than it is today.

After 2010, however, the size of the workforce relative to the population will begin to shrink. In the ensuing decades, the ability of the baby bust generation to support the retired generation above it without a significant reduction in the living standards of either group will depend to a large extent on whether growth in capital and technological innovation continues and on the productivity of the workforce. If each worker in the future can produce a significantly larger volume of goods and services than he or she does today, the problems of population aging can be contained.

We have, roughly, the period between now and 2010—less than twenty-five years—to create an environment in which that high level of productivity can be achieved. It is a *one-time chance* to create economic conditions and a system of social supports that will allow working-age people of the future to shoulder the responsibilities of caring for the elderly without dramatically reducing their standard of living, or neglecting other important priorities.

From this perspective, the United States is currently doing one thing right and several other things that are very harmful. The right thing was to increase the rate of Social Security retirement contributions in 1983, so that the Social Security trust fund will run an increasingly large surplus in the years to come. Indeed, as noted, it is estimated that by about 2020 the surplus funds will result in the Social Security system owning a large part of the national debt.[31] This growing surplus is indirectly a form of enforced investment in the national economy by today's workers. Properly managed, large amounts of surplus funds placed in government securities may be able to reduce the need for the federal government to go to private money markets (that is, to issue bonds and notes to private investors in competition with corporate securities), and this should free up capital for business investment. As a result, more capital should be available for machines, materials, and new processes that can make workers of the future more productive.

But two harmful trends could well offset this influx of capital. In brief, we appear to be issuing too many tickets out of the workforce and not enough tickets in, at least for skilled workers who can make the greatest contribution to productivity growth.

Retirement

The most alarming increase in tickets out of the workforce is the trend toward early retirement. Today, only a minority of workers stay on the job until age sixty-five. Overall, the labor force participation rates of men fifty-five to sixty-four decreased steadily from the 1970 rate of 83 percent to the 1984 rate of 68 percent.[32] And while some early retirees have health problems that may prevent them from working, this is not true of the great majority of those who retire in their late fifties and early sixties.

The trend toward early retirement has been steadily increasing in the postwar decades. A number of factors have contributed to it. Growing affluence has been the underlying cause. As the nation has become wealthier, more Americans have been able to select leisure over employment earlier in their lives. The greater availability of private pensions has allowed them to exercise this option more easily. The federal government has been particularly generous in this respect: all of its 3 million civilian and military employees have long been entitled to retire after thirty years of service. Another factor at work is the eagerness of many companies to shed their older employees and their reluctance to retrain or hire anyone over about the age of fifty. Too often older workers are faced with a choice between early retirement and unemployment or a dead-end job.

Whatever its causes, the trend toward early retirement is both senseless and damaging as far as the long-term health of the American economy is concerned. It does not, as many people believe, clear the dead wood out of the labor force. A large body of research shows that in most occupations older workers in their fifties, sixties and even seventies are as capable as their younger counterparts.[33] And, if experience and maturity of judgment are considered, many are more capable. Most workers who retire at fifty-five have at least ten or fifteen potentially productive years ahead of them. Rather than clearing out dead wood, we are scrapping valuable seasoned timber.

Looking to the future, early retirement will increasingly be a luxury the nation cannot afford as the number of younger workers declines and particularly the number of well-educated, highly skilled younger people. Qualified older workers will be needed in considerable numbers both to maintain a thriving economy and to share the burden of supporting the very old.

For the time being, many firms will no doubt continue, wherever possible, to substitute young people for older employees, in the traditional belief that the former are less expensive and more likely to have the skills needed in a rapidly changing economy. Easing older workers out, however, can be a costly practice, both for employers and for society at large.

For companies, a retrained older employee who remains on the job for ten or fifteen more years may be a far better investment than a succession of younger workers who must be put through an initial training period but who then soon leave the organization to take other positions. There is also the matter of the heavy costs involved in paying retirement and health benefits over long periods to early retirees who are no longer helping to earn these benefits.

From society's point of view, the costs involved in losing the productive capacity of early retirees are enormous—they consume far more than they produce, rather than producing more than they consume. And the effect on the Social Security system of people both drawing Social Security benefits earlier than they otherwise would and also no longer paying Social Security taxes is obviously to increase significantly the burden on active workers. Although there is little definitive research on the matter, there is good reason to believe that the most sensible policy for both employers and society would be continuous, periodic retraining of all workers over their *entire* work lives.

Children

But even canceling many tickets out of the workforce will not solve future problems of an aging society unless we start issuing more good tickets in. To a large extent, whether or not the United States can afford the costs of an aging population and maintain its overall high standard of living will depend on whether today's young people are well prepared for the world of work and whether they can find jobs. Unless members of the baby bust generation are highly skilled, well motivated, and properly placed, they will not stand a chance of achieving the productivity gains that will be required in the coming decades.

Unfortunately, the United States today is squandering a large portion of its youth. In many cases it is not giving them the background that will serve as a ticket into the workforce at all, as the high rates of youth unemployment testify. In many other cases it is not giving them *good* tickets—they can find jobs, but they are not prepared for the kind of high opportunity employment that leads to increased productivity.

Given the critical role that today's children will have to play later as adults in maintaining the nation's economic well-being, their welfare, which is important in any event, should be our highest priority. Both for families and for the nation as a whole, children are a short-term expense and a long-term investment. In fact, in the long run they are the *only* investment that really matters, since all the other resources we invest in as a people will be useless unless the next generation of workers, who will soon be our younger colleagues and will eventually be our guardians, know how to use them effectively. They *are* the long-range future of the American economy.

There is abundant evidence, however, that the nation does not yet understand that its children are its greatest resource.[34] Large numbers of young people are growing up in severe poverty. Many lack adequate nutrition or health-care coverage; many live in dilapidated, poor quality housing; and they attend run-down, often dangerous schools where they get, at best, an inferior education. As a result, large numbers of children, as they approach adulthood, have not acquired even the most rudimentary skills. They are virtually unemployable. Many others who are perfectly capable of holding down a job can find no work. At least a quarter of our young people are getting off to a severely disadvantaged start in life. Viewed only in humanitarian terms, this is a scandal in a nation as rich as ours. Viewed in relation to the nation's future well-being—its standard of living, its security, and its domestic stability—this neglect of our children is profligate beyond belief.

Optimists about the future workforce often assume that the need for more skilled workers in the future will lead employers to invest more in training programs and other measures to make up for the effects of a disadvantaged background. The level of investment may increase. But it is hard to imagine that private efforts by themselves will be adequate to bring the large number of children who are getting off to such a poor start up to the level of productivity needed to support an aging society.

Common Concerns

The combination of issuing too many tickets out of the workforce and too few good tickets in can have calamitous effects on our national well-being, but like the increasing cost of health care, these trends are not foreordained. It is not too late if we act now to improve the health, education, and personal environment in which today's children are reared. But these and other effects of societal aging call for a quality that has too often been missing in American public policy: foresight. Problems posed by demographic change call for dramatic actions now to fend off what are almost certain adversities in the future.

The nation has already made one important adjustment in anticipation of future problems: the 1983 reforms in the Social Security retirement system. This was brought about by a perceived crisis in Social Security financing. Most experts expect that the Medicare system will face a crisis of solvency in the 1990s, and this may lead to health care reforms.[35]

But we cannot wait for a crisis to draw attention to the needs of our children, and we should not wait for crises to address our other problems. Each year lost makes the problems of an aging society far harder to resolve.

Tremors

What do all these social and economic problems add up to? As a nation we have been standing still while the earth has moved beneath us:

- Employment and the benefits that come with it are no longer as secure as they once were.
- Family supports—economic and personal—are no longer as reliable as they used to be.

- All the many aspects of childrearing have become more difficult than they were in the past.
- Support for the elderly has become far more problematical and expensive.
- Education for people of all ages has become more important as the means for attaining it have become less satisfactory.
- Health care has become more expensive for everyone and ruinously expensive for many.

To some degree, all of us share these problems—from average Americans to members of the underclass. They define many of our most urgent common concerns today. They have many causes, but for one reason or another they are likely to be with us for the indefinite future and their effects are very severe indeed. Collectively, they mean that all of us are less secure in very important respects than we were a few decades ago, and certainly less secure than most of us would like to be. If any one of these problems manifests itself in a serious way in the lives of any one of us, it is a crisis. If we lose our jobs or benefits, if our income stagnates, if we have a serious illness not covered by insurance, if our children are ill educated or poorly cared for, if our aged relatives are incapacitated, or opportunities for economic advancement pass us by—it is an earthquake. And the odds are that each of us will experience one or more of these earthquakes at some time. When things are going well—as they usually are for most of us—these problems seem only distant tremors. But the forces of social and economic change have made the supports of our lives more fragile: if and when the earthquake hits, there is less to protect us.

From the perspective of individuals these trends add up to less security and less opportunity to build the kinds of lives we would like for ourselves and our children. From the perspective of the nation as a whole they add up to waste. It is much more than a platitude that our human resources are our most important resources. Human capacities are critical to enhancing our economic productivity. People who are unemployed or underemployed, people whose skills are outmoded, people who are frustrated by lack of opportunity and uncertainty, people who are retired while they could still have active years ahead of them, children who get off to a bad start physically, educationally, and psychologically, people burdened by debt and responsibilities they cannot meet—all these are wasted resources. In a nation that aspires to an ever increasing standard of affluence, they are resources we cannot afford to waste.

Because unresolved social and economic problems affect us all, at least as tremors and eventually as earthquakes, and because they affect the well-being of the nation as a whole, they are common concerns calling for common solutions, and government at the national level must play a large role in finding these solutions.

Presently, the federal government contributes very little to solving these problems. We have become used to defining the limits of the federal social role in terms of the major concerns it has addressed and the programs that have comprised it for a great many years. The present stalemate in social policy has neglected the fact that federal activism evolved into its present form to meet strongly felt common needs. All over America today people are searching for help with new sets of problems, as they once searched for help with the problems of income support in old age or the development of a national infrastructure. Americans are improvising as best they can, but their improvisations are not satisfactory: their situations are becoming worse rather than better. What too many policymakers seem to have forgotten is that solving common problems, whatever they are, is what we have government for. And it may well be that this myopia has led many Americans to regard political issues as irrelevant—the debate has too little to do with many of their most pressing concerns.

But even people who agree that current problems require a more vigorous public response may well ask what form that response should take. What can national government actually *do* to overcome past stalemates and resolve the problems that have emerged from recent decades of social and economic change? That is the subject of the following chapters.

II

Priorities
for the Social Role

The outstanding priority of the federal social role for the first
century of our national life was economic development; for
the second century it was economic security; and for the third
century it must be human resource development.

Levers

It is easy to feel overwhelmed by the problems of the federal
social role. Its inequities, half-measures, neglect, and undue deference to privilege are troublesome enough. If we add to these
the unmet needs that have assumed growing importance due to
recent decades of social and economic change, the result is a list
of issues that seems hopelessly long. This, at least, proves there
is no shortage of work for activist government in the years to
come. But the sheer magnitude of the federal agenda is itself a
deterrent to getting on with the job. It is difficult to know where
to begin, and it is also hard to believe that any first steps will
make much of a difference.

What the American people and their leaders need is not more
lists of issues. These are produced in abundance by think tanks,

lobbies, political parties and others. We need a sense of priorities: an indication that some things matter more than others, that by pulling the right levers we can move mounds of specific problems.

In particular, what we need is a set of priorities that will allow the nation to confront the longstanding inadequacies of the federal social role as well as the problems that have emerged from recent decades of economic and social change. And, to be realistic, those priorities must be compatible with the American style of activism. New policy directions must be able to overcome the limits that tensions between individual and collective values and between attachments to group and nation, respectively, have placed on the social role.

The Missing Middle

The best way to discern what directions for the future matter most is to focus on the weak points of present policy. Politically, economically, and socially, government in the United States is an extremely conservative institution. This means that attempts to rebuild the federal social role from the ground up are certain to be dismissed as utopian, however rational they may be. It also means that successful reform is likely to grow out of attempts to overcome the shortcomings of programs now in place.

Looking at American social policy as a whole, it is easy to see why the federal role has failed to measure up to the nation's needs— why it has been plagued by inadequacies in the past and has not provided a strong enough response to the problems created by economic and social change. There has always been a neglected element in the federal social role—an element so central to its design that it can be called the "missing middle" of American domestic policy. That element is an effective employment policy.

Activist government is the United States has always been structured around employment, in the sense that its measures have been designed to benefit individuals, directly or indirectly, through their participation in the world of work. For example, policies to promote economic development are intended to improve the lives of average Americans by providing them with opportunities to make a good living, and access to most federal programs for economic security depends on steady attachment to the workforce. Furthermore, access to those programs depends on holding a *good* job: one that pays a decent wage, provides opportunity, and offers sound benefits. Subsidies, tax preferences, and even most of business regulation ultimately are intended to help people make a good living and enjoy the fruits of their labors.

Even the areas of neglect in the social role make sense if we accept certain assumptions about employment. It makes sense, for example, for the nation to do less for the working poor, the long-term unemployed, welfare mothers, and poor children than it does for average Americans, if we assume that disadvantaged individuals should, and eventually can, make their own way in the world of work—that they can become average Americans.

In these circumstances, it is only a slight exaggeration to predict that if everyone had a good job the underclass would disappear, the working poor would rise to the economic condition of middle-income Americans, public and private programs would protect us against the costs of ill health and old age, economic growth would overcome the problems associated with population aging, working families would have the necessary income to solve their problems, and so forth. And our individualist values would be satisfied, because all of us would have solved our most serious problems by our own efforts. The design of the federal social role would make perfect sense, and each of us would be living a far better life, if only we could all be assured of a good job.

But, of course, we don't have that assurance. And this should come as no surprise to anyone. The New Deal architects of social activism realized that their design would only meet the nation's needs if employment problems could be overcome. The first recommendation of the Committee on Economic Security of 1935 was for a full employment policy.[1] The committee expected that, even in times of economic recovery, large numbers of people would be without work, and they realized that neither social insurance nor other public protections would be adequate by themselves to sustain those people at a decent level or maintain overall prosperity for long. Only jobs would do, because only jobs would provide continuing security in the prime of life and access in times of distress to the kinds of programs designed by American social activists. The New Deal architects did not take employment for granted: they called for measures to ensure that it was available.

The United States has never adopted a full employment policy. Attempts to introduce it were deferred in 1935 and defeated by the business community in a monumental battle over the Full Employment Bill in 1945.[2] Opponents were successful in arguing that full employment would be too costly, too disruptive of the labor market, and, in general, un-American and socialistic. The Humphrey-Hawkins Act of 1978 was the nation's most recent review of the issue. It resulted in a statement of laudable goals but no reliable mechanism for achieving them.

As a result, we are left with a system of public policy and a set of social values that are based on the assumption that virtually all Americans can and do hold good jobs, when this is clearly not the case.

And the missing middle of public policy has become larger and more serious with the passage of years. As the preceding chapters demonstrate, employment has become less secure for all of us at the same time that our individual economic circumstances have become more tenuous and the increased costs of an aging society are bearing down on us. Moreover, the things that we must do to gain and hold good jobs are becoming more difficult. We must develop and maintain a high level of skills, follow the ever-changing labor market, and protect ourselves against a wide range of other threats to our wages, benefits, and conditions of employment.

In doing these things we largely are thrown back on our own personal resources because the United States has never developed effective public or private systems to help us adjust to the effects of economic and social change on our prospects for employment. In short, we have developed a system that makes no sense unless we assume that what are manifestly major problems for many Americans are no problems at all.

If we are looking for a realistic way to make order out of the longstanding problems of the federal social role and the difficulties that have emerged from recent decades of change, we would do well to concentrate on the missing middle of the federal social role. A major priority for inaugurating the third century of federal activism should be assuring every American who is willing and able to work not only the chance to hold a job but the chance to hold a *good* job—one with decent pay, good benefits, and a reasonable prospect of security and advancement.

Another Path

Of course, this is not the only way to deal with problems that arise from the missing middle. Generations of public policy experts have advocated decoupling economic security programs from work by recasting those programs as some form of a guaranteed minimum income that would be provided by government to everyone in need, regardless of their past or present employment status.[3] This is one way of starting to redesign the federal social role from the ground up.

There is no doubt that the idea of a guaranteed income has considerable intellectual merit, but it has been rejected repeatedly by Congress and voters, and it is likely to be rejected in the future. It involves a radical change in the structure of policy, to which Americans have always been averse. More importantly, it seems to reject the individualist work ethic—the idea that public and private benefits should largely be a matter of earned right. With two strikes against it, a guaranteed income appears to be a less promising way than full employment to fill the missing middle of social policy.

Moreover, full employment, unlike a guaranteed income, is a form of national investment rather than expenditure. And it is the form of investment that we most critically need today: a commitment to upgrading the quality and productivity of our workforce. Unless we make this commitment on a massive scale, the pressures of domestic and international competition, together with the costs of an aging society, almost certainly will drive down our standard of living.

In short, public values and economic rationality coincide when it comes to the issue of employment. Americans believe that they and everyone else should work. To accomplish this all Americans will have to work more efficiently—they will have to gain the skills and make other adjustments that allow them to hold good jobs. The future well-being of the nation depends critically on whether they can realize their aspirations in this way.

Human Resources

In broad terms, at least, the measures required to address employment problems are no mystery. A truly effective employment policy must not only create jobs. It must also remove the impediments that prevent individuals from achieving their full potential in the world of work. In particular, it must ensure that more people are prepared to hold good jobs, that those jobs are available, and that workers can stay employed long enough to earn security against the threats of old age, ill health, and other personal problems.

This means that a full employment policy suited to our times must go beyond the job creation proposals of 1935 and 1945 and beyond the general commitments contained in the Humphrey-Hawkins Act. It must contain the ingredients of what is often called a "human capital" or "human resource" strategy for meeting the nation's needs. In particular, it must contain three major elements: security, education, and jobs.

Security

We cannot expect people who are without adequate food, shelter, clothing, health care, child support, and protection against the hazards of old age to be productive workers or good citizens. Employment and the present programs of the federal social role will provide these elements of security for most people, but for those who are without them, whether adults or children, building a baseline of security is the first step toward enhancing human resources.

A baseline of security is also required for those who are unable to make the many transitions required by a fast-changing economy. Without it, they will be less willing to take the kinds of risks that lead to greater opportunities for themselves and enable them to make their greatest contribution to society as a whole.

Security also means safety in the most ordinary sense of the term: safety on the job, safety from environmental hazards, safety from dangerous products and shaky services, such as banks that fail or poor quality health care. We cannot expect people to be productive workers and good citizens unless they are secure in these ways as well. And security means confidence that the rights of our citizens will be protected and that equal opportunities will be afforded to all. Discrimination on any grounds creates a withering of the spirit incompatible with the full development of our nation's human resources.

Education

High quality elementary and secondary education for all children, high quality daycare for preschool children of working parents, and access to higher education without incurring crippling debts are key ingredients in enhancing the prospects for each generation of Americans in all aspects of their lives. And, obviously, better education is essential to create the skills employers need to boost productivity and economic growth.

Opportunities for retraining and career change at all stages in life also are required if individual Americans are to keep up with the pace of economic and social change. For those young people and adults who have missed the chance to gain high quality education by the usual means, remedial training programs and help with job placement are the surest way to avoid wasted lives— wasted both for them and for society at large.

Jobs

Well prepared members of the workforce will only meet with frustration unless there is an adequate labor market to receive them. Improving the labor market is no easy task, but it is possible. We must stimulate employers to create more good jobs—jobs that pay a decent wage, provide adequate benefits, and hold out opportunities for advancement—and encourage them to seek productivity gains through upgrading labor, not by cutting its cost. Further, we must reduce needless unemployment or underemployment that results from irresponsible business practices, we must match jobs with workers more efficiently, and we must provide public employment if private opportunities are unavailable.

Why Should it Work?

Why should this approach to reform of the federal social role succeed when others have failed? In part, it should succeed because it provides precisely the type of leverage needed to move social policy off dead center in the United States. It asserts a strong sense of national priorities: the three goals of human resource development would set clear directions for federal policy in the years to come. And a program aimed at achieving those goals would address the most pressing common concerns of the American people today.

A human resource program would be a national commitment to deal with areas of longstanding neglect in public policy by closing gaps in the present system of income security and filling in the missing middle of the federal social role. And it would be a commitment to expanding federal activism to confront the major adverse effects of economic and social change. A program of human resource development would combat threats to employment, provide more adequate care for children, and shore up families in a variety of other ways. In addition it would help us to build the highly productive workforce needed to support an aging society, and it would contain stronger measures to control the costs of demographic change—both the rising costs of health care and the increasing burden of providing adequate income for the elderly.

Finally, a policy of enhancing human resources would attack the problems of the underclass, and of the disadvantaged, generally, by providing better services to both children and adults, and also by a national commitment to helping them break the cycle of poverty—to become self-sufficient through work. The nation would be getting at the root causes of poverty by investing in improved education, health, living conditions, and job prospects for the poor. In contrast, most of our present antipoverty programs are limited to providing income supports. At best, they can only alleviate the symptoms of poverty, not attack the disease.

In short, a program of human resource development should succeed because it would directly confront some of our most pressing common concerns on an issue-by-issue basis. And it would also address those concerns by creating benefits across the board. If the quality of our workforce is, in fact, among our most important economic resources, then a policy aimed at upgrading it should bring gains in terms of increased economic productivity that will make all of our public and private problems easier to solve. A human resource policy should help to make our national economic pie bigger. Almost everyone benefits from this.

Moreover, policies aimed at enhancing the productivity of all workers elude two of the most common (and most mistaken) criticisms of social spending: that it harms the economy and that it perpetuates dependency. Spending on human resources is clearly national investment, not consumption.

Finally, a human resource policy would benefit us all because its various measures should help each of us to withstand whatever problems social and economic change may bring in the years to come—whether by helping us to make transitions in employment, to deal with the stresses of two-earner households, or to shoulder the burdens of an aging society. The ultimate goals of such a policy should be to create a more favorable environment within which individuals can respond to the forces of change and to give each of us a better set of personal skills with which to work.

Autonomy

But as important as these pragmatic reasons why a human resource policy should succeed are the values that it embodies. A program aimed at enhancing the abilities of each of us to function more effectively in today's complex society is more than just a response to problems of employment and other immediate economic and social concerns. It expresses a larger social ideal: what theorists have called the value of individual "autonomy."

For centuries, advocates of democracy have stressed the central importance of the individual as a social, political, economic, and moral being. According to this view, the success of a democratic society and government can be measured in large part by whether it creates conditions that will enable all citizens to make choices and engage in the activities that allow them to lead their lives successfully, by their own lights and up to their own capacities.

To put it differently, democratic government and social life are in serious jeopardy when people are blocked from pursuing options that are within their abilities—when there are second-class citizens of any sort. We cannot expect any of our institutions to operate well if large numbers of people are unable to read a newspaper, hold a job, care for their families, or participate in society up to their full capacity.

If we accept this view of democratic principles, then institutions—governments, businesses, families—are means to the end of individual self-fulfillment. It is to the well-being of individuals, not institutions, that we owe our first allegiance. Our primary goal must be to create conditions that will allow all citizens to lead autonomous, self-directing lives.

But democratic autonomy also has another face. None of us would be such a great enthusiast for individual choice and opportunity if we believed that most people would choose to lead lives of idleness, dissipation, and neglect of their families, friends, and communities. We don't want to ensure that everyone can read so that they can learn to become embezzlers. We don't want to give them a hand up in the job market so that they can loaf. The other face of democratic autonomy is individual responsibility.

Economic self-sufficiency is only one aspect of individual responsibility, although it is the aspect most often discussed in public policy debates these days. We expect individuals to make their own best efforts rather than to depend on government, charity, or other sources of help. But we are also concerned with other aspects of responsibility. For example, political scientist James Q. Wilson believes that Americans are rediscovering the importance of some old-fashioned values, which he calls "character."[4] We expect people to take responsibility for their families, if they can, to be prudent about personal finances, and not to engage in activities that would be harmful to others. Obviously, too, the types of individual responsibility we expect depend on the opportunities that individuals enjoy. We expect wealthy people to use some of their affluence for projects that benefit society, and we expect powerful people—leaders of business, politics, and opinion—to take an active interest in the well-being of their fellow citizens.

There is every indication that this version of democratic principles—an emphasis on autonomy, opportunity, and responsibility—fits well with the values that Americans actually hold. Recent studies of American belief systems by sociologist Sidney Verba and political scientist Jennifer Hochschild reveal that equality, fairness, freedom, and many other positive words in the democratic vocabulary tend to be equated with opportunity.[5] Americans generally do not condemn unequal outcomes in the race of life, but they do believe that everyone should have a fair and equal chance. This is what we would expect from a nation of individualists: everyone is expected to make it on his own, but nobody should be held back by circumstances beyond his control.

Setting a high priority on policies that promote human resource development obviously would advance the value of individual autonomy. People who are more secure, better educated, and more able to realize their potential in the world of work will not only be better employees; they will also be better able to achieve their own personal goals, by their own lights, in all aspects of their public and private lives.

A human resource policy stands a good chance of winning public acceptance, in part, because these are goals to which we all aspire. Using government to achieve them would be harnessing its energies to some of our most strongly felt common values.

They are mainstream American values that resonate throughout our history. After all, it was Lincoln who argued that "the leading object" of our form of government should be "to lift artificial weights from all shoulders; to clear the paths of laudable pursuit for all; to afford all an unfettered start, and a fair chance in the race of life."[6] And Theodore Roosevelt urged us to use government in the same way. "Help any man who stumbles," he declared. "If he lies down, it is a poor job to try to carry him; but if he is a worthy man, try your best to see that he gets a chance to show the worth that is in him."[7]

The values of autonomy, opportunity, and a fair chance are also values that liberals and conservatives share. Advocates of both political persuasions have always argued that their agendas would lead to greater opportunity for individual self-reliance. Liberals have sought to reach this goal by measures that enhance individual security. Virtually every major extension of the federal social role in this century—from the time of Theodore Roosevelt, to the New Deal, to the Great Society—has been justified, at least rhetorically, as a way of enlarging opportunity. Conservatives have sought to reach the same goal by clearing away needless government interference with individual choice.

But neither liberals nor conservatives have fully come to grips with the fact that, through no fault of their own, large numbers of people are unable to achieve their full potential. As a result, there is a tendency for liberal policies to reduce to promoting security of and by itself and for conservative policies to promote freedoms that many people find empty.

A human resource program would reach beyond traditional liberal and conservative measures to open up greater opportunities and help individuals develop the capacity to take advantage of them. This is a common ground on which both liberals and conservatives can meet. By directly confronting the barriers to individual opportunity, a human resource program should help the nation to achieve goals that adherents of both political persuasions have sought by indirect means. And by emphasizing values that most Americans share, it should help overcome the present stalemate about the future directions of the federal social role.

Resolving Tensions: Individual and Nation

For many of the same reasons that it would create a common ground for liberals and conservatives, a human resource policy should also help resolve the two basic tensions in American political life. This is probably the most important reason why it is likely to succeed.

It should reconcile the tension between individualism and national values because it is a truly inclusive policy. As mentioned, everyone would benefit from its measures both directly and indirectly. Divising inclusive programs—such as Social Security—has always been the easiest way to overcome the ambivalence most Americans feel about activist government. Because it fits the requirements of our inclusive political style, a human resource policy should not only be supported, but supported strongly, by the American people.

Moreover, such a policy is even better suited than Social Security or other income transfer programs to resolve the tension between individual and collective values. Its goal is greater self-sufficiency, both for the disadvantaged and for other Americans. It aims to help all of us help ourselves. In the old cliché, it would teach people how to use a fishing pole, rather than give them a fish. Because it emphasizes autonomy (freedom and opportunity), rather than emphasizing security alone, a human resource policy is the perfect bridge between individualism and collectivism. It is a means of using common resources to help each of us achieve supremely individualist goals: self-direction and self-support.

But a human resource policy can only bridge the gap between individual and collective values if it is designed in a way that pays due respect to the importance of individual responsibility. This means, for example, setting high standards for students and schools, expecting both employers and employees to take an active interest in upgrading skills, expecting parents to provide adequate support for their own children (where possible), expecting older workers to make their greatest contribution to the labor force and firms to help them do so, and expecting the poor and the unemployed to make their best efforts to become self-supporting through work.

A nation of individualists should be ready to support the use of collective means to enhance personal opportunities only if the means employed place responsibility on everyone who benefits from such measures to make their own best efforts to take advantage of those opportunities. We should be giving fishing poles only to people who are willing to fish.

This is not a harsh requirement. There is every indication that most Americans are seeking greater opportunity and freedom in many aspects of their lives: most of the poor and unemployed want to become self-supporting; both companies and workers want to solve the problems of outmoded skills; and everyone appears to want better performance from our educational system. Requiring that measures to implement a human resources policy contain a strong element of individual responsibility is not harsh, but it is necessary if our individualist values are to be satisfied by collective measures.

Resolving Tensions: Nation and Group

A human resource program should also reconcile the tension between national and group attachments in at least two different ways. First, it would focus the national debate in this area on the most important question: what the effect of federal policy is on individuals, not on institutions.

Clearly policies that would extend the federal role into areas such as education, child welfare, and the terms of employment—areas that traditionally have been dominated by other levels of government and by business—could be accused by localists of overreaching. In a nation that values institutional diversity, a program of this scope might be expected to meet with opposition, as have other attempts to impose stronger federal priorities. But if the goal of a more extensive federal role is greater autonomy through human resource development, the force of any opposition should be blunted by public values that are at least as strong as diversity. In an individualist democracy, it should be possible for everyone to agree that policies which promote greater individual freedom must have higher priority than the prerogatives of institutions.

In fact, the growth of the federal social role, in this century at least, has frequently required states, localities, and businesses to give up some of their prerogatives in the interest of federal initiatives that serve the strongly felt needs of individuals. This has been true in spending programs, where the federal government assumed responsibility for providing income security that had formerly been the almost exclusive prerogative of other levels of government, business, and charities. And it has been true in the areas of regulation, civil rights, and other aspects of the social role.

Today many of the most strongly felt needs of individuals can be best addressed by a program of human resource development. If those needs are, in fact, as urgent as they appear to be, there is no reason to expect that institutional prerogatives will stand in their way now, any more than they have in the past when public problems became severe and a federal solution was clearly required.

But, of course, other institutions have never entirely given way to new federal initiatives. A truly accurate account of the growth of activist government must recognize that each stage of its expansion has been less a reduction in the importance of other institutions in providing for public needs than a change in the types of responsibilities that the federal government and other institutions have assumed for meeting common problems. At each stage national priorities have been asserted more strongly, but the means of achieving them have continued to depend on states, localities, businesses, the voluntary sector, families, and other institutions. And in many cases, as described in previous chapters, greater federal activism has led to a larger role for other institutions as well.

This brings us to the second way in which a human resource policy should be able to reconcile the values of nationalism and localism. There is no reason why it should obviate the need for other institutions to play an active role in upgrading education, enhancing income security, improving the prospects for employment, and achieving other national purposes. On the contrary.

The nation's needs are too great and too many to squander either public or private means. The federal government must do what it does best, and other institutions must perform the roles to which they are suited if we are to improve the opportunities of all our people.

A national commitment to human resource development, like other federal initiatives, would simply mean that all institutions in society would assume new responsibilities for achieving common purposes. Who should decide what those responsibilities are? In the end, the federal government must decide. As the representative of all the people it alone has the final responsibility to see that common problems are solved and that all sectors of society contribute to solving them. This is what asserting national priorities has meant in the past and what it means today.

But, by themselves, federal initiatives that assert a stronger sense of national priorities are not enough. Successful activism also requires a careful balancing of national standards for institutions and individuals with efforts to help them achieve those standards. Simply demanding adherence to the common interest is a recipe for failure. It casts the federal government in the role of a common scold. Activists have always recognized that individuals and institutions may have real difficulties in assuming new responsibilities.

More specifically, the need to assert priorities and ease the way to progress is a matter of closing and opening doors. At its best, activist government has found ways to discourage practices that harm the public interest and to encourage those that promote it. Hamilton's economic policies made speculative behavior difficult and investment in productive activities profitable. The social insurance plans of the New Deal, with their mandatory employer contributions, made it impossible for companies to neglect the welfare of their employees, but they also helped open the door to negotiations between business and labor about exactly what form job-related benefits should take. The civil rights policies of the 1960s closed the door on legally segregated schools, but the federal government helped pay the cost of integration through grants-in-aid to the states.

Examples could be multiplied. The point is that federal activism should help all sectors of society achieve a better future, and this involves devising measures that will minimize the cost of change. It involves opening opportunities for a better life as well as closing doors on problems of the past.

There are, then, two strong reasons why a program of human resource development should be able to overcome the objections that advocates of institutional diversity might raise against a greater extension of the federal social role. First, it appeals to common values of enhanced individual opportunity, which should have the highest priority in a democratic society. Second, although it calls on the federal government to assert those values more strongly, it does not preclude other institutions from playing a large role in achieving national purposes. On the contrary, it calls on all sectors of society to make more vigorous efforts to solve common problems.

Partners

In addition to these more or less theoretical reasons why a human resource program is likely to succeed, there are more tangible straws in the wind that indicate such an initiative would meet with strong support.

Many of our largest and best-managed businesses are already turning their attention to the benefits they can reap from improving the prospects of their workers and from a national workforce that has greater opportunities. In recent years, many companies have been improving retention, equal opportunity, retraining, and benefit plans and allowing greater participation in workplace management. They believe they can boost production by developing a more loyal, more highly skilled, and more stable workforce. Through placement, training, and relocation programs, companies have also shown increased concern for workers who have lost their jobs. The vogue for Japanese labor relations techniques is another indication of the growing concern for more creative use of human resources.

Progressive corporate managers also are looking for partnerships with states, communities, and the voluntary sector to develop programs that will improve the skills of young people and meet the midcareer needs of older employees. Many states and communities, in turn, have acted vigorously to upgrade schools, colleges, and other institutions that help enhance human resources. In virtually every state efforts have been made to give disadvantaged people—typically poor children, welfare mothers, and displaced workers—a second chance to become self-sufficient. In the last few years, counseling, retraining, placement, public employment, and other activities intended to get people off welfare and to help them become self-sustaining have been emphasized at all levels of government.

Individuals have responded enthusiastically to corporate and governmental initiatives. Programs offering training, opportunities for greater involvement in company decision making, and a second chance for the disadvantaged have found no shortage of would-be participants. Individual Americans clearly are willing to assume their share of reponsibility for achieving success in life, given the opportunity.

A consensus is emerging—a consensus of deeds not words—that all institutions of American society, and all individuals, must do more to enhance the capacities of our people to lead more productive and satisfying lives. To date, the sum total of these efforts has been fairly small. But the direction for national effort to which they point is clear. The federal government will not lack willing partners in designing and implementing initiatives to enhance human resources.

Disclaimers

Although we can and should expect a great deal from a program of human resource development—both as a solution to particular public problems and as a means of reviving activist government more generally—we should also recognize that there are limits to its proper scope and probable effectiveness.

The most obvious limit is in the area of public values. A human resource policy would advance the principle of individual autonomy. But, important as it is, that principle is not the only cardinal value that should guide a democratic society. We must strive to maintain basic rights and liberties, to ensure fair and equal treatment of individuals by all institutions, and to secure a decent standard of living for all of our people, as well as to enlarge opportunity. The values embodied in these other goals are important in their own right, and a democratic society must devote at least some of its energies to advancing them.

In addition, those values should guide the way in which any human resource policy is implemented. For example, we should make every effort to ensure that measures to advance opportunity are available on the same terms to all of their intended beneficiaries and that they contain provisions to ensure due process for appeals against adverse government actions. And we must face up to the fact that a program aimed at both enlarging opportunity and demanding responsibility will inevitably create some serious dilemmas. What if some people do not want to take advantage of the opportunities afforded or to accept the responsibilities they entail? Do we still have a commitment to help them secure a decent standard of living? This is the type of question for which there is probably no satisfactory answer across the board. We will have to wrestle with it in different ways as we develop different measures.

There are also at least two important practical difficulties that face a human resource policy. First, in a great many cases, we either do not know how to help individuals and institutions become more self-sufficient, or the cost of doing so would be prohibitively high. This is one reason why policymakers have backed away from some efforts that might fall under the umbrella of human resource policy in the past. The abandonment of some of the more ambitious programs of the War on Poverty is a case in point. It is simply very hard, for example, to help a teen-aged mother who has been reared in a culture of poverty—who has few skills, low self-esteem, and a defeatist attitude—to become a self-supporting member of society. We must realize that, because of limits on our present knowledge about human behavior and how to make social programs work, there are limits to how much a human resource program can accomplish, in the near term at least.

Second, because the goal of enhancing human resources is so easily generalized—because all of us could use a hand up in some aspect of our lives—there is a real danger that a commitment to greater public efforts in this area could squander public resources by scattering them too widely. Clearly if we are to place a stronger emphasis on human resources, we also need to discipline it with an equally strong sense of which problems are most important and which people are most in need of help.

None of these difficulties is fatal. It is certainly possible to keep measures aimed at enhancing human resources within the bounds of our other public values. And it is possible both to improve our social technology and to focus federal initiatives on the areas of greatest need. To solve longstanding problems and meet the challenges of economic and social change, we not only can but must overcome these difficulties. But we will never do so unless we both admit that the difficulties exist and make a firm commitment to overall directions of policy that require us to come to grips with them.

12

―――――

Measures

B ecause the American style of activism requires consulta-
tion—and in the end, partnership—between the federal government and all sectors of society, devising specific measures to
make a human resource policy work calls for patience and inge-
nuity. In all probability, major initiatives will have to await another
presidential election, and perhaps more than one. In part, this is
because Congress and any administration must wrestle the federal
budget deficit to manageable proportions in the late 1980s. But
federal deficits are not the major reason why large-scale new initiatives can only be produced by a new administration. Because
the agenda of domestic problems that has accumulated over a
decade of stalemate is very long, developing specific proposals
that cut across a great many areas of policy in a coordinated way—
as a human resource program must—will require an extensive
planning exercise that only new leadership has the time and political resources to mount.

   The Committee on Economic Security of 1935 provides at least
one model for how to proceed. That committee was composed of
the principal officers of government who would be responsible
for carrying out its decisions—the Secretaries of Labor, Treasury,

Agriculture, the Attorney General, and the Federal Relief Administrator. It was supported by a phalanx of consultative groups whose members represented virtually every interest that might be affected by its work. And it was given a wide-ranging mandate: to look across administrative and programmatic boundaries in search of new solutions to the leading issues of the times.

The program that the Committee on Economic Security developed, the Social Security Act, has been easily the most successful piece of domestic legislation in our nation's history. In no small part its success has been due to the fact that the act forged proposals for dealing with a large number of concerns into a coherent whole. The scope of the undertaking allowed its architects to balance conflicting institutional and individual concerns—issues of who benefits and who pays—around an integrated series of actions from which, on net, most Americans clearly derived some advantage.

Any new administration should seriously consider convening one or more groups like the Committee on Economic Security. But this time it should give the members an even larger mandate: to examine how all aspects of the federal social role—spending, taxes, incentives, regulations, and national economic management—can be used to advance the goals of human resource development. Inevitably the members of such a group will be troubled by fiscal constraints. (While it is a myth that the nation cannot afford to spend more for public purposes, it obviously cannot afford to spend infinitely more.) And they will be troubled by practical constraints as well: the limits of our knowledge about how to effect large-scale social change, and the difficulties of balancing the various strands of the American style of activism.

To imagine what the future of the federal social role will and should be requires imagining what a group of committed public servants—a Committee on Human Resources (CHR)—operating within these constraints would produce. It would be the sheerest speculation to try to predict the result. And even if it were possible, detailing all the specific measures required to make a human resource policy work is beyond the scope of this or any other single book. Still, it is at least possible to indicate some of the priorities that a prospective CHR should have and to mention some of the measures it should consider. In particular, if its mission is to achieve the three goals of a human resource policy—security, education, and jobs—the recommendations of a CHR should clearly differ from those of the 1935 committee in at least two important respects.

Children

The New Dealers concentrated primarily on creating safeguards for retirees, widows, and the unemployed and made only a start in dealing with the problems of children. If it is insightful, a CHR will make children its highest priority. The reason is partly that programs for the elderly and unemployed are already in place. And, inadequate as they may be, the chances of greatly improving them over the long run depend on the future contributions that today's children will make to our economy and society. Moreover, the most serious difficulties with programs now in place are not likely to arise for a decade or more, whereas the problems of today's children can only be solved now—before their health and attitudes are permanently damaged.

Some aspects of an increased national investment in children are easy to discern. Obviously, support for maternal and child health, nutrition, and early childhood education should be increased to the point where these services reach the entire population in need. Repeated studies have shown that getting all of our children off to a good start in life is not only humane but also cost-effective in terms of future savings in health care, education, and other areas.

But approaching the reform of social policy from the perspective of children also means plunging into some of the most vexed issues of the federal social role: national policy on daycare, the federal role in education, and what to do for children whose prospects are damaged by their home environments.

Clearly the nation must invest more in education, and it must get better results. One of our highest national priorities must be to ensure that all children in all parts of the country receive the best possible basic education and training in specialized skills. Today this responsibility is largely in the hands of state and local governments, and although many are making exemplary strides, many are not. We cannot afford a patchwork quilt of investment in education. The resources of the federal government must be brought to bear to supplement, encourage, and, if necessary, require more vigorous efforts on a nationwide basis.

Funding should be targeted to the areas of greatest need: those parts of the country where the performance of children is lagging and the resources of local authorities are limited. Proposals for national core curricula, teacher certification, and a longer school year should be carefully evaluated and implemented, if their effectiveness can be shown. No price should be too high and no standards too rigid to achieve educational excellence. We can and must build public schools for all of our children that are as good or better than the best private alternatives.

The debate over whether the federal government should make a larger investment in daycare has been going on for some years. Clearly, with so many two-worker households, there is an enormous national need to ensure proper supervision of children, both in their preschool years and during after-school hours. This is a concern that cuts across all social classes—from welfare parents who would like to get a job but are tied down by their children, to the working poor who cannot afford adequate daycare, to middle-class people who find they must spend large sums to acquire it. Virtually all parents and everyone else who has close contact with children share the concern.

With such widespread interest, the foundation may have been established for a comprehensive, contributory program of daycare, provided either through the public school system or by private vendors. Such a system might be financed by a small addition to the payroll tax paid by both employers and employees, and it might also be supplemented by parental contributions, scaled according to each family's means. Alternatively, we might treat child care in the same way that we treat public schooling—as a necessary investment by the community as a whole and a service to which all children are entitled. In this case, we would simply expand existing educational systems to accommodate preschool children and to provide after-school supervision. And we would fund this expansion from general revenues, as we now fund elementary and secondary education. Some states and cities are already beginning to adopt this approach by lowering the age of kindergarten enrollment.

Finally, we might adopt a combination of incentives to employers and nonfederal levels of government, together with an enhanced child care tax credit for middle-income people and greater funding for existing programs that provide daycare to the poor. This approach would result in a less orderly and efficient system than comprehensive programs would create. It would be more prone to abuse and cutbacks, and its results would be harder to monitor and control, but it would be more consistent with our traditional practice of using multiple means to solve public problems.

In the end, it probably does not matter much which approach is chosen. The important thing is to assert a stronger national interest in child care in some form.

To young people who are enrolled in higher education we owe an unencumbered start in the race of life. The present system of student aid relies far too heavily on loans. Too many young people begin their careers heavily in debt. We need their full productive potential in the years to come more than we need their loan payments. The federal student aid system should rely far more heavily on *grants* to low-income students, and the total resources available to them should be fully adequate to finance their education. We should continue to offer loans for middle-income students, but with the strong presumption that their parents have the responsibility to provide them with an education where possible. The parent, not the student, should incur the debt, to the extent that this responsibility can be enforced.

Beyond these measures, the nation must remain open to any and all new ideas for improving the prospects of its children— such as the controversial concept put forward by Mayor Bradley of Los Angeles to offer boarding school education to youngsters who are so much at risk from their home environments that failure in life is all but inevitable.[1]

The mayor's suggestion is not as farfetched as it might seem. Educators believe they can detect which students are in serious danger of becoming school dropouts or underachievers. The numbers are, thankfully, fairly small—perhaps two hundred thousand for each birth cohort. We also know that the crime rate among this group is high. The cost to society of sending someone to prison is on the order of $50,000–$70,000 per year—far more than the tuition at even the best boarding schools.

Wealthy and middle-class people commonly adopt the expedient of sending troubled youngsters to schools where their exposure to dangerous influences is controlled. Why should the parents of poor children not have the same option—assuming that they are allowed freedom of choice in the matter—particularly when society would be the net beneficiary? One need not imagine "ghettoized" reform schools. High-quality private preparatory schools are a more appropriate model. It may be that this is one area in which the public sector can and should compete more vigorously with private alternatives. Perhaps we should move toward creating a new form of institution—a residential "magnet school"—where youngsters of all backgrounds who need intensive supervision could receive the education that is now beyond their reach.

Health Care

The second respect in which the efforts of a CHR should differ from the efforts of the group in 1935 is that it should complete the work begun then, and continued in 1965, to develop a comprehensive national health care policy. Measures to accomplish this should have high priority, because the inadequate coverage and rising cost of health care programs make them the most troubled of our major provisions for individual security.

There are clear indications that most Americans know what they want when it comes to health care: virtually unlimited access on demand to the best available service. The clearest indication is that, except when health care services are physically inaccessible or denied to them for financial or other reasons, Americans consume these services as if they had a natural right to them. And they are clearly willing to pay for unlimited access—preferably on the installment plan, by insurance. The mounting national medical bill testifies to this.

In these circumstances, politicians should stop fighting the preferences of the American people and give them what they want—along with measures to keep the cost as low as possible. This involves two major changes in present policy: developing a combination of public and private systems for the 35 million uninsured, and reversing the present approach to health care cost containment. The former could be achieved by a variety of means— most simply by extending Medicaid coverage to everyone uninsured by other means and charging a premium to wage-earners, and / or their employers. Once broader coverage is achieved, the task is then to improve the adequacy of both public and private medical insurance—by gradually extending Medicare and Medicaid to cover *all* health care costs, starting with catastrophic illness, and requiring private plans to provide more adequate coverage as well.

Whatever mechanism is adopted for broadening the coverage of health care insurance, special measures will be required to finance the growing cost of long-term care. Former Social Security Commissioner Robert Ball estimates that this can be accomplished by a fairly small increase in Medicare premiums (0.5 percent) if Social Security retirement benefits are diverted to pay the room and board costs of nursing home patients.[2] Other plans to finance long-term care are also under development. Many, like the plan described in the next chapter of this book, include incentives for state and local governments to develop more effective systems of noninstitutional care. Clearly, the long-term care problem can be solved by measures that are within our means, although it is not yet clear exactly what combination of policies make for the best solution.

The other major change needed to provide more adequate health care protection—a better system of cost containment—requires accepting the fact that price is no object for most Americans when they are ill. As a result, present approaches to restraining costs are swimming against the tide. The basic idea behind present systems is to limit demand by requiring individuals to pick up some of the bill for their health care—deductibles and copayments in the case of Medicare. If price is no object, however, this can only result in imposing large costs on individuals when they are in distress without having much effect on overall expenditures.

There are at least two more promising approaches to cost containment. The first is for government at all levels, and other large institutions, to act, in essence, as "consumer cooperatives" for the purchase of health care.[3] Like other "co-ops," government, corporations, and large unions would use their enormous purchasing power to drive hard bargains in the health care marketplace. They would negotiate with providers to obtain the best possible comprehensive care at the lowest possible price. Institutional diversity would be an advantage. If, for example, the federal government found that the steelworkers' union had made a better deal in securing health care for its members than the Department of HHS had been able to obtain in negotiating prices and service for Medicare recipients, there would be a strong incentive for federal officials to go back to the bargaining table. The growth of health maintenance organizations (HMOs) illustrates this "consumer co-op" approach, and, to some extent, so do the restrictions imposed on Medicare reimbursement in the 1980s.

The other possible approach is to assume that bargaining in the marketplace for health care services will not work because the various components of the health care system—hospitals, doctors, nursing homes, and so forth—in essence operate as monopolies. If we make this assumption, then we would expect that even the most aggressive bargaining will only lead health care providers to dig in their heels on issues of price, artificially inflate their costs, or reduce their level of service. If these fears are justified, the most promising approach to cost containment would be to treat the health care system in the way that we treat public utilities and other monopoly providers of services. Government should regulate both prices and investment. And it should ensure adequate access for the public as a whole, while at the same time allowing providers a fair return on capital.

In all likelihood, the United States will adopt a combination of approaches to health care cost containment, just as it has adopted a combination of approaches to providing pensions, creating jobs, encouraging home ownership, and attaining other public goals. One key to success in any approach is comprehensiveness—controlling the costs of medical, hospital, and long-term care, so that controls in one area are not circumvented by increased costs in other areas. Finding a combination of approaches that accomplishes this and protects all of the American people should be high on the list of priorities for any CHR. If comprehensive coverage is combined with a comprehensive strategy of cost containment, there is a good chance that the national bill for health services will not be exorbitant, in the near term at least. The "big spenders" on health care are those who would maintain the present system of partial protection and runaway costs, rather than those who would design a system of adequate protection within which costs can be restrained.

It must be admitted, however, that no one can be sure how effective various cost control measures will be over the long term. It is possible that, despite our best efforts, the pressures of an aging society may increase the nation's medical bill to a level most Americans would find unacceptable. In these circumstances, we may decide that we no longer want a system that provides unlimited access to health care. For example, we may conclude—as the British have—that we must restrict the access of people in the last years of their lives to certain forms of interventionist medicine.

Hopefully events will not develop in this way, and we should certainly begin by adopting an optimistic approach. But because there are many unknowns, we should take precautions to structure our system of health care so that the American people are kept aware of the national health bill. We should also make sure that any decisions to restrict access are made in the full light of public debate and applied in a fair and uniform way.

The federal government is the best source of continuing public education about medical costs and the best forum for public debate on what to do about them. Among the benefits of extending federal financing for health care and federal controls over costs is the fact that national officials would be held responsible for reporting on their efforts to keep the system affordable. Moreover, any debate over restricting access, if it develops, would take account of all views in the nation, including the full range of views about the issues of human rights involved. And it should be a careful and protracted debate.

If, after public deliberation, the American people were to decide that they must restrict health care in some way, federal control of the system would make it possible to apply restrictions fairly and uniformly. Or, at least, a system that is publicly controlled would be more likely to restrict access in a fair and uniform way than our present fragmented system does. Today the wealthy and the well-insured have unlimited care, and people with less ability to pay are often denied costly procedures. It is conceivable that the American people might choose the present system of limiting access, but there are certainly strong grounds for arguing against it.

In any event, the American people as a whole should have the right to choose, if cost containment measures prove ineffective. And one reason for imposing those measures at the federal level is to create a health care system in which the American people can make that choice through open public debate, rather than have it imposed on them by the laws of the marketplace or the professional judgments of the medical community. First, however, we should try all possible measures to avoid having to make such a choice at all. And the most important measure is a strong system of cost containment.

Jobs

There is, however, at least one important respect in which a CHR should emulate the priorities set forth in 1935: it should restate a national commitment to full employment and ratify that commitment by a program of public service jobs. Full employment should have high priority because it is the missing middle of present federal policy—all of our existing programs would be more effective if it could be achieved. And it is the one achievement that, more than any other, would ease the strains caused by social and economic change.

Broadly speaking, measures to achieve full employment should take two tracks: programs to deal with the problems of the unemployed and programs to prevent the loss of jobs.

Most of the unemployed already fall into two natural "catchment areas" of public policy: AFDC and Unemployment Insurance (UI). That is, sooner or later most people who are experiencing hardship from unemployment end up applying for benefits from one or the other of these programs. At present, the programs simply tide them over for a period of time, in the expectation that they will find jobs on their own. And most do. But, at present, those who remain unemployed are dropped by UI after a period of time and maintained indefinitely by AFDC. This is waste. A more constructive policy must be developed.

There are probably many sound ways to combat the waste that results from unemployment. A fairly direct approach that combines a selection of ideas from recent discussions of employment problems runs along the following lines.

We should begin by making benefits for both AFDC and UI more uniform on a nationwide basis, so that the unemployed can concentrate on finding jobs rather than on coping with immediate financial emergencies. After a reasonable period of time, job search, placement, and, if necessary, retraining assistance should be provided to those who remain unemployed. Participation in these programs should be mandatory. Those who will not try to help themselves should lose benefits. Finally, if, despite their best efforts, some individuals cannot find employment at a decent wage, public service jobs should be offered. We can debate endlessly about what sorts of jobs they should be. There is an enormous amount of public improvement needed in our society, and no shortage of ideas about how to organize the unemployed to carry out this work. For example, Senator Paul Simon has developed a plan for creating 3 million new jobs that would use our idle manpower to upgrade the quality of social services, protect the environment, and improve our physical infrastructure.[4] Alternatively, we might create jobs by expanding recruitment in the armed services. Or we might adopt the simple expedient, once suggested by Senator Moynihan, of reinstating twice-a-day mail delivery. In the end it matters less how we do it; what matters most is that a nation with a strong work ethic should live up to its principles.

What about unemployed young people? Often they are not eligible for UI or AFDC. A simple approach would be to make any young person living in poverty who applies to a federal job-search center automatically eligible for UI, if he can demonstrate that he has actively sought employment for a certain period of time. The same progression of job search, placement, and training, followed by the offer of a public service job, if all else fails, would be available to unemployed youth as to UI and AFDC recipients. In some cases, such a system could be used to pay school dropouts to continue their education.

To increase the chances of success in placing the unemployed, and to ease labor mobility generally, the nation must develop an improved job-search information system. The United States Employment Service, which is currently responsible for performing this function, lists only a small percentage of all job openings, and the openings it lists tend to be either highly specialized or minimum-wage jobs in the service sector. Also, Employment Service offices often lack the information needed to refer applicants across state lines. Either the capabilities of the Employment Service should be upgraded or private firms should be offered "head hunter" fees for placing the long-term unemployed.

These and other full employment ideas clearly could have unintended effects. They could end up discouraging some people from looking for jobs, but we do not know this. They might increase the cost (and wages) of labor at the lower end of the income scale—which might not be a bad effect. We should not be timid about measures to increase employment. These and other ideas are clearly worth a try, at least on an experimental basis, and if they do not work, the nation must keep trying until it finds a system that does work.

Measures to prevent unemployment should include the programs to help young people get off to a better start in life already mentioned. But a CHR should also direct its attention to retraining people now on the job, particularly those working in troubled industries and middle-aged employees whose skills are becoming outmoded. Ideally, we should seek to upgrade skills whenever possible. But we should also offer workers who have reached a dead end in their present fields the chance to gain training in new technical specialties where there is an increasing demand for labor. A great deal of unemployment can be avoided, productivity can be enhanced, costs to the public for Unemployment Insurance, welfare, and Social Security can be reduced, and lives can be enriched if the nation vigorously addresses the need for retraining.

Again, many approaches are possible. Greater tax incentives to employers or regulations mandating retraining of employees about to be terminated in some circumstances would place much of the responsibility in the hands of business. A revolving loan fund, retraining vouchers, or a direct grant program organized along the lines of the GI bill would place responsibility on individuals to take the initiative in upgrading their skills. Because many displaced workers have been employed in troubled industries which tend to be unionized, support for unions to provide stronger retraining and placement services to their members should also be considered. In all likelihood, the right approach is a combination of these different ideas. At present the federal government does little to help solve the retraining problem: surely some more adequate response can be devised.

Good Jobs

In addition to adopting measures to combat unemployment, we should insist that business create more *good* jobs. After all, the adverse effects of recent economic change include not only the loss of jobs, but also changes in the terms of employment that threaten an increasing number of Americans.

One element in a good job is adequate private benefits. Part-time, intermittent, and temporary employees should not be denied fringe benefits. A comprehensive national health care system would solve the problem of providing medical coverage. The other major problem, ensuring that workers receive adequate pensions, could be solved by requiring employers to create full vesting rights for all employees in company pension plans that are fully portable when people change jobs. For those businesses unwilling to establish plans, or too small to do so, employer and employee contributions to a public plan—perhaps a supplementary fund managed by the Social Security Administration—should be mandatory.

In addition, loopholes in existing law that allow companies to dump or misuse pension plans should be closed. And federal policies that discourage older people from continuing to work should be amended. One example is the provision in the ERISA regulations that allows companies to discontinue pension benefits to retirees who work forty hours or more per month. Clearly this creates a disincentive for older people to engage in the type of work they most prefer: part-time employment.

Another element of a good job is a good income. The federal minimum wage has not been raised for many years, and inflation has so eroded its value that many full-time employees working at the minimum wage earn incomes below the poverty line. There may well be some truth to the argument that raising it would lead employers to lay off some marginal workers, although there is no firm evidence that this effect would be large. On the whole, it seems a matter of simple justice that people who work full time should be able to earn a living wage. And it seems hypocritical that an affluent nation with a strong work ethic should be unwilling to guarantee this. The minimum wage should be raised to a level that allows the millions of people at the bottom of the economic ladder who are doing "the right thing"—going to work rather than living at public expense—to earn incomes that at least reach the poverty line.

But whatever we do with the minimum wage, we will inevitably have to rely more on increasing the skills and productivity of workers, and on other measures to stimulate economic growth and improve the terms of employment, rather than of federal wage regulation to raise the living standards of most Americans. It would be folly to try to legislate a solution to the problems of stagnant real income across the board, just as it would be folly not to adopt measures that address the underlying causes of that problem. All of the measures of a human resource program would contribute toward the goal of improving incomes, although major improvements are likely to come only gradually,

A good job also means security of employment. Firms should not be able to discard workers like disposable parts. They must extend loyalty to their employees if they expect loyalty in return. The trend toward looser labor contracts—more part-time and contract work—seems to point in the opposite direction. But it is not clear exactly what to do about the problem. Requirements for advanced notification of layoffs, assistance in placement, and continuation of fringe benefits after termination would seem to be the least that can be asked, but they do not get to the heart of the issue. More flexible wage structures, restrictions on the export of jobs, and job-sharing arrangements may provide part of the answer.

But no one has come up with a wholly convincing case for where the full answer lies. The experience of European countries indicates that too much job security can hamper job creation—firms are unwilling to hire when they must make what they regard as too great a commitment to their workers. There must be a happy middle ground. In the United States too little attention has been devoted to searching for it. We must search harder and find some means of enhancing employment security.

The Economy

A greater national investment in children, a comprehensive health care system, and improved employment policies would carry the nation a long way toward a meaningful program of human resource development. Yet both the need for those measures and their success depends ultimately on the overall health of our economy. In a prosperous economic environment, the problems of children, providing adequate health care, and employment will all be less acute. And if we are to spend more to solve these problems by public means, we will have to raise more taxes. Our ability to do this will be greatly enhanced if our economy is growing and, in particular, if productivity can be increased.

Although investing in human resources is by itself a means of increasing productivity, we must seek other means as well. Responsible fiscal and monetary policy obviously are essential. We must reduce the federal budget deficit and all of its attendant ills. A larger investment in *civilian* research and development, where the results have a direct bearing on economic growth, is also critical. And it is essential for the United States to develop a more effective trade policy. Taken together, a stronger federal emphasis on trade, R&D, and better macroeconomic policy are the essentials of a realistic "industrial policy."

But the federal government should not become just another business booster. We have or can readily develop the regulatory tools to clamp down on irresponsible and wasteful speculative behavior. We should use them against nonproductive mergers and acquisitions and against shady practices such as "green-mail." We should also examine whether federal tax and credit policy encourages this type of waste and make the appropriate changes. And we should adopt measures to reduce the mounting level of corporate as well as individual debt—perhaps by tax disincentives, by regulations limiting consumer credit and corporate borrowing, or by cutting back on federal credit activities that encourage borrowing in certain sectors of the economy.

In addition, there are also growing indications that the loosening of federal regulation in recent years, particularly in the financial industry, has not, on net, served the public interest well. The large number of bank failures, as well as questionable loans and possibly overly aggressive expansion by major banks, together with revelations of poor management and shady practices in other financial institutions, not only endangers the funds of large numbers of individuals but also endangers the stability of our economy as a whole. It is becoming apparent that new and more vigorous approaches to regulation are required.

We should also thoroughly reexamine the federal government's role as a source of credit. In addition to evaluating the effect of credit programs on speculative behavior and on the total level of public and private debt, we should ask ourselves other questions. Do we want to continue policies that channel a large part of our GNP into housing and agriculture, rather than other sectors of the economy? Even if we do, is it best for the federal government to perform the functions of banker, insurer, and underwriter in the ways that it now performs them? Would more reliance on private credit markets with stronger federal supervision achieve a better allocation of capital? Or, in the case of student loans, should we cut out the private middlemen and make direct government loans or grants to individuals? Should we continue to accept losses on federal credit activities that exceed federal spending on AFDC? These and other questions suggest that a floor-to-ceiling review of the future federal role in credit markets is in order. And such a review should give high priority to assessing whether we have struck the right balance among credit, taxes, regulation, and spending as ways to achieve public purposes.

But we should expect even more of the business community and of the federal social role regarding it than simply an orderly and responsible conduct of business affairs. There are indications that federal regulations protecting individuals against unsafe products and working conditions also need to be strengthened, or at least better enforced. And we should expect business to stamp out discrimination on the basis of race, sex, or age, as well as to live up to its responsibilities to protect the environment.

Affordable Goals

These and other measures to achieve the goals of a human resource policy cannot be put in place overnight. It will take years to gather the public resources needed to finance them and to test different approaches. Also, in some cases, they must be phased in gradually to avoid serious and unfair disruption of institutional plans and individual expectations. But these are the directions in which we should be moving, and the time to get moving is now.

Most of the measures just suggested would be very expensive, but they are not beyond our national means if our economy continues to grow. Tripling the federal investment in elementary and secondary education would cost an additional $17 billion. It has been estimated that major progress could be made toward a more adequate daycare system by an additional federal investment of about $5 billion.[5] All at-risk youngsters could be provided with intensive remedial education for several years in public "boarding schools" of the sort now operated by the Job Corps program for $10–15 billion. Extending Medicaid coverage to the 4 million pregnant women and pre-teen-aged children living below the poverty line—most of whom presently have no health-care insurance—would cost less than $5 billion. Properly managed, a comprehensive health-care system should actually save the nation money in the years to come, compared with the present trends in health care spending. The net cost of 2 million public service jobs for the hard-core unemployed at the minimum wage would be between $10 billion and $15 billion.

All of these estimates are almost certainly off the mark to some degree, because the nation has not looked closely at what could be done in most of these areas for years. But they are not wrong by an order of magnitude. They are almost certainly "in the ballpark." And if we add them up, they fall well within the amounts that a $4 trillion economy that is growing at current rates can afford—well within the range of devoting 2–3 percent more GNP to the federal social role over the coming decades, even allowing for the inevitable increase in the cost of public programs that will result from an aging society. Indeed, if we do not make these investments during the window of opportunity between now and the early decades of the next century, our ability to deal with the problems created by societal aging will be severely restricted.

To the extent that economic growth does not provide the resources we need, we may have to look at the priorities embedded in our tax code and credit policies. Should we continue to forgo tens of billions of dollars through tax exemptions that support the purchase of second homes by middle-income people and that support state and local bonding authority, when those revenues might be used to improve the prospects of our children or to create greater security against unemployment and the costs of ill health? How would we trade off the present subsidies to large, corporate farms against the goals of a human resource policy, and should we be channeling so much of our credit into housing, as opposed to business research and development? Now that the Internal Revenue system exempts most low-income people from taxation, is there any reason not to tax Social Security benefits fully? Surely the goals of a human resource policy are more important than some, if not all, of these other commitments.

We can find the money, and we must. Spending on human resources is not a luxury, it is an investment that we must make if our economy is to grow and we are to be true to our public values in the years to come. It is a form of pulling ourselves up by our own bootstraps. We can find the money, if we can find the will.

It is, of course, possible that the privileged institutions of our society, as well as ordinary taxpayers, will balk at this type of expense. Perhaps the present modest strides toward human resource development are acceptable to business and nonfederal levels of government, but more ambitious measures would be rejected. Still, it would be wrong to assume the worst on this score before we even try out the idea of a greater federal role. As indicated, businesses, states, and localities have come to realize that they have a large stake in upgrading human resources. And many of the measures just suggested, such as comprehensive health care, greater investments in children, and improved treatment of the unemployed, would lift financial and other burdens from their shoulders.

In the end, however, whether these investments should be made will depend on the American people. The federal government is their government, to do with as they want. If they perceive their common interest in a new burst of activism to meet the problems raised by economic and social change, they can override privileged institutions and vested interests. It is the task of public leadership to help them find where their interests lie and to appeal for their support. And it is also the task of leadership to find combinations of policies that close and open doors in ways that make it easier for both the privileged and the public to act on the interests they have in common.

The Better and the Good

Some leaders may be reluctant to subscribe to the measures suggested above, because they are "old ideas." Many of them have been advanced before without success. The recent period of reassessment in public policy has encouraged a great deal of defeatist thinking, and one form that thinking takes is a demand for "new ideas" that will magically cut the gordian knots of difficult public problems. Anyone who has those sorts of ideas should certainly become a national hero, but major innovations in public policy usually appear at the rate of three or four a century—and even then some clever scholar generally finds that they are ultimately derived from an obscure source in the past.

Hopefully the deliberations of a CHR or whatever other process leads to the detailed formulation of a human resource policy will spark ideas that are wholly new. But the nation cannot afford to insist on novelty for its own sake. What we need are not new ideas or old ideas but good ideas—ideas that meet the nation's needs. And there is every reason to believe that the forces of economic and social change have created an environment in which measures such as those outlined above—or others pointed in the same direction—are ideas whose time has come.

But what is even more important than these specific measures are the goals they are intended to achieve. It is critical that the nation vigorously pursue the goals of a human resource policy. The measures just suggested indicate that this is possible. They are not a detailed blueprint for action, but they indicate that a blueprint can be developed—at least for policies that address our most urgent national needs. If there are better measures, let them be adopted. We cannot afford to be paralyzed by arguments about measures. That would be letting the better become the enemy of the good. The outstanding priority for the United States right now is *not* finding better measures for a program of human resource development. There are plenty of workable measures already on the table. The outstanding priority is to launch such a program by the best means available.

We must accept the fact that large initiatives inevitably involve a great deal of uncertainty. "It is common sense to take a method and try it: If it fails, admit it and try another. But above all, try something," Franklin Roosevelt said.[6] That is the spirit of pragmatic activism that we must apply if the nation is to overcome the major problems that face it today.

The Inflation Issue

There is, however, one final "ghost at the banquet" of any human resource policy that must be exorcised. Retraining, public service jobs, and other measures to enhance the opportunities of our people should benefit the nation in many different ways. But one of the most important goals of these measures must be truly full employment: every able-bodied adult who is willing to work must be employed at a living wage under good conditions, with due allowance for transitional periods between jobs. If the goal of human resource policy is only *fuller* employment—reducing the number of jobless or marginally upgrading the terms on which people work—then a large number of our fellow citizens will still suffer from problems of limited income and opportunity.

For many different reasons, the goal of truly full employment may prove to be unattainable. Still, it is important to know where we are trying to go in the coming decades if we are ever to get there. Unless we put full employment at the top of our list of national priorities, it is certain that we will never achieve it.

It is essential, however, to face up to one major problem that stands in our way. Because the idea of full employment is not new, ample arguments have been mustered both for and against it over the years. The most telling opposition in recent decades has come from economists, who argue that full employment would result in increased inflation. In the words of economist Isabel Sawhill, a friend of full employment, "It would be relatively easy to increase employment if there were no worries about inflation."[7]

The economists' argument takes two forms: a concern about labor supply, and a concern about consumer demand. The supply argument is based on the theory that, in a situation of unemployment, the number of job openings available at current wages may be less than the number of qualified employees looking for work. More precisely, the number of vacancies that, if filled, would allow employers to make an acceptable profit at current prices may be less than the number of unemployed people qualified to fill these vacancies. Hence, if employers were forced to hire everyone who is without a job, they would have to raise their prices to cover the increased cost of labor.

The demand argument, in its simplest form, is that if everyone were suddenly employed at a good wage, there would be such a massive increase in purchasing power that the existing supply of goods and services would be used up. Prices would rise as the newly employed competed with everyone else for a limited pool of consumption items.

Most economists support some version of these inflation arguments, and unless their concerns are put in proper perspective they are perfect stoppers to discussions of full employment. To begin with, few economists seem confident about how many more workers the economy could absorb without an increase in inflation. Generally they talk about the "natural rate of unemployment," the lowest rate to which unemployment could fall without prices going up. Estimates of this "natural rate" have increased from 4 percent in the 1960s, to 5 percent in the 1970s, to 6 percent in the 1980s—always about a percentage point below the actual unemployment rate in periods of recovery. Economists seem to assume that the nation could always do a little bit better in fighting joblessness, but they cannot say exactly how much better. Nor can they say very precisely how much inflation would be created by full employment. Estimates vary widely.

The reason for the fuzziness in these estimates is obvious. If we accept the labor supply argument, the effect of full employment on inflation will depend on the qualifications of workers, the directions of business development, how well workers are matched with jobs, the overall rate of economic growth, and a variety of other factors. And economists are frank in admitting that, to the extent the economy is expanding and skilled workers are matched with good jobs, inflationary forces will be reduced.

If we accept the demand argument, inflationary forces will depend both on what is being demanded and on how quickly the newly employed add to the quantity of goods and services. For example, if the majority of the newly employed are poor people in low-wage jobs, their demand is likely to be for the essentials of life: food, housing, clothing, etc. And if there is a surplus of some of these goods, as there often is, then inflationary pressures are not likely to be strong. Or, to take the extreme case, if the newly employed previously have been subsisting on welfare benefits and they achieve only low-wage jobs, then there should be practically no inflationary effect. Their disposable income will remain about the same. Only one thing will have changed: they will be contributing to the economy rather than remaining idle.

In short, although economists can demonstrate that full employment would result in some inflationary pressures, it is impossible to say how strong those pressures would be, because that depends on a host of details about the general state of the economy and the work force that change over time. Conceivably, inflationary effects could be trivial. In any event, the ways to minimize those effects are also among the ways to create full employment, in the broadest sense of the term: creating an environment that fosters economic growth, training workers to fit the jobs available, helping them find jobs, and giving special priority to people who are poor or hard to place. And, in addition to a well-designed employment policy, we have other means to fight inflation: federal monetary policy, better enforcement of antitrust policies against oligopolies, and, as a last resort, price and wage constraints, administered either by regulatory means or through the tax system. It is also possible that we can reduce the trade-off between inflation and employment by encouraging firms to link wage increases more closely to increases in productivity. This idea has been elaborated by economists Martin Weitzman and

Lester Thurow in their proposals for developing a "share-economy."[8]

By all estimates, however, full employment would lead to some increase in inflation—at least in the short term—even though the increase might be small. Is this any reason to oppose a full employment policy? In the end that question comes down to a moral issue. Inflation is, in effect, a tax—like a sales tax—that increases the price of everything we buy. If the only way that we can avoid paying that tax is for some of our fellow citizens to be doomed to idleness, then it is a tax that we should feel morally obliged to pay. Otherwise, our prosperity is attributable to their distress. We are standing on their shoulders, holding them down.

Most of us are willing to accept some level of taxation to support the poor and indigent. We live in a country that spends billions of dollars on welfare payments to tide people over periods of financial distress. An inflation tax that would result from these same people working and contributing to the economy and that would also increase our own prospects and security would seem more worthwhile.

It is not clear that the tax needs to be large, and certainly every effort should be made to keep it as small as possible. Obviously high, sustained rates of inflation would wreck the American economy and, like any excessive tax, should not be paid. But we have no solid ground for believing that an inflation tax resulting from full employment must be excessive. As mentioned, we can moderate it by a variety of means. And, in the end, if *not* paying a moderate inflation tax allows us to prosper while others are left helpless, then it is a tax we should gladly pay.

13

The Near Term

Because of spending constraints imposed by the federal deficit and the need to allow time for new policies directions to mature, it may not be possible to mount a full-fledged human resource policy for some years to come. But delays in major reform do not mean that public leaders can or should be idle. There are measures that can be taken now, even within the constraints of deficits, and in the waning days of a long administration, to prepare the way for a full-scale revival of the activist tradition and a major human resource program.

Division of Labor

An essential preliminary for major reform in the social role is sorting out responsibility for the system of public policy now in place. We need to clear the decks for future action by deciding which of the many problems the federal government now addresses truly require attention at the national level and which can be handled as well or better by other institutions.

Finding better answers to these questions is also a way to leap-frog at least some current policy hurdles. Once certain problems are clearly acknowledged to be the primary responsibility of the federal government, there is less excuse for half-measures in dealing with them. Policymakers will have to confront the challenge of developing programs that are commensurate with high priority needs; they will no longer be able to assume that some other institution can make up for shortcomings in the federal government's response.

Even within the constraints of deficit reduction, Congress and the President can begin the process of sorting out issues of the division of labor between the federal government and other institutions. And they can do so in the next few years, because there is a growing consensus about what at least some aspects of the division should be.

A Model for Reform

Evidence of that consensus is the Report of the Committee on Federalism and National Purpose, which the authors of this book established and with which they were closely associated. The committee, cochaired by Senator Daniel Evans of Washington and Governor Charles Robb of Virginia, was an independent group of twenty-five prominent Americans, representing all shades of opinion and sectors of society, which was convened in July 1984 and issued its report in December 1985. Its goal was to consider what changes are required in the division of labor between the federal government, on the one hand, and states and localities, on the other. The committee's report, *To Form a More Perfect Union*, is a principled and practical blueprint for near-term action on some of the most troubled issues of social policy.[1] Equally important, both the committee and its report are models for the type of wide-ranging, bipartisan thinking about national priorities that will be essential for any future efforts at reform.

The committee focused its attention on one particular aspect of federalism: the areas of shared responsibility between the federal government and states or localities. In 1986 the federal government spent over $100 billion on more than three hundred shared intergovernmental programs. These programs run the gamut from multibillion-dollar welfare systems such as AFDC and Medicaid to small grants for local development projects. Responsibility for them is "shared" in the sense that both the federal government and states or localities play a role in determining funding levels and the policies that guide program operations.

Typically, the federal government determines how much funding it will make available for each shared program and sets general guidelines for how its funds should be distributed and used. States and localities generally administer operation of the programs. Also, they are generally required to supplement federal support, and the amount of federal funding they receive often depends on how large a contribution they are willing to make. For example, in the AFDC program, each state decides what level of benefits should be paid to recipients, and the federal government reimburses states for some portion of the total cost. States and localities are also allowed considerable leeway in formulating the policies that guide shared programs. They determine many aspects of eligibility for AFDC and Medicaid. Also, directly or indirectly, they set priorities for how federal assistance for community development, aid to education and other shared programs will be distributed.

Shared programs are, thus, prime examples of how institutional diversity affects national decision making in the United States. They take a different form in virtually every state and city. Benefits for AFDC are five times higher in some states than others. Mass transit and housing funds are heavily concentrated in a few cities, and community development programs vary enormously in different parts of the country.

The essence of the recommendations of the Committee on Federalism and National Purpose is that the number of *shared programs* should be *greatly reduced*. The committee argued that in a great many areas where funding and policy responsibility is now divided, it should be more heavily concentrated at either the federal or the state and local level.

In particular, it argued that the federal government should establish uniform nationwide standards for eligibility and benefit levels in the two major intergovernmental welfare programs: AFDC and Medicaid. The federal government should also provide almost all of the funding for these programs. States should continue to manage welfare systems because they already have the administrative apparatus in place. And they should continue to pay 10–20 percent of the program costs to give them a stake in sound administration.

At the same time, the committee proposed that states and localities should assume full financial and policy responsibility for most community development and local infrastructure programs—programs for purposes such as urban renewal, mass transit, and waste-water disposal. Federal funding for these programs would be terminated. The net result of the committee's proposals would redirect over $20 billion in federal funding from localized purposes to an enhanced national welfare system.

In effect, the committee proposed a Madisonian division of labor between the federal government and other levels of the American political system. It declared that combatting the effects of poverty was what Madison called "a great and aggregate" issue requiring uniform policies and funding levels on a nationwide basis. The level of benefits available to poor people and their access to those benefits should not depend on the accident of where they are born or happen to reside.

The committee also declared that community development and local infrastructure programs address what Madison called "local and particular" problems. The problems of community development and local infrastructure differ in each state and city. The nation will be best served if state and local governments have authority to determine what level of funds should be devoted to each problem area and to set priorities among those areas—for example, to choose how much they should invest in mass transit as opposed to urban renewal, and what form those investments should take.

Rationale

The committee believed that establishing a new division of labor along these lines is critical for several reasons. To begin with, it argued that the existing discrepancies between states in welfare benefits and eligibility are unfair and prevent the nation from providing adequate solutions to the problems of poor people. The only way to eliminate discrepancies is to establish uniform standards and benefit levels supported by the federal government. With responsibility goes discretion. As long as states retain a large role in funding or policy, uniformity and adequacy on a nationwide basis will be almost impossible to achieve.

In short, the committee believed that federalizing welfare programs would improve the service they provide. Seen as a blueprint for antipoverty policy, its report recommends a sharp change in direction at the federal level. Since the high tide of interest in problems of poverty during the Johnson and Nixon years, the federal government has pursued three strategies in this area:

• An income strategy—represented by AFDC, Food Stamps, Medicaid, and other programs that transfer income in cash or in kind.
• A service strategy—represented by personal social services, education, and training programs.
• An urban strategy—represented by grants to states and cities aimed at improving the environment in which poor people live and promoting economic development from which they and others will benefit.

Programs in all three of these areas have suffered from the budget cutters' axe in recent years. The committee's recommendations would, in essence, phase out much past federal participation in the urban strategy, focus the service strategy primarily on measures to help the poor become self-sufficient through work, and shore up the income strategy.

But the committee's recommendations were not intended to be only a program for reducing the effects of poverty. The committee believed that concentrating responsibility for community development and local infrastructure at the state and local level also would result in better service. Many members of the committee were, or had been, state and local officials. They were convinced that the regulations, spending limits, and red tape entailed in shared programs frequently stand in the way of sound decision making. Governors, mayors, and county executives know the needs of their communities far better than the federal government does, and those needs differ widely.

Unfortunately, local officials are too often induced to overinvest in projects for which federal matching funds are available and underinvest in other projects that, in their judgment, should have higher priority. State and local officials also have difficulty developing sensible long-range plans when many of their decisions depend on annual appropriations from Washington. And they spend too much time fulfilling reporting requirements and shoehorning their needs into federal regulations.

The committee believed that state and local governments are, on the whole, as well managed and responsive to public views as government at the national level. Committee members were particularly impressed by the strides that states have made in recent years to upgrade their administrative capacities and adopt constitutional amendments that have modernized their political systems. And they were impressed by state and local initiatives in education, health care cost containment, and economic development. In these and other problem areas, state and local government has shown far greater innovation and responsiveness in recent years than has government at the national level. For example, while federal investment in elementary and secondary education has remained stagnant, investments by states and localities increased from an average of $1,317 per pupil in 1975 to $3,222 in 1986.[2] And New Jersey, Massachusetts, and other states moved to control health care costs several years before the federal government took its first tentative steps in 1984.

In short, members of the federalism committee believed that the nation would make far better investments in community development and local infrastructure programs if decisions about those investments were solely in state and local hands, and they believed that state and local officials are fully competent to take on this responsibility.

The final reason why the committee advocated a Madisonian division of labor was that its members were concerned about the problem of decision-making overload at the federal level. Shared community development and local infrastructure programs place a particularly heavy burden on federal officials. Because these programs take a different form in every community, federal oversight is extremely time-consuming and, in the end, almost impossible. Nonetheless, members of Congress are forced to spend a large share of their time making sure that the needs of their states and congressional districts are accommodated. An army of Washington lobbyists enforces responsiveness in this respect. The federalism committee believed that national leaders should be able to concentrate their attention on the highest national priorities. Relieving the federal government of responsibility for major community development and local infrastructure programs would be a large step toward redirecting efforts and priorities in Washington.

Cost and Responsibility

This new division of labor can also be achieved at no cost to government at the national level. Analysis by the committee's staff and consultants showed that the cost to the federal government of largely federalizing AFDC and Medicaid, together with other committee recommendations, would be approximately equal to the savings that would be achieved by discontinuing localized programs. Because of the way in which funding formulas for those programs are presently structured, however, states and localities would receive somewhat less from the federal government than they currently receive, if the committee's recommendations were adopted. As a result, they would be faced with a three-way choice: raise additional revenues to replace a portion of federal funds now devoted to urban renewal, mass transit, waste-water treatment, and similar purposes; cut costs by more efficient management and better targeting of funds; or reduce service.

This is exactly the choice that the federalism committee believed states and communities should face. They, not the federal government, should decide how much of the taxpayers money should be invested in local projects and how that money should be used.

They are in a position to know what projects merit public support and how to manage those projects most efficiently. And their decisions on localized projects can be more carefully scrutinized by ordinary citizens. The citizens of New York, for example, will be much more interested and informed about whether their taxes should be raised to provide operating subsidies for subways than are federal officials who now decide on mass transit subsidies, or than the citizenry of the country as a whole, whose taxes pay for those subsidies.

But while it carefully examined the effects of its proposals on states and localities, the federalism committee warned against evaluating proposals for reform in terms of "winners and losers" among institutions. In the end, its report declared, "it is far more important to assess whether the people, rather than particular levels of government are 'winners' or 'losers' from any system of federalism."[3] In other words, the first priority of government must be the well-being of individuals, not institutions.

Other Measures

Among other committee recommendations was a proposal to "turn welfare programs into jobs programs"—to mount a national effort aimed at making AFDC beneficiaries self-supporting through work. All able-bodied recipients of AFDC benefits should be required to accept retraining and job placement assistance and to accept work if offered. The federal government should greatly increase support to state-managed programs for training and placement assistance, particularly for those welfare recipients with the most severe employment problems. And it should reduce the red tape in this area of shared responsibility. The major criterion for federal funding should be success in finding jobs for welfare recipients. States should be encouraged to experiment with many different ways to achieve that goal.

The committee also proposed a first step toward dealing with the rising costs of long-term care. States should continue to manage long-term care programs for Medicaid beneficiaries, but the federal government should gradually assume most financial responsibility for those programs. The present bias in the Medicaid system, which makes it difficult for states or health care providers to be reimbursed for any form of long-term care other than expensive and often unnecessary institutionalization, should be eliminated.

Finally, the committee recommended that the federal government come to grips with a problem that has haunted the American system of federalism since its inception: the differences among states in fiscal capacity. Just as there have always been poor and rich individuals in the United States, there also have been poor and rich states and communities. Some areas have strong economies; others suffer from short- or long-term economic distress. States and communities with serious economic problems cannot possibly offer the level of services available in more affluent areas.

It is clearly in the national interest for all parts of the United States to enjoy an adequate level of police and fire protection, education, local transportation, and other community services, even if those services are best financed and managed at the state and local level. To address the problem of differing fiscal capacities, the committee proposed that the federal government provide general assistance grants to the dozen or so poorest states and to local governments with severe limits on their ability to raise resources that are commensurate with their needs. These grants would be large enough to level out the major disparities in resources across the nation.

State and local governments would be free to use the grants for any purpose, and funds would be made available by a formula that would discourage them from reducing tax efforts. Targeted fiscal capacity grants would, in effect, replace the recently discontinued General Revenue Sharing Program, which distributed funds to virtually every community in the country. And they would help poor areas adjust to the termination of federal programs for community development and local infrastructure.

Even when the costs of an expanded "work-welfare" program, long term care block grants, and fiscal capacity grants are added to the cost of federalizing AFDC and Medicaid, the federalism committee's recommendations would still be fiscally neutral for the federal government. The savings realized by terminating localized programs would be approximately equal to the cost of federalizing welfare programs plus the cost of these other measures.

Lessons

The Report of the Committee on Federalism and National Purpose is a model for activism in a great number of ways. It asserts a strong sense of national priorities: poverty is a national problem that deserves a large commitment of resources at the federal level, whereas many localized problems should be dealt with by other levels of government. It makes constructive use of the principles of both uniformity and diversity: certain problems require uniform nationwide solutions; others require different solutions in different parts of the country; still others require a mixture of both approaches. The report also asserts national values:

- All Americans deserve the same measure of economic security from government; all should have the opportunity to become self-sufficient through work.
- The ultimate goal of government is to benefit individuals, not institutions.
- Government at the national level is ultimately responsible for arranging institutional responsibilities to meet that goal.

And, the report contains the elements of any successful partnership between the federal government and other institutions: it closes some doors—to unfairness and neglect in welfare programs; and it opens other doors—to greater discretion for states and localities in managing a wide range of responsibilities. It provides both incentives and direct assistance to help other levels of government assume their responsibilities in ways that will further the overall national interest.

The committee's recommendations are particularly valuable because they are forward-looking. Not only would the nation provide more adequate welfare services under existing programs, but it would begin to make headway in reforming those programs to meet the problems of the future: by transforming income programs into jobs programs and taking a first step toward solving the problem of long-term care. The report is also forward-looking in the sense that the measures it proposes would make a large contribution to relieving the problem of overload at the federal level. The social role would be less wide and thin: time and resources would be freed to deal with the highest-priority issues.

Finally, the committee proposed major institutional reform. But the problems on which it focused are different from those that have commanded the attention of would-be reformers in the past. For the most part, they concentrated on improving the structure and mechanisms of the federal establishment. Yet the fact that we have a multi-layered system of government is a fundamental part of our constitutional design. The committee proposed a major reassignment of responsibilities among the various layers. This version of institutional reform is at least as important, and probably more feasible in the near term, than proposals of the past. Institutional reformers may have been neglecting the obvious by concentrating too much on Washington and too little on the opportunity to make major gains in other ways.

These and other achievements of the report were made possible by the structure of the committee and the way in which it proceeded. Representatives of all levels of government and many different shades of opinion were brought in on the ground floor. The experience of the committee indicates that on issues of major national importance, there is enough common ground and good will in the United States for a cross-section of national leadership to agree not only on public priorities but also on how to attain them.

The committee's experience also indicates that the present stalemate in federal policy can be broken if the right issues are raised in the right way. The committee met, not to discuss the narrow area of welfare reform, but to discuss broad concerns about the relationship between different levels of government. This allowed it to adopt a wide-ranging agenda. In the end, the package of proposals that the committee endorsed was both realistic and acceptable to its members in large part because it cut across program areas to link changes in the welfare system to changes in localized programs and other reforms.

Human Resources

The recommendations of the Committee on Federalism and National Purpose are, thus, important in a great many ways. But in the long run, the committee's most important contribution may have been to recommend a number of first steps toward establishing a comprehensive program of human resource development in the United States. If the measures proposed by the committee were adopted, large numbers of people living in poverty would benefit from a greater measure of economic security. For example, over 4 million poor children and pregnant women who are not covered by any form of health insurance would fall under the protection of Medicaid. Both they and their parents would have a stronger base from which to build productive lives. And a more vigorous work/welfare program would help adult beneficiaries of programs for the poor to become self-supporting in the future.

States and localities would have greater discretion to tailor programs of economic and social development to their varying needs. Medicaid would become a federal responsibility and this would provide national officials with greater leverage in attempts to control the growth of health care costs across the board. We would begin to develop an approach to long-term care that is arguably more efficient than the present system, and certainly more humane.

But the most important contribution that recommendations of the federalism committee would make toward developing a human resource program would be to help improve the process of federal decision making. By shifting responsibility for community development and local infrastructure programs to state and local officials, measures proposed by the committee would free up the federal government to concentrate on the type of major new initiatives that a human resource program will require. And by showing that substantial progress can be made toward meeting national needs even in a time of fiscal stringency, those measures would help to revive confidence in activist government—confidence that is essential if the nation is to meet the challenges of today and of the decades to come.

14

Government
for the People

It is time for the authors to step from behind the scenes and speak with their readers in a more personal voice.

In one way or another, we spent over three years preparing to write this book. We traveled to all parts of the United States and talked with literally hundreds of people—scholars, public officials, businessmen, journalists, and others—asking them and ourselves one simple question: What should be the federal social role? Two experiences illustrate our sense of where the answer lies.

In late August of 1986, we met for a few days at a rented house in Vermont to revise the early chapters of our manuscript. One afternoon when cabin fever had set in, we sought an hour's escape by driving to the nearest point of interest: the village of Plymouth Notch, lifelong home of none other than Calvin Coolidge.

Quite simply, we were enchanted. There, in what William Allen White called "the museum that was Vermont," we were wrapped in the peaceful splendor of spacious, white clapboard houses, tidy streets, deep blue mountains, and cozy valleys cut by hedgerows already painted by the year's first frost. And although we found little to admire in the thin-lipped little Puritan whose rubbers are still in the family barn, we were forced to admit an irrational longing for this to be the defining vision of America. And we left it with regret.

Later that day we recalled another excursion some months before. Tough-minded, barrel-chested Mike Sviridoff invited us to visit some housing reclamation projects that his organization, the Local Initiatives Support Corporation, had helped to finance in a section of the South Bronx. There, in the clutter, dirt, and drabness of a worn-out city, we met the leaders of community groups with names like Banana Kelly and the South Bronx Desperadoes. Here were the prototypes of a new late-century type of civic activist—realistic, hard-working, patient, ingenious beyond belief. Drawn largely from backgrounds in human services, they had suddenly been cast up against the world of big banks, insurance companies, construction firms, and the most frustrating tangles of bureaucracy at all levels of government. Yet they had somehow managed to build or refurbish hundreds of units of low-income housing. There was nothing pretty about what they created—just solid, clean, honestly run blocks of small apartments where decent people could live on decent terms.

We said to each other that day in Vermont that one of the great misfortunes of our times is how many people believe Plymouth Notch is not only what America is, but what it should be: safe, smug, and static—whereas we thought that Sviridoff's more muscular, shirtsleeves world, moving into the future while fighting off constraints from the past, was closer to the reality of late-century American life. Progress on a human scale seemed more virtuous than nostalgia, and it seemed to contain more of what we could find pride in as Americans.

But, of course, we realize that we were wrong. America encompasses both Plymouth Notch and the South Bronx Desperadoes. And in that realization we found the answer to the question we had been asking. The emotional, economic, and social distance between rural Vermont and New York City is enormous. But the United States is a great nation in large part because it has been able to bridge that distance by common laws, common purposes, and common understandings. It is great because it has woven from these divergent strands a whole that is much greater than the sum of its parts—greater because there *are* so many strands to enrich the fabric.

We believe that, above all else, the purpose of the federal social role is to keep the national fabric intact: to preserve the Union. Whatever else it does or does not do, maintaining a sense of nationhood—keeping our people at peace with one another and reinforcing their sense of common purpose—is its primary charge and major accomplishment. And it is an accomplishment too easily taken for granted. A monument in Woodstock (just up the road from Plymouth Notch) commemorates the sacrifice of local men who marched out of those mountains to die for the cause of Union on the battlefields of the South. What was the Union to them, those self-reliant farmers dwelling in their mountain paradise? Yet the sense of common purpose was strong enough to claim their lives. And Sviridoff's projects in New York stand side by side with areas bombed out by the race riots of the 1960s. It took an enormous effort to maintain the Union in those days, too—an effort that could only have been organized by national government.

Neither event was so very long ago. We are both old enough to have clasped the hands of Civil War veterans and to remember the riots vividly. We count among our friends not only people who have served the public in recent years, but members of the Roosevelt, Truman, and Eisenhower administrations, as well as a man who knew President Harding. Each generation of Americans has had to overcome threats to the Union in its time. It has been imperiled over and again in living memory.

How great an accomplishment our national Union is was repeatedly dramatized for one of us during the years in which we were preparing to write this book. Pifer had cause to make several visits to South Africa, which he has known well for over a quarter of a century. There he witnessed the tragic disintegration of what should be one of the most fabulous nations in the world. And the fundamental reason for that tragedy was the lack of a sense of common citizenship and common purpose among its people.

We firmly believe the United States cannot take national union for granted, at any time or in any circumstances. It is the precondition for everything else that is good in American life.

Yet our nation has become careless. The stalemate and neglect of American public life in recent years have cast the cause of Union adrift. When millions of our fellow citizens are members of a hopeless "underclass" who have little to gain and little to lose, there is disunion. When we are divided between those who are secure at home, on the job, in their youth or in their waning years, and those who live under constant threat of financial distress, there is disunion. When we are so divided over race, religion, and class that we lose sight of the goal of providing our children with a decent education, there is disunion. When business wastes lives and resources through greed and speculation rather than productive activity, there is disunion. When states and communities develop an ineffective hodgepodge of responses to some of their citizens' most fundamental needs, there is disunion.

Above all else, there is disunion when there is neglect of the common problems that face us as a nation: when a large number of our people are effectively left out of the protections afforded to average Americans. Neglect leads to frustration; people no longer make their best efforts as workers, friends, or citizens. It leads men and women to be careless of both their own good and the greater good. In large or small ways it leaves each of us isolated, defensive, and frightened: a nation of antagonistic parts rather than a nation that can act as a whole.

The centrifugal forces of American life have always been with us and they always will be. But the simple fact is that they have become stronger in recent years. They have been strengthened in no small part by the doctrines of leaders who have preached distrust of national government, decentralization, and privatization and encouraged a destructive philosophy of everyone for himself. They have been strengthened, too, by the myth that there are severe limits on what we can accomplish as a people—that we are helpless to solve many of our common problems.

History teaches us what happens when centrifugal forces become too strong: like a speeding car on a sharp turn, the nation crashed in 1861, 1929, 1965, and at various other times as well. Each time the signs were everywhere, but we were too careless to read them. Then as now we thought we could get by on luck alone. Then as now it was impossible to plot exactly how much disunion would be too much. All we could say for certain, as we can certainly say today, was that the trends were bad.

They are particularly bad now because we need the Union far more today than the Vermont men who died for its cause needed it a century ago. Social and economic changes have created a more complex and interdependent society than they ever could have imagined. We have more common problems, the nation is more of a common enterprise, our fates are more interdependent than ever before. We simply cannot maintain our standard of living or the quality of our lives by walling ourselves up behind our individual interests. Like misers, we can count our short-term gains, but the coin we count is depreciating in value.

Yet how does the nation react to its growing interdependence? An example of how badly it reacts is the growing popularity of the concept of "generational equity."[1] It is a concept that means many things to many people, but for at least some of its promoters it has a very definite meaning. They have noticed the aging of American society and the neglect of our nation's children and decided to put the two problems together. Under the banner of "generational equity" they claim that the fair and necessary way for the United States to react to these twin problems is to reduce public spending for the elderly and invest the savings in programs for children.

This is disunion: a divisive response to common problems. It is a response that would set old against young rather than concentrate the nation's energies on the stake we all have in the welfare of all generations. And it is a response motivated by the myth that the nation's resources are so limited that we cannot afford to invest in causes of the highest priority.

To unite the nation, we must meet the needs of both children and the elderly. We must develop strategies that will enlarge the economic pie by boosting the productivity of tomorrow's workers and helping today's employees make their best efforts. At the same time we must find more effective ways to honor our commitment to the needs of the growing number of elderly. A common effort of this sort—not a mean-spirited system of winners and losers—is our only safe road. If we don't look for it, we will never find it.

Another example of how badly the nation responds to its problems is the debate over school vouchers.[2] A generous version of the case for vouchers holds that since middle-class people can escape inadequate public schools by sending their children to private institutions, poor people should have the same option. Government should give every low-income parent a voucher to purchase education in either a public or a private institution.

But middle-class people will, by definition, always have more resources than poor people. As a result, whatever the value of the vouchers, middle-class parents will always be able to outbid others for the more prestigious and better-quality institutions. We will have reinforced a two-class educational system in the United States, one school system for the rich and one for the poor. People who advocate vouchers advocate responding to the problems of divisiveness in education by creating more divisiveness.

In a democracy, common institutions—institutions where people of all sorts can rub shoulders with each other, where they can get to know their fellow citizens on an equal basis—are among our most precious undertakings. We have too few of them. Public schools are among the oldest and most important of all common institutions. They are valuable beyond measure because the experiences and attitudes of youth form the character of a nation. The path to Union is not to dismantle public schooling in the United States but to bend all our energies toward making it work: to create schools in which children from all backgrounds will receive the best education attainable anywhere in the world.

We readily admit that government cannot solve all the nation's problems. In fact, it cannot solve the most important problems: it cannot make us kinder, more responsible, wiser, more insightful, and more loving people. It cannot teach us what is right or true. And it should not try.

The Founding Fathers knew their history well. They viewed with dismay the needless wreckage that has always resulted when issues of faith and morals become public issues. In a large and diverse nation, agreement, compromise, and consensus are never possible on such issues. Conflict is only encouraged when government steps in. Religious fundamentalists and other groups who would inject sectarian views into our schools and other public institutions are advocating the surest route to disunion.

What government at the national level can do is to solve those common problems on which the nation as a whole finds it possible to agree—both about the nature of the problem and about the right solution. These are generally practical, material problems. But they are work enough for any institution. And in solving them as one united people, we practice the values that are most fundamental to all religions and moral systems: we learn to put ourselves in each other's shoes. Democratic morality unites rather than divides, and the only way to practice and refine that morality is through continuing efforts to meet the problems that affect people in all walks of life. Among its virtues, activist government focuses the attention of all of us on how much we have in common with our fellow citizens—in the end, on our common humanity.

All of this requires leadership. Thoreau expressed the attitude of many Americans when he said, "I came into the world not chiefly to make this a good place to live in, but to live in it."[3] A sense of community is always a sometimes thing in a busy, diverse nation. We look to our national leaders to remind us of common problems and opportunities. Recently too many have abdicated that high charge. Too many politicians have sought advancement by trying to satisfy the narrow interests of every pressure group, rather than speaking out for the common interest. And they have tried to cover their tracks by explaining that, after all, government is just the process of slicing up the pie of national wealth among its many claimants.

This, too, is the path to disunion. All claims are not equal. Some go to fundamental common concerns and some do not. It is the task of leadership not only to sort out claims but to define issues in ways that bind us together rather than drive us apart—to have a larger vision of the common good than each of us can possibly have if we calculate the wisdom of public policy in terms of our checkbooks.

We need a leadership of integrity—one that establishes principles for the long-range good of all the people and sticks by its guns. At a rhetorical level, the Reagan presidency was highly successful in this respect. A large part of its public support came from the belief that the man in the White House was a man of principle. Until international events cast a large shadow over his administration late in 1986, the American people were reassured by a president who projected an image of foresight, courage, and compassion.

Unfortunately, his policies served the nation less well than his image. Policies of the Reagan years attempted to roll back the protections of the federal social role, neglected emerging problems, and encouraged beliefs that we cannot and should not act together as a nation. They strengthened the centrifugal forces of our national life and fostered disunion. And, if David Stockman's memoirs are to be believed, at a critical point in the 1984 election, the president and his advisors deliberately misled the American people about the most salient economic issues of the day.

But the powerful appeal of the president's image should teach us something. Integrity and vision count for a great deal in American politics. Yet by themselves, they are not enough. To preserve the Union, Americans need government for the people: practical, activist government that can be trusted to address their common concerns. They have a right to it; they should demand it; they should lend their full support to leaders who will give it to them. If they do, there are no limits to what the American republic can achieve.

Notes

FOREWORD

1. Princeton University Press has been offered a series of seven volumes. Six of these are based on the Project's group activities, and the seventh is a manuscript on family policy specially prepared for the Project. Two volumes are in press: Margaret Weir, Ann Shola Orloff and Theda Skocpol, eds., *The Politics of Social Policy in the United States*, and Amy Gutmann, ed., *Democracy and the Welfare State*. Five volumes are in preparation: Alfred J. Kahn and Sheila B. Kamerman, eds., *Privatization and the Welfare State;* Theodore R. Marmor and Jerry L. Mashaw, eds., *Social Security in Contemporary American Politics;* Peter Edelman, ed., *Rights in Transition;* Lee Bawden, ed., *Employment Policy: Lessons for the Future;* and Theodora Ooms and A. Sidney Johnson, *Taking Families Seriously*.

CHAPTER 1

1. Theodore Roosevelt, *The New Nationalism* (1910; rept. ed. Gloucester, Mass.: Peter Smith, 1971), p. 36.
2. Inaugural Address, January 20, 1981.
3. See E. S. Savas, *How To Shrink Government: Privatizing the Public Sector* (Chatham, N.J.: Chatham House, 1982); Jack Kemp, *An American Renaissance: A Strategy for the 1980s* (New York: Harper & Row, 1979); George Gilder, *Wealth and Poverty* (New York: Basic Books, 1981); Martin Anderson, *Welfare* (Stanford: Hoover Institution, 1978).
4. See, for example, Alice Rivlin, "Comment," in *Emerging Issues in American Federalism* (Washington, D.C.: Advisory Commission on Intergovernmen-

tal Relations, 1985); "Godkin Lectures: Government Needs To Improve Decision Making," *Harvard Gazette* (March 24, 1984); "A System Overload," *Intergovernmental Perspective* (Winter 1980); Fred Hirsch, *Social Limits of Growth* (Cambridge: Harvard University Press, 1976).

5. Arthur M. Schlesinger, Jr., *The Cycles of American History* (New York: Houghton Mifflin, 1986), chap. 2.

6. See Albert O. Hirschman, *Shifting Involvements* (Princeton: Princeton University Press, 1982); Samuel P. Huntington, *American Politics: The Promise of Disharmony* (Cambridge: Harvard University Press, 1981).

7. See Hugh Heclo, "The Political Foundations of Anti-Poverty Policy," in Sheldon Danzinger and Dan Weinberg, eds., *Antipoverty Policy: What Works?* (Cambridge: Harvard University Press, 1986); Stanley Kelley, Jr., "Democracy and the New Deal Party System," in Amy Gutmann, ed., *Democracy and the Welfare State* (Princeton: Princeton University Press, forthcoming); "Most Americans Oppose Reagan Budget Priorities," *Washington Post*, February 14, 1986; Seymour Martin Lipset and William Schneider, *The Confidence Gap* (New York: Free Press, 1983); Thomas Ferguson and Joel Rogeres, *Right Turn* (New York: Hill and Wang, 1986).

CHAPTER 2

1. Jefferson to James Madison, December 20, 1787, in Albert Fried, ed., *The Essential Jefferson* (New York: Collier Books, 1963).

2. First Inaugural Address, March 4, 1801, in Fried, *Essential Jefferson*, p. 404.

3. Hamilton to James Duane, September 3, 1780, in Henry Cabot Lodge, ed., *The Works of Alexander Hamilton*, vol. 1 (New York: Knickerbocker Press, 1904), p. 217.

4. Jefferson, Article on Conciliation with the Federalists, June 1, 1803, and First Inaugural Address, March 4, 1801, in Fried, *Essential Jefferson*, pp. 403, 436.

5. Quoted in Washington Irving, *Life of George Washington in Three Volumes*, vol. 3 (New York: Putnam, 1855), p. 139.

6. Jefferson, First Inaugural Address, p. 403.

7. Lincoln, Message to Congress, July 11, 1861.

8. Isaac Max Rubinow, *Social Insurance, with Special Reference to American Conditions* (New York: Holt, 1912), p. 407.

9. Roosevelt, Radio Address on the Third Anniversary of the Social Security Act, August 15, 1939, in *50th Anniversary Edition: The Report of the Committee on Economic Security* (Washington, D.C.: National Conference on Social Welfare, 1985), p. 148.

10. Roosevelt, Message to Congress Reviewing the Broad Objectives and Accomplishments of the Administration, June 8, 1934, in *50th Anniversary Edition*, p. 136.

11. Roosevelt, First Inaugural Address, March 4, 1933.

12. "Report of the Committee on Economic Security," in *50th Anniversary Edition*, pp. 21–70.

13. *Marbury* v. *Madison*, 1 Cranch 137 (1803).

14. *Brown* v. *Board of Education,* 347 U.S. 483 (1954).

15. Jefferson, Opinion on the Constitutionality of a National Bank, February 15, 1791, in Fried, *Essential Jefferson,* p. 299.

16. *Steward Machine Company* v. *Davis,* 301 U.S. 548 (1937); *Helvering* v. *Davis,* 301 U.S. 619 (1937).

C H A P T E R   3

1. Alexis de Tocqueville, *Democracy in America,* 2 vols. (1835, 1840; rept. ed., New York: Random House, 1945).

2. Madison, *The Federalist Papers,* no. 10 (New York: New American Library, 1961), p. 83.

3. Washington, Farewell Address, in Washington Irving, *Life of George Washington in Three Volumes,* vol. 3 (New York: Putnam, 1855), p. 360.

4. William James, *The Varieties of Religious Experience* (1902; rept. ed., New York: New American Library, 1958), p. 284.

C H A P T E R   4

1. Except where indicated, these and other figures used in this chapter to describe dimensions of the federal social role are derived from the president's budget submission for fiscal year 1988 and other recent years, and in particular from the exploratory volume, *Special Analyses of the Budget of the United States Government,* prepared by the Office of Management and Budget.

2. Executive Office of the President, Office of Management and Budget, *Historical Tables: Budget of the United States Government* (Washington, D.C.: Government Printing Office, 1986) pp. 15.2 (1)–15.2 (6).

3. U.S. House of Representatives, Committee on Ways and Means, *Background Material and Data on Programs Within the Jurisdiction of the Committee on Ways and Means* (Washington, D.C.: Government Printing Office, March 1986).

4. U.S. Department of Commerce, Bureau of the Census, *Economic Characteristics of Households in the U.S.—1st Quarter, 1984,* Survey of Income and Pension Participation, Series P-70 (Washington, D.C.: Government Printing Office, April 1985).

5. U.S. Senate, Committee on the Budget, *Tax Expenditures* (Washington, D.C.: Government Printing Office, September 1978 and March 1982).

6. For an excellent discussion of federal credit activity, see Dennis Ippolito, *Hidden Spending* (Chapel Hill: University of North Carolina Press, 1984). Also see Office of Management and Budget, *Special Analyses of the Budget of the United States* (Washington, D.C.: Government Printing Office, 1986), section F.

7. Frank Newman, *Higher Education and the American Resurgence* (Princeton, N.J.: Carnegie Foundation for the Advancement of Teaching, 1985), p. 6.

8. The standard text on regulatory theory is Alfred E. Kahn, *The Economics of Regulation,* 2 vols. (New York: Wiley, 1970). For an analysis of recent developments in regulatory practice, see George C. Eads and Michael Fix, *Relief or*

288 NOTES

Reform (Washington, D.C.: Urban Institute Press, 1984). For problems of regulation, see James Q. Wilson, ed., *The Politics of Regulation* (New York: Basic Books, 1980).

9. See Thomas K. McCraw, *Prophets of Regulation* (Cambridge: Harvard University Press, 1984).

10. Murray Weidenbaum, "On Estimating Regulatory Costs," *Regulation* (May–June 1978): 17. For a critique of Weidenbaum's estimates, see Eads and Fix, *Politics of Regulation*, pp. 28–44.

11. For a discussion of the interchangeability among policy tools, see Thomas D. Hopkins, *Social Policy and the Regulatory Process*, Project on the Federal Social Role Working Paper, no. 9 (Washington, D.C.: National Conference on Social Welfare).

CHAPTER 5

1. Robert J. Lampman, *Balancing the Books: Social Spending and the American Economy* (Washington, D.C.: National Conference on Social Welfare, 1985), p. 4.

2. Ibid., p. 18.

3. Robert Kuttner, *The Economic Illusion* (Boston: Houghton Mifflin, 1984).

4. Lampman, *Balancing the Books*, p. 32.

5. Martin S. Feldstein, "Social Security, Induced Retirement and Aggregate Capital Accumulation," *Journal of Political Economy* (Fall 1974): 905–926. For criticism of Feldstein, see Henry J. Aaron, *Economic Effects of Social Security* (Washington, D.C.: Brookings Institution, 1982); Alicia H. Munnell, *The Economics of Private Pensions* (Washington, D.C.: Brookings Institution, 1982).

6. Edward F. Denison, *Accounting for Slower Economic Growth* (Washington, D.C.: Brookings Institution, 1979).

7. Lampman, *Balancing the Books*, p. 27.

8. Moses Abramovitz, "Welfare Quandaries and Productivity Concerns," *American Economic Review* (Spring 1981): 1.

9. John E. Schwarz, *America's Hidden Success* (New York: Norton, 1984). Many of the examples in this section are drawn from Schwarz and from Christopher Jencks, "The Hidden Prosperity of the 1970s," *Public Interest* (Fall 1984): 37–61.

10. U.S. Department of Commerce, Bureau of the Census, *Estimates of Poverty Including the Value of Non-cash Benefits: 1985*, Technical Paper no. 56 (Washington, D.C.: Government Printing Office, 1986), p. 52.

11. U.S. Department of Commerce, Bureau of the Census, *Current Population Report*, Survey P-60, no. 154, *Money Income and Poverty Status of Families and Persons in the United States: 1985* (Washington, D.C.: Government Printing Office, 1986), p. 3.

12. U.S. House of Representatives, Committee on Ways and Means, *Background Material and Data on Programs Within the Jurisdiction of the Committee on Ways and Means* (Washington, D.C.: Government Printing Office, 1986), p. 90.

13. National League of Cities, *Federal Housing Assistance: Who Needs It? Who Gets It?* (Washington, D.C.: National League of Cities, 1985) p. 11.

Notes 289

14. U.S. Department of Commerce, Bureau of the Census, *Student Enrollment: October 1955*, Current Population Survey, P-20, no. 66 (Washington, D.C.: Government Printing Office, 1955); U.S. Department of Commerce, Bureau of the Census, *School Enrollment: Social and Economic Characteristics: October 1985*, Current Population Survey, P-20, no. 409 (Washington, D.C.: Government Printing Office, 1985).

15. U.S. Department of Commerce, Bureau of the Census, *Statistical Abstract of the United States: 1985* (Washington, D.C.: Government Printing Office, 1985), table 259, p. 155.

16. U.S. House of Representatives, Select Committee on Children, Youth and Families, *Opportunities for Success: Cost-Effective Programs for Children* (Washington, D.C.: Government Printing Office, August 1985), pp. 6–9.

17. *Statistical Abstract: 1985*, pp. 68, 72.

18. "Aid to Poor Seen as Cost Effective," *Washington Post*, August 19, 1985.

19. Paul W. Portney, "Air Pollution Policy," in Paul W. Portney, ed., *Environmental Regulation in the United States* (Washington, D.C.: Resources for the Future, forthcoming).

20. Committee on Ways and Means, *Background Material: 1986*, p. 102.

21. William Graham Sumner, *Social Darwinism* (selected essays, 1911–1919) (Englewood Cliffs, N.J.: Prentice-Hall, 1963).

22. Charles Murray, *Losing Ground* (New York: Basic Books, 1984).

23. U.S. Department of Health and Human Services, National Center for Health Statistics, *Vital Statistics: U.S.* (Washington, D.C.: Government Printing Office, 1977), tables 1-31, 1-32. U.S. Department of Health and Human Services, *Advanced Report of Final Natality Statistics, 1984* (Washington, D.C.: Government Printing Office, 1986), table 18.

24. Mary Jo Bane and David T. Ellwood, "Slipping into and out of Poverty: The Dynamics of Spells," Working Paper, no. 1199 (Cambridge, Mass.: National Bureau of Economic Research, September 1983).

25. For summaries of the case against Murray, see Sara McLanahan, Glen Cain, Michael Olneck, Irving Piliavin, Sheldon Danzinger, and Peter Gottschalk, "Are We Losing Ground?" *Focus* (University of Wisconsin Institute for Research on Poverty) (Fall–Winter 1985): 1–12; Robert Greenstein, "Losing Faith in 'Losing Ground,' " *New Republic* (March 25, 1985): 12–17.

26. For a concise discussion of the effect of taxes on income distribution, see Joseph A. Peckman and Mark J. Mazur, "The Rich, the Poor and the Taxes They Pay: An Update," *Public Interest* (Fall 1984): 28–36.

27. Robert J. Lampman, *Social Welfare Spending* (New York: Academic, 1984).

28. Beth Stevens, "Blurring the Boundaries: How Federal Social Policy Has Shaped Private Sector Welfare Benefits," in Margaret Weir, Ann Shola Orloff, and Theda Skocpol, eds., *The Politics of Social Policy in the United States* (Princeton: Princeton University Press, forthcoming).

29. U.S. Congressional Budget Office, *The Federal Budget for Public Works Infrastructure* (Washington, D.C.: Government Printing Office, July 1985), p. 57.

30. For discussions of the history of "privatization" and current ideas about

it, see Alfred A. Kahn and Sheila B. Kamerman, eds., *Privatization* (Princeton: Princeton University Press, forthcoming). We are indebted to the authors of essays in this volume for many of the ideas on which the following discussion is based.

31. "Studies Rebut Hospital Cost Theories," *Washington Post*, December 17, 1985.

32. Alfred A. Kahn and Sheila B. Kammerman, "Child Care Services and the Reagan Administration" in Kahn and Kammerman, eds., *Privatization*.

33. "Filling the Gaps in Medicare Coverage," *New York Times*, August 18, 1985. R. E. Merritt and D. B. Potemkin, eds., *Medigap: Issues and Update* (Washington, D.C.: Intergovernmental Health Policy Project, George Washington University, June 1982).

34. Lester M. Salamon, *Partners in Public Service: Toward a Theory of Government-Nonprofit Relations* (Washington, D.C.: Urban Institute, 1985), pp. 40–49.

35. For a discussion of other major revisions in the social security retirement systems, see Robert M. Ball, "The 1939 Amendments to the Social Security Act and What Followed," in the *50th Anniversary Edition of the Report of the Committee on Economic Security* (Washington, D.C.: National Conference on Social Welfare, 1985), pp. 161–172.

36. Alicia H. Munnell and Lynn E. Blais, "Do We Want Large Social Security Surpluses," *New England Economic Review* (September–October 1984): 5–21.

CHAPTER 6

1. James Fenimore Cooper, *Home as Found* (Chicago: Belford, Clarke, 1838), p. 5.

2. U.S. Department of Commerce, Bureau of the Census, *Economic Characteristics of Households in the U.S.: 4th Quarter, 1983*, Survey of Income and Program Participation, series P-70 (Washington, D.C.: Government Printing Office, February 1985).

3. Alicia H. Munnell, "Ensuring Entitlement to Health Care Services," *New England Economic Review* (November 12, 1985).

4. American Hospital Association, *Cost and Compassion: Recommendations for Avoiding a Crisis in Care for the Medically Indigent* (Chicago: American Hospital Association, 1986), p. 5.

5. Statement of Jack Owen, Executive Vice President, American Hospital Association, to the Subcommittee on Health of the Committee on Ways and Means of the U.S. House of Representatives, March 2, 1987. *Healthcare USA 1* (October 1984): 10.

6. Children's Defense Fund, *A Children's Defense Budget: An Analysis of the FY86 Budget and Children* (Washington, D.C.: Children's Defense Fund, 1985), p. 263; Children's Defense Fund, "States Monitoring Medicaid Eligibility Levels for a Family of Four, as a Percentage of the Federal Poverty Level" (Washington, D.C.: Children's Defense Fund, April 29, 1985).

7. American Hospital Association, *Cost and Compassion*, p. 5.

8. "Trends in Physician Assignment Rates for Medicare Services," *Healthcare Financing Report* (Winter 1985): 70; Robert M. Ball, "Gaps in Healthcare Coverage for the Elderly," Testimony presented at a hearing of the Senate Labor

and Human Resources Committee on Health Goals for the Nation, January 12, 1987, pp. 6–7.

9. Ball, "Gaps in Healthcare Coverage," p. 10.

10. Ibid., p. 14.

11. "Nursing Costs Force Elderly to Sue Spouses," *New York Times*, February 6, 1986; "Elderly Couples Rearranging Assets To Anticipate a Need for Medicaid," *Wall Street Journal*, November 13, 1986.

12. Leon Wyszewski and S. E. Borki, "Families with Catastrophic Health Care Expenditures," *Health Services Research* 21, no. 5 (December 1986): 617–634.

13. ICF, Inc., *The Role of Medicare in Financing the Health Care of Older Americans* (Washington, D.C.: ICF, July 1986).

14. National Health Care Campaign, *Facing Facts: A Statistical Profile of Health Care in the United States* (Washington, D.C.: National Health Care Campaign, December 1986).

15. "The Inadequately Insured," *A Health Care Agenda for the States* (Washington, D.C.: Conference on Alternative State and Local Policies, 1985), p. 9.

16. *State Programs of Assistance for the Medically Indigent*, Intergovernmental Health Policy Project, George Washington University: November 1985, p. vii.

17. U.S. House of Representatives, Committee on Ways and Means, *Background Data on Programs Within the Jurisdiction of the Committee on Ways and Means* (Washington, D.C.: Government Printing Office, 1985), p. 85. U.S. Department of Health and Human Services, Social Security Administration, *Social Security Bulletin*, Annual Statistical Supplement, 1986 (Washington, D.C.: Government Printing Office, December 1986), table 7, p. 73.

18. Commerce Clearing House, *Handbook of Pension Statistics* (Washington, D.C.: Commerce Clearing House, 1985); Emily Andrews, *Changing Profiles of Pensions in America* (Washington, D.C.: Employee Benefit Research Institute, 1985).

19. Executive Office of the President, Office of Management and Budget, *Budget of the United States Government: Appendix—FY1988.* (Washington, D.C.: Government Printing Office, 1987), p. I-10.

20. U.S. House of Representatives, Committee on Ways and Means, *Background Material and Data on Programs Within the Jurisdiction of the Committee on Ways and Means* (Washington, D.C.: Government Printing Office, March 1986), p. 476.

21. U.S. Department of Commerce, Bureau of the Census, *Money Income and Poverty Shares of Families and Persons in the United States: 1985*, CPR: Consumer Income series P-60, no. 154 (Washington, D.C.: U.S. Department of Commerce, August 1986), p. 25.

22. Alan Fox, "Earnings Replacement Rates and Total Income: Findings from the Retirement History Study," *Social Security Bulletin* (October 1982): 21, table 11.

23. Susan Grad, *Income of the Population 55 and Over, 1984*, U.S. Department of Health, Education and Welfare (Washington, D.C.: Government Printing Office, 1965), p. 76.

24. "A Fifty-Year Report Card on the Social Security System." National

292   N O T E S

survey conducted by Yankelovitch, Skelly and White, Inc., August 1985, for the American Association of Retired Persons, table 8.

25. Sandra J. Newman and Ann B. Schnare, "HUD and HHS Shelter: America's Two Approaches to Housing the Poor," *Journal of Housing* 43, no. 1 (January–February 1986): 29.

26. Committee on Ways and Means, *Background Material,* pp. 371, 383.

27. Ibid., p. 305.

28. Children's Defense Fund, *A Children's Defense Fund Budget: An Analysis of the FY87 Federal Budget and Children* (Washington, D.C.: Children's Defense Fund, 1986), pp. 186, 303.

29. Public Voice (for the Ford Foundation), *Rising Poverty, Declining Health: The Nutritional Status of the Rural Poor* (Washington, D.C.: Public Voice for Food and Health Policy, February 1986), pp. 51–73.

30. Ward Sinclair, "Many Quit Farming as Credit Crisis Dims Hopes," *Washington Post,* June 3, 1986.

31. George Eads and Michael Fix, *Relief or Reform?* (Washington, D.C.: Urban Institute Press, 1984), pp. 235–263.

32. U.S. Department of Labor, Bureau of Labor Statistics, *Monthly Labor Review* (November 1986): 73; U.S. Department of Commerce, Bureau of the Census, *Money Income and Poverty Status of Families and Persons in the United States: 1985,* CDR Series P-60, no. 154. (Washington, D.C.: Government Printing Office, August 1986), p. 3.

33. See Jennifer Hochschild, "Race, Class, Power and Liberal Democracy," in Amy Gutmann, ed., *Democracy and the Welfare State* (Princeton: Princeton University Press, forthcoming).

CHAPTER 7

1. Theodore J. Lowi, *The End of Liberalism* (New York: Norton, 1969).

2. David A. Stockman, *The Triumph of Politics* (New York: Harper & Row, 1986), p. 388.

3. "Report of the Committee on Economic Security" (1935), in *50th Anniversary Edition* (Washington, D.C.: National Conference on Social Welfare, 1985), pp. 21–30.

4. "A Fifty-Year Report Card on the Social Security System," National survey conducted by Yankelovitch, Skelly and White, Inc., August 1985, for the American Association of Retired Persons, table 19.

5. See, for example, Peter J. Ferrara, *Social Security: The Inherent Contradiction* (Washington, D.C.: Cato Institute, 1980), pp. 351–397.

6. Charles E. Lindblom, *Politics and Markets* (New York: Basic Books, 1977), esp. pp. 344–356.

7. See Theodore R. Marmor, *The Politics of Medicare* (New York: Aldine, 1970).

8. See James T. Patterson, *America's Struggle Against Poverty* (Cambridge: Harvard University Press, 1982), p. 69.

9. See Martha Derthick, *Policymaking for Social Security* (Washington, D.C.: Brookings, 1979); Jerry Cates, *Insuring Inequality* (Ann Arbor: University of Michigan Press, 1983).

10. See the various essays in Margaret Weir, Ann Shola Orloff and Theda Skocpol, eds., *The Politics of Social Policy in the United States* (Princeton: Princeton University Press, forthcoming).

CHAPTER 8

1. *The Hoover Commission Report on Organization of the Executive Branch of Government* (New York: McGraw-Hill, 1949); President's Committee on Administrative Management, *Report with Special Studies* (Washington, D.C.: Government Printing Office, 1937); Commission on Intergovernmental Relations, *A Report to the President for Transmittal to Congress* (1955; rept. ed. New York: Arno Press, 1978).

2. See Edwin Amenta and Theda Skocpol, "Redefining the New Deal: World War II and the Development of Social Provision in the United States," in Margaret Weir, Ann Shola Orloff and Theda Skocpol, eds., *The Politics of Social Policy in the United States* (Princeton: Princeton University Press, forthcoming).

3. Joseph A. Califano, Jr., *Governing America* (New York: Harper & Row, 1986), pp. 376–377.

4. For an excellent discussion of these and other institutional reform ideas, see Arthur Maas, *Congress and the Common Good* (New York: Basic Books, 1983).

5. Alice Rivlin, "Economics and the Political Process," presidential address at the 99th meeting of the American Economics Association, December 29, 1986.

6. David A. Stockman, *The Triumph of Politics* (New York: Harper & Row, 1986), pp. 376, 377.

CHAPTER 9

1. Robert Z. Lawrence, *Can America Compete* (Washington, D.C.: Brookings Institution, 1984).

2. U.S. Department of Labor, Bureau of Labor Statistics, *Employment and Earnings* (Washington, D.C.: Government Printing Office, January 1987), table B-1.

3. "Many Economists Hold Federal Policies Have Contributed to Farm Crisis," *New York Times*, February 26, 1986; "Upheaval in U.S. Food Industry Forces a Hard Look at Its Future," *New York Times*, October 9, 1986.

4. Janet L. Norwood, "The Growth in Service Jobs," *New York Times*, August 28, 1985; "Shift to Service Economy Grows," *Washington Post*, November 11, 1985.

5. See, for example, "Employment," Project on the Federal Social Role, Working Paper, no. 8 (Washington, D.C.: National Conference on Social Welfare, 1986); Sar Levitan, ed., *The Feds in the Workplace* (Washington, D.C.: National Council on Employment Policy, 1985); William L. McKee and Richard Fraschle, *Where the Jobs Are* (Kalamazoo, Mich.: W. E. Upjohn Institute, 1985); Herbert Darnes, ed., *Policy Issues in Work and Retirement* (Kalamazoo, Mich.: W. E. Upjohn Institute, 1982); Donald Bauman and Carl E. Van Horn, *The Politics of Unemployment* (Washington, D.C.: Congressional Quarterly Press, 1985); Anthony Patrick Carnevale, *Jobs for the Nation* (Alexandria, Va.: Amer-

NOTES

ican Society for Training and Development, 1985); Ray Marshall, "Selective Employment Programs and Economic Policy," *Journal of Economic Issues* (March 1984): 117–142.

6. Paul O. Flaim and Ellen Seghal, "Displaced Workers of 1979–83: How Well Have They Fared?" *Monthly Labor Review* (Washington, D.C.: Government Printing Office, June 1985); U.S. Congress, Office of Technology Assessment, *Technology and Structural Unemployment: Reemploying Displaced Adults* (Washington, D.C.: Government Printing Office, February 1986). For a discussion of various estimates of the number of displaced workers, see Charles F. Stone and Isabel V. Sawhill, *Labor Market Implications of the Growing Internationalization of the U.S. Economy* (Washington, D.C.: National Committee for Employment Policy, 1986).

7. Robert Pear, "Millions Bypassed as Economy Soars," *New York Times,* March 16, 1986.

8. U.S. Department of Labor, *Employment and Earnings,* vol. 33, no. 1 (Washington, D.C.: Government Printing Office, January 1986), pp. 155–156.

9. Ibid.

10. "Area Businesses Trimming the Fat," *Washington Post,* September 14, 1986.

11. "The New Unemployed," *Washington Post,* September 14, 1986.

12. James Barrow, "Gaps in Retaining Are Seen in an Era of Industrial Changes," *New York Times,* August 10, 1986.

13. Jonathan Kozol, *Illiterate America* (New York: Doubleday, 1985).

14. Steven Morrison and Clifford Winston, *The Economic Effects of Airline Deregulation* (Washington, D.C.: Brookings Institution, 1986), pp. 24–36, 44–45.

15. Barry Bluestone and Bennett Harrison, *The Great American Job Machine* (Washington, D.C.: Joint Economic Committee, 1986).

16. William Serrin, "New Job Trend: Temporary Workers," *New York Times,* July 9, 1986.

17. Bluestone and Harrison, *The Great American Job Machine.*

18. U.S. Department of Labor, Bureau of the Census, *Monthly Labor Review* (Washington, D.C.: Government Printing Office, November 1986), p. 72.

19. U.S. Department of Commerce, Bureau of the Census, "Standard Statistical Establishment List: Basic Items, no. 94, August 1986.

20. U.S. Department of Commerce, Bureau of the Census, *Money Income and Poverty Status of Families and Persons in the U.S.: 1985,* P-60, no. 154 (Washington, D.C.: Government Printing Office, August 1986).

21. For a discussion of varying estimates, see Lindley H. Clark, Jr., "The Baby Boomers Say They're Doing Pretty Well," *Wall Street Journal,* March 18, 1986; see also Frank S. Levy and Richard C. Michel, *Family Income in America,* analysis prepared for the Joint Economic Committee of the U.S. Congress (Washington, D.C.: Government Printing Office, November 28, 1985).

22. Bluestone and Harrison, *The Great American Job Machine.*

CHAPTER 10

1. Economic Policy Panel of the Economic Policy Committee of UNA-USA, *Work and Family in the United States* (New York: United Nations Association of the United States of America, December 1985), pp. 43–44.

2. U.S. Department of Labor, Bureau of Labor Statistics, "Rise in Mothers' Labor Force Activity Includes Those with Infants," *Monthly Labor Review* (October 1985), p. 62.

3. U.S. Department of Commerce, Bureau of the Census, *Statistical Abstract of the United States: 1986* (Washington, D.C.: Government Printing Office, 1986), p. 62.

4. Ibid., p. 47.

5. U.S. Department of Commerce, Bureau of the Census, "Housing Vacancy Survey," series H-111, 3rd quarter 1986.

6. U.S. Department of Commerce, Bureau of Economic Analysis, *National Income and Public Account of the United States, 1929–82: Statistical Tables* (Washington, D.C.: Government Printing Office, 1985). U.S. Department of Commerce, Bureau of Economic Analysis, *Survey of Current Business* (Washington, D.C.: Government Printing Office, July 1984, July 1986).

7. U.S. Department of Education, Center for Statistics, *Educational Statistics: A Pocket Digest* (Washington, D.C.: Government Printing Office, 1986).

8. U.S. Department of Labor, Bureau of Labor Statistics, "Part-Time Workers: Who Are They?", *Monthly Labor Review* (February 1986): 16.

9. Thomas Long and Lynette Long, *Handbook for Latch-Key Children and Their Parents* (New York: Arbor House, 1983); U.S. Department of Commerce, Bureau of the Census, *After School Care of School Aged Children* (Washington, D.C.: Government Printing Office, February 1987).

10. U.S. Department of Commerce, Bureau of the Census, *Household and Family Characteristics*, series P-20, no. 411 (Washington, D.C.: Government Printing Office, August 1986).

11. U.S. Department of Commerce, Bureau of the Census, *Money Income and Poverty Statistics of Families and Persons in the United States: 1985*, series P-60, no. 154 (Washington, D.C.: Government Printing Office, August 1986).

12. See, for example, Nicholas Lemann, "The Origins of the Underclass," *Atlantic* (June 1986): 31–55; Staff of The Chicago Tribune, *The American Millstone* (Chicago: Contemporary Books, 1986); Isabel V. Sawhill, "Anti-Poverty Strategies for the 1980s" (Washington, D.C.: Urban Institute, 1986), pp. 6–9.

13. Michael Harrington, *The Other America* (New York: Bantam Books, 1968), p. 1. See Daniel P. Moynihan, *The Negro Family: The Case for National Action* (Washington, D.C.: U.S. Department of Labor, 1965); *Report of the National Advisory Commission on Civil Disorders* (New York: Bantam, 1968). For discussion of the various "Moynihan Reports," see Daniel P. Moynihan, *The Politics of a Guaranteed Income* (New York: Random House, 1973), pp. 1–112.

14. U.S. Department of Commerce, Bureau of the Census, *Money Income and Poverty Status of Families in the United States: 1985*, CPR, series P-60, no. 154 (Washington, D.C.: Government Printing Office, 1986, p. 23); U.S.

Department Labor, Bureau of the Census, "Current Labor Statistics: Employment Data," *Monthly Labor Review* (October 1986): 57.

15. Sawhill. "Anti-Poverty Strategies," p. 9; Dorothy Gilliam, "Debate on the Underclass," *Washington Post*, July 10, 1986.

16. See, for example, Lemann, "Origins"; Chicago Tribune, *American Millstone;* Sawhill, "Anti-Poverty Strategies."

17. William Julius Wilson, "Cycles of Deprivation and the Underclass Debate," *Social Service Review* (December 1985): 541–559; Robert Aponte, Kathryn M. Neckerman and William Julius Wilson, "Race, Family Structure and Social Policy," in *Race and Policy*, Project on the Federal Social Role Working Paper, no. 7 (Washington, D.C.: National Conference on Social Welfare, 1985).

18. Jacob S. Siegel and Cynthia M. Taeuber, "Demographic Dimensions of an Aging Society," in Alan Pifer and Lydia Bronte, eds., *Our Aging Society* (New York: Norton, 1986).

19. U.S. Department of Commerce, Bureau of the Census, *Historical Statistics of the United States: Colonial Times to 1970, Bicentennial Edition, Part 1* (Washington, D.C., Government Printing Office, 1975) p. 55; and National Center for Health Statistics, unpublished estimates, 1986.

20. U.S. Department of Commerce, Bureau of the Census, *Projections of the Population of the United States, by Age, Sex, and Race: 1983 to 2080*, CPR, series P-25, no. 952 (Washington, D.C., Government Printing Office, 1984), p. 7: table E.

21. *Historical Statistics of the U.S.: Colonial Times to 1970*, p. 19: series A 143–157; and *Projections of the Population of the U.S. . . . 1983 to 2080*, pp. 46, 86.

22. *Historical Statistics of the U.S.: Colonial Times to 1970*, p. 15: series A 119–134; and *Projections of the Population of the U.S. . . . 1983 to 2080*, p. 8: table F.

23. *Historical Statistics of the U.S.: Colonial Times to 1970*, pp. 15, 16: series A 119–134; and *Projections of the Population of the U.S. . . . 1983 to 2030*, p. 45.

24. *Historical Statistics of the U.S.: Colonial Times to 1970*, p. 49: series B 1–4; p. 15: series A 119–134; p. 50: series B11–19; and U.S. Department of Commerce, Bureau of the Census, *Statistical Abstract of the United States: 1985* (Washington, D.C.: Government Printing Office, 1984), p. 57.

25. U.S. Department of Health and Human Services, *HHS News: Press Releases July 29, 1986*; and Office of the Actuary, Health Care Financing Administration, *Medicare Data* (Baltimore, Md.: HCFA, July 1986), table 2.

26. John L. Palmer and Stephanie G. Gould, "Economic Consequences of Population Aging," in Pifer and Bronte, eds., *Our Aging Society*, p. 381.

27. Ross H. Arnett, David R. McKusick, Sally T. Sonnefeld and Carol S. Cowell, "Projections of Health Care Spending to 1990," *Health Care Financing Review*, 7, no. 3 (Spring 1986): p. 9, table 7.

28. Joseph A. Califano, Jr., *America's Health Care Revolution: Who Lives? Who Dies? Who Pays?* (New York: Random House, 1986), p. 168; unpublished data from Health Care Financing Administration; Health Care Financing Administration, *Health Care Financing Review: Statistical Report on Medical Care—Eligibility, Recipients, Payments and Services*, HCFA-20-82 (Baltimore: HCFA, Office of Actuary, Division of Medicaid Cost Estimates, 1985).

29. Robyn Stone, Gail Cafferata and Juaim Sangl, *Caregivers of the Frail Elderly* (Washington, D.C.: National Center for Health Services Research, March 1986).

30. We are indebted to John Palmer and Stephanie Gould for many of the basic ideas on which this section is based. See "Economic Consequences of Population Aging," in Pifer and Bronte, *Our Aging Society*, p. 373.

31. Alicia Munnell and Lynn E. Blais, "Do We Want Large Social Security Surpluses?" *New England Economic Review* (September–October 1984): 16.

32. U.S. Department of Labor, Bureau of Labor Statistics, *Employment and Earnings* (January 1986): 154.

33. See Matilda White Riley and John W. Riley, Jr., "Longevity and Social Structure: The Potential of the Added Years," and Malcolm H. Morrison, "Work and Retirement in an Older Society," in Pifer and Bronte, *Our Aging Society*, pp. 53–78, 347–366.

34. Children's Defense Fund, *A Children's Defense Budget: An Analysis of the FY 1987 Federal Budget for Children* (Washington, D.C., Children's Defense Fund, 1986); and *Statistical Abstracts 1985*, p. 455.

35. Karen Davis, "Paying the Health Care Bills," in Pifer and Bronte, *Our Aging Society*, p. 308.

CHAPTER 11

1. "Report of the Committee on Economic Security" (1935), in *50th Anniversary Edition* (Washington, D.C.: National Conference on Social Welfare, 1985), p. 23.

2. The classic description of that battle is Stephen Kemp Bailey, *Congress Makes a Law* (New York: Columbia University Press, 1950).

3. See Daniel P. Moynihan, *The Politics of a Guaranteed Income* (New York: Random House, 1973).

4. James Q. Wilson, "The Rediscovery of Character: Private Virtue and Public Policy," *Public Interest* (Fall 1985): 3–16.

5. Sidney Verba and Gary R. Orren, *Equality in America* (Cambridge: Harvard University Press, 1985); Jennifer L. Hochschild, *What's Fair* (Cambridge: Harvard University Press, 1981). See also Lawrence M. Mead, *Beyond Entitlemen* (New York: Free Press, 1985); Herbert McCloskey and John Zaller, *The American Ethos* (Cambridge: Harvard University Press, 1985).

6. Lincoln, Message to Congress, July 11, 1861.

7. Theodore Roosevelt, *The New Nationalism* (1910; rept. ed. Gloucester, Mass.: Peter Smith, 1971), p. 34.

CHAPTER 12

1. Confirmed by telephone interview with Donna Bojarsky of Major Bradley's office, December 16, 1986.

2. Robert M. Ball, "Gaps in Health Care Insurance Coverage," statement presented at hearings of the Senate Labor and Human Resources Committee on Health Goals for the Nation, January 12, 1987.

3. We are indebted to Professor Robert G. Evans of the University of British Columbia for this analogy. Robert G. Evans, unpublished luncheon speech,

Washington, D.C., September 12, 1986, at symposium: "Our Children, Our Parents," sponsored by Yale University Institution for Social and Political Studies and Bush Center.

4. Paul Simon, *Let's Put America Back to Work* (Chicago: Bonus, 1987).

5. Alfred A. Kahn and Sheila B. Kammerman, *Childcare: Facing the Hard Choices* (Dover, Mass.: Auburn House, 1987).

6. Franklin D. Roosevelt, *The Public Papers and Addresses of Franklin D. Roosevelt, 1928–1932* (New York: Random House, 1938), p. 646.

7. Isabel V. Sawhill, "Rethinking Employment Policy," in *Employment, Project on the Federal Social Role Working Paper, no. 8* (Washington, D.C.: National Conference on Social Welfare, 1986).

8. See Martin Weitzman, *The Share Economy* (Cambridge: Harvard University Press, 1984): Lester C. Thurow, *The Zero Sum Solution* (New York: Simon and Schuster, 1985).

CHAPTER 13

1. Committee on Federalism and National Purpose, *To Form a More Perfect Union* (Washington, D.C.: National Conference on Social Welfare, 1985).

2. National Education Association, *Estimates of School Statistics, 1975–76, and 1985–86,* (Washington, D.C.: National Education Association, 1976 and 1986).

3. Committee on Federalism and National Purpose, *To Form a More Perfect Union,* p. 27.

CHAPTER 14

1. See, for example, Paul Taylor, "The Coming Conflict as We Soak the Young To Enrich the Old," *Washington Post,* January 5, 1986.

2. For recent initiatives on education vouchers, see "Administration Drafts 3rd Plan for School Vouchers," *New York Times,* December 1, 1986; "Reagan Proposes Vouchers To Give Poor a Choice of Schools," *New York Times,* November 14, 1985. For a more extensive discussion of educational vouchers, see Edward G. West, "Tuition Tax Credit Proposals," *Policy Review* 3 (1978): 61–75.

3. Henry David Thoreau, *Civil Disobedience* (New York: Modern Library, 1950), p. 645.

Index

abortion rights, 44
Abramovitz, Moses, 90
activist government. *See* federal
social role
activist philosophy:
"common solutions to common
problems," 19, 34
Constitution and, 32, 37–38
democratic government and, 19–
20
freedom and, 34
general welfare and, 33–34
historical prevalence of, 34–35,
41–42
origins of, 31–32, 34
pragmatic activism, 29, 41–42,
45–56
principles of, 45
Adams, Charles Francis, 76
Adams, John Quincy, 35
adverse selection, 112
AFDC. *See* Aid to Families with
Dependent Children
affirmative action programs, 131,
152
aged, the. *See* elderly, the
Agricultural Adjustment Act, 40
agriculture, job losses in, 172
Aid to Families with Dependent
Children (AFDC), 40
abuse of program by clients, 96–
98

children as focus of, 99, 153
client use patterns, 97–98
dependence fostered by, 98–99
expenditures on, 64, 65
inadequacy of payments, 95–96,
130
job training for clients, 270
Reagan administration reforms,
97
reform proposals for, 249, 250,
265–66, 270
as shared program, 265
the underclass served by, 204,
206
uniform eligibility standards,
265–66
work effort, impact on, 98
airline industry, labor cost reduction by, 179–80
Alabama, Medicaid benefits in, 123
Alaska, Medicaid benefits in, 123
American government, principle of,
45
American Indians as "hard case"
for the social role, 153
American Plan for economic development, 35
American political style, 133–34
diversity of institutions at federal
and local levels, 134–36
"hard cases," inability to deal
with, 151-53

American political style (*continued*)
   inclusiveness, 136–39
   individualism, 139–45
   privileged institutions, 146–51
   reform of the social role and, 167
Amtrak, 109
Arkansas, AFDC payments in, 130
Articles of Confederation, 156
autonomy of individuals:
   American attitudes toward, 229–
      230
   democracy dependent on, 228
   liberal-conservative agreement
      on, 230
   responsibility and, 228–29, 231

baby boom generation:
   income stagnation experienced
      by, 182–83
   as percent of the population, 208
   retirement years, potential prob-
      lems of, 117, 211–12
   Social Security reforms to deal
      with, 116–18, 212
baby bust generation:
   age groups of, 208
   baby boomers, support of, 117,
      211–12
   income expectations, 183
Ball, Robert, 245
Bananna Kelly and the South Bronx
   Desperadoes, 278
Bane, Mary Jo, 97
banking industry, insuring and regulating of, 81, 147, 254
Bill of Rights, 30
blacks:
   as "hard case" for the social
      role, 151–52
   See also underclass the
Blue Cross, 125
boarding school for at-risk
   children, 243–44, 256
Bradley, Tom, 243

Brandeis, Louis, 76
Britain, health care in, 210
Brownlow Commission, 156
Brown v. Board of Education, 44
Bryce, James, 54
budget deficit, 239
   credit programs and, 70
   social spending and, 92
budget process as national planning
   mechanism, 161
Bureau of Labor Statistics (BLS),
   174, 180
business:
   affirmative action, opposition to,
      152
   corporate welfare system, 104
   federal social role as counterpoint
      to, 51–52
   "gaming" of the federal system
      by, 149
   health care programs operated
      by, 125
   human resource development by,
      235–36
   industrial policy and, 254–55
   job skills training by, 178
   labor cost reduction by, 179–82
   part-time and contract workers,
      use of, 180
   as privileged institution, 146–48,
      149, 150
   regulation of, 78–79
   subsidies for unproductive indus-
      tries, 147–48, 149

Califano, Joseph, 159
California, AFDC payments in, 130
Canada, health care in, 210
capital punishment, 44
Carter, Jimmy, 41
catastrophic illness, 123–24
Census Bureau, U.S., 208
centrifugal forces of American life,
   280–81, 284

child care. *See* daycare

children:

AFDC program and, 99, 153

at-risk children, programs for, 243–44, 256

future prosperity dependent on, 214–16

as "hard case" for the social role, 153

as human resource policy priority, 241–44

inadequacy of programs for, 131, 215

as percent of the population, 208

population changes, 26

See also education; families and children, threats to

China, cultural diversity in, 50

CHR. *See* Committee on Human Resources

civilian work force, federal, 60

Civil Rights Act of 1964, 75, 79

Civil Rights Commission, 79

civil rights laws, 38

achievements of, 94

inadequacy of, 131–32

origins of, 79

civil rights movement, 41, 44

Civil War, 36–37

Clay, Henry, 35, 36

Clayton Anti-trust Act, 75

Clean Air Act amendments of 1970, 94

Clean Water Act, 75

Cohen, Wilbur, 144

commercial activism, 35, 38

Committee on Economic Security, 162

members and mandate, 239–40

Report of, 40, 140, 196, 221

Committee on Federalism and National Purpose, 11

assessment of recommendations, 272–75

recommendations of, 264–72

structure and procedures, 273

Committee on Human Resources (CHR), proposed, 240–41

Commodity Credit Corporation, 71

commodity insurance, 73

common institutions, 282

community development and local infrastructure programs, 266, 267–68

comprehensive programs:

Americans' preference for, 143

argument for, 142

the poor inadequately served by, 143–44

Comptroller of the Currency, 79

Congress:

budget process of, 161

local governments, sympathy for, 148–49

regulatory agencies, establishment of, 76–77

regulatory legislation, 75–76

Congressional Budget Office, 159

"conservative revolution" in American politics, 20

conservatives:

federal social role, attitude toward, 20–21

human resource policy, support for, 230

social policy reform, approach to, 164, 165

Constitution, the:

activist view of, 32, 37–38

general welfare clause, 45–46

as institutional change, 156

"limited government" view of, 30

consumer cooperatives for purchase of health care, 246

consumer debt, 197

consumer electronics industry, 187

contract workers, increase in number of, 180
contributory systems, Americans' preference for, 140–41
Coolidge, Calvin, 277
Cooper, James Fenimore, 54, 119
corporate welfare systems, 104
Council of Economic Advisors, 160, 162
credit programs, 69–70
  activities favored by, 70
  budget deficit, impact on, 70
  changes since 1977, 82
  direct loans, 71
  economic importance of, 71
  goals of, 70
  government-sponsored enterprises, 73
  loan guarantees, 72–73
  origins of, 70–71
  privatization of, 109–10
  reassessment of, 254–55
cyclical views of American politics, 21–22

daycare:
  federal investment, need for, 242–43
  multi-institutional approach to, 243
  problems of, 199–200
dedicated taxes, 138
Democracy in America (Tocqueville), 47
democratic government:
  activist philosophy and, 19–20
  individual autonomy and, 228
  synthesis with the social role, 37–38, 40
democratic morality, 283
Dennison, Edward, 89
deregulation, 131, 132
desegregation, 152
Dickens, Charles, 54
Disability Insurance, 140

discrimination, destructive effects of, 225
displaced workers, 174, 175
District of Columbia:
  AFDC payments in, 130
  Medicaid benefits in, 123
diversity in America, 49–50
division of labor between federal and local institutions:
  blueprint for, 264
  cost-effectiveness of, 269–70
  decision-making overload avoided through, 269
  decision on, need for, 263–64
  local control, programs appropriate for, 266, 267–68, 269–70
  Madisonian division of labor, 266
  rationale for, 266–69
  shared programs, reduction of, 264–66
  uniformity of standards and benefits through, 265–66, 267
divorce rates, 196–97, 199

early retirement, problems created by, 212–14
earned right to federal benefits, 141
Eastman Kodak company, 179
economic impact of military spending, 92
economic impact of social spending:
  budget deficit and, 92
  economists' views on, 86–90
  harmful impact, supposed, 85–86
  historical record, 87
  international comparisons, 87–89
  misunderstandings regarding, 91–92
  positive impact, 89
  rerouting of money, 91
  taxes and, 89–90

theoretical observations, 89–90
work effort reduction, 9
economic management:
  employment problems addressed
    by, 190
  industry policy, 254–55
  mixed results of, 132
  stability promoted through, 81–
    82
education:
  boarding school for at-risk chil-
    dren, 243–44, 256
  employment problems addressed
    by, 190
  expenditures on, 66–67
  as federal responsibility, 241–42
  in human resource policy, 225
  improvements in, 93–94
  parallel institutions for, 50
  privatization of public schools,
    110
  public education as common
    institution, 282
  public school enrollment, decline
    in, 197–98, 200
  school vouchers, 282
education loans, 71, 72, 243
Eisenhower, Dwight D., 44
elderly, the, 24–25
  expenditures on programs for,
    62, 64, 209–11
  family support for, 198, 200
  health care for, 120, 121–22,
    124, 209–11
  home-based care for, 210
  life expectancy increases, 207
  parallel institutions for, 50
  as percent of the population,
    207–9
  population changes, 25
  privatization of medical insur-
    ance for, 111
  universal benefits of programs
    for, 64
  See also pension system

Ellwood, David, 97
Emancipation Proclamation, 36
emergency room treatment, 122
Employee Retirement Insurance
    Security Agency (ERISA),
    74–75, 79
  regulation by, 127, 128, 189,
    252
employment contract in America,
    change in, 181–82
employment policy (full employ-
    ment):
  absence of, 220, 222
  consumer demand concerns, 260,
    261
  good jobs, creation of, 251–53
  guaranteed income alternative,
    223
  inflation concerns, 259–62
  job-search information system,
    250
  labor supply concerns, 260–61
  New Deal precedent for, 221–22
  as proper focus of the social role,
    220–21, 248–49
  public service jobs, 248, 249–
    250, 256
  retraining of workers, 251
  unemployment problems, pro-
    grams to deal with, 249–50
  unintended effects, possible, 250
  See also human resource policy
employment problems, 25
  average American's susceptibility
    to, 172–73
  avoidance of, 192
  corporate supports, inadequacy
    of, 188–89
  economic management as
    response to, 190
  economic sources of, 171–72
  education assistance as response
    to, 190
  federal protections, inadequacy
    of, 189–91, 192

employment problems (*continued*)
    as federal responsibility, 193
    income stagnation, 182–83
    job mobility, 183–85
    job skills, increased demand for,
        176–78
    labor cost reduction efforts, 179–
        182
    local institutions' response to,
        192–93
    part-time and contract work, 180
    recession as complicating factor,
        185–86
    scope of, 187–88
    small businesses and, 180–81
    transitions of worklife, 191–93
    uncertainty regarding the future,
        186–87
    of working women, 198–99
    See also unemployment
Environmental Protection Agency,
    79–80
environmental protection laws, 79–
    80
    achievements of, 94
ERISA. *See* Employee Retirement
    Insurance Security Agency
Evans, Daniel J., 11, 264
export loans, 73

Fair Labor Standards Act, 40
families and children, threats to, 25
    average American family,
        changes in, 195–96
    connections to community, loss
        of, 197–98
    consumer debt, 197
    daycare problems, 199–200
    divorce, 196–97, 199
    elderly members, support for,
        198, 200
    federal response to, 201
    financial vulnerability, 200
    home owning, decline in, 197

illegitimacy, 197
    mobility of families, 198
    smaller families, 197
    working women and, 196
    families as source of social assis-
        tance, 105, 106–7
farm credit policies, 71, 131
Farmers Home Administration, 71
federal administrators, privilege
    accorded to, 151
Federal Aviation Administration,
    75, 79
Federal Civil Code, 61
Federal Communications Commis-
    sion, 74, 78
Federal Deposit Insurance Corpora-
    tion, 81
federal government, capacities of,
    21, 51
Federal Home Loan Mortgage Cor-
    poration (Freddie Mac), 73
Federal Housing Administration
    (FHA), 72
federalism, 148
Federal National Mortgage Associ-
    ation (Fannie Mae), 73
Federal Power Commission, 74, 78
Federal Register, 61
Federal Reserve Board, 79, 81, 162
federal social role (activist govern-
    ment):
    achievements of, 18–19
    as business counterpoint, 51–52
    changes since 1977, 82–83
    civilian workforce required by,
        60
    commercial activism, 35, 38
    comprehensive *v.* needs-based
        programs, 142–44
    conservative attitude toward, 20–
        21
    as conservative institution, 166
    contributory systems used in,
        140–41

cyclical nature of activism, 21–22
definition of, 66
democracy, synthesis with, 37–38, 40
democratic morality of, 283
as diverse enterprise, 66–67
employment as focus of, 220–21
general welfare served through, 44–46
growth in the 20th century, 19, 38–39, 40–44
growth process, 60
inadequacy of, 24, 119–20, 129–32. *See also* health care programs; pension system
inclusiveness of, 57–58, 99–100, 103
initiation under Hamilton, 31–32
internal dynamic of, 43
Jefferson-Hamilton debate on, 32–34
leadership for, 22, 283–84
Lincoln's influence, 36–38
local alternative, 50–51
local institutions, coordination with. *See* parallel institutions
measurement of, 59–60
middle-class orientation, 100–101, 103, 139–40, 145
misunderstandings regarding, 60
modern problems, need to address, 24–27
national capacities required to solve national problems, 51–52
as national idea of government, 43–44, 106
overload of institutional capacities, 21
periods of decline, 35–36, 41
policy structure, modern, 61

policy tools, 61–62
interchangeability of, 83–84
judicial social policy, 80–81
See also economic management; incentives for favored activities; regulation; spending policies
pragmatic approach to, 29, 41–42, 45–46
preservation of the Union and, 279–82
priorities for, 219–20. *See also* employment policy; human resource policy
public skepticism regarding, 20, 22–23
public support for, 23, 106–7, 114–15
reassessment of, 17–18, 19–26, 84
redistributive impact, 101–2
schools of thought on. *See* activist philosophy; "limited government" philosophy
shape of the economy changed by, 91
stalemate in public policy, 23–24
Supreme Court decisions and, 44, 45, 80–81
tensions created by:
  individualism *v.* nationalism, 48, 54–56
  local attachments *v.* national concerns, 48, 49–54
See also limiting factors on the social role; myths of the social role; reform of the social role
Federal Trade Commission, 78, 79
Federal Trade Commission Act, 75
Feldstein, Martin, 89
female single parents, 26
  welfare's impact on, 96, 97
fertility rates, 197

fiscal capacity grants, 271
Food and Drug Administration, 74,
    79
Food Stamp program, 64, 206
Ford Foundation, 131
foreign countries:
    competition and investment
        from, 171
    social spending in, 87–89
freedom of the individual, 34
full employment. *See* employment
    policy
Full Employment Bill of 1945, 222

"gaming" of the federal system,
    149
General Accounting Office, 159
General Revenue Sharing Program,
    271
general welfare:
    Constitution's clause on, 45–46
    federal social role in service to,
        44–46
    Jefferson-Hamilton debate on,
        33–34
generational equity, 281
Gettysburg Address, 37
good jobs, elements of, 251–53
Government National Mortgage
    Association (Ginnie Mae),
    72
government-sponsored enterprises,
    73
Gramm-Rudman-Hollings budget
    act of 1985, 161
Great Society era, 166
Greece, social spending in, 88
"green-mail," 254
Greenspan, Alan, 117
Greenspan Commission, 117–18
Greyhound company, 181
guaranteed income policy, 223
Guaranteed Student Loan Program,
    72, 83

Hamilton, Alexander:
    activist philosophy, 31–32
    on freedom of the individual, 34
    general welfare, views on, 33–34
    Jefferson, rivalry with, 32–34
    pragmatism of, 41–42
    republican attitudes, 36
Harrington, Michael, 202
Head Start program, 94, 131
health care costs, 126
health care policy, comprehensive,
    211
    consumer cooperatives and, 246
    cost containment system, 245–48
    costs of, 256
    as federal responsibility, 247–48
    financing of, 245
    long-term care measures, 245,
        270–71
    mechanisms for, 245
    public preference for, 244–45
    restrictions on access, 247, 248
health care programs, 120
    able-bodied workers excluded
        from, 135
    achievements of, 94
    catastrophic illness and, 123–24
    corporate programs, inadequacy
        of, 125
    cost containment system, 245–46
    eligibility requirements, varia-
        tions in, 122–23
    emergency room alternative,
        122
    expenditures on, 125–26, 209–
        211
    health care costs, impact on,
        126, 210–11
    home-based care systems, 210
    limited coverage, 123
    long-term care, 210
    nursing home care not covered
        by, 124
    payment systems of, 126

preventive medicine not promoted by, 126
quality of medical service, variations in, 123
supplemental programs, 124–25
types of, 120–21
uninsured population, 121–22, 125, 135
See also specific programs
health care system, regulation of, 246
health maintenance organizations (HMOs), 246
Hepburn Act, 77
high-technology industries, employment in, 183, 187
Highway Trust Fund, 139
Hirschman, Albert, 21
Hispanics:
as "hard case" for the social role, 151–52
See also underclass, the
Hochschild, Jennifer, 229
home-based health care systems, 210
home buying, decline in, 130, 197
homeless, increase in number of, 130
Hoover Commissions, 156
House of Representatives:
Select Committee on Children, Youth, and Aging, 94
housing, improvements in, 93
housing asssistance, 70–71, 72
expenditures on, 65, 67
human capital, investment in, 89
human resource policy:
advisory committee for, 240–41
autonomy encouraged by, 228–230
business sector involvement, 235–36
children as top priority, 241–44
costs of, 255–56
discipline needed for, 238
economic health as prerequisite for, 253–55
education, 225
employment concerns, 248–51
as federal responsibility, 234
funding sources, 256–57
good jobs, creation of, 251–53
health care aspects, 244–48
individualism-nationalism tensions addressed by, 231–32
individuals as focus of, 231–33
inflation issue, 259–62
institutional diversity, possible threat to, 232–35
as investment, 227
job security measures, 253
labor market improvement, 225–226
launching of programs, importance of, 258–59
leadership necessary for, 239, 257–58
limits of, 236–38
local-national coordination, 233–235
local opposition to federal role, possible, 232–33, 257
New Deal model for, 239–40
"new ideas" for, 258
political support for, 230
the poor benefitted by, 226–27
public support for, 229–30, 231
responsibility encouraged by, 231–32
retraining of workers, 251
security-building measures, 224–225
success, likelihood of, 226–27, 231
universal benefits of, 227
values embodied in, 236–37
human resources, waste of, 217–218

Humphrey-Hawkins Act of 1978, 222
Huntington, Samuel, 21

ICF, Inc., 124
illegitimacy:
    as threat to families, 197
    welfare's impact on, 96, 97
immigrants as "hard case" for the social role, 153
"implied powers," principle of, 32
incentives for favored activities, 61
    credit programs, 69–73
    regulation of, 77
    tax expenditures, 67–69
inclusive political style, 136
    costliness of, 138
    financing problems due to, 138–139
    functioning of, 137
    overcommitment resulting from, 136–37
    perpetuation of programs due to, 137–38
    programs favored by, 136
    in the social role, 57–58, 99–100, 103
    in spending policies, 64, 66
income security protections, inadequacy of, 189–91
income stagnation, 182–83
indebted society, 197
individualism of Americans, 54–55
    comprehensive and needs-based programs to satisfy, 142–43
    contributory systems and, 140–141
    human resource policy and, 231–232
    hypocrisy of, 145
    as limiting factor on the social role, 139–45
    middle-class working ideal, 139–140

the poor disadvantaged by, 143–145
industrial policy, 254–55
inflation:
    full employment and, 259–62
    health care costs and, 210
    measures for dealing with, 261–262
inflation tax, 262
Interstate Commerce Act of 1887, 38
Interstate Commerce Commission (ICC), 76–77, 78
"iron triangles" as barriers to reform, 158–59

Jackson, Andrew, 35–36
James, William, 57
Japan, social spending in, 88
Jefferson, Thomas, 44
    activist administration, 35
    on freedom of the individual, 34
    on general welfare, 33–34, 45
    Hamilton, rivalry with, 32–34
    "limited government" philosophy, 30–31, 47–48
    republican attitudes, 36
Job Corps, 256
job mobility, problems of, 183–85
job placement services, 225
job-search information system, 250
job security measures, 253
job skills:
    company training for, 178
    older workers and, 177
    service sector requirements, 176
    specialization of, 177–78
    workers' lack of, 176–77, 178
Jobs Training Partnership Act (JTPA), 190–91
job training for welfare clients, 270
Johnson, Lyndon B., 19, 38, 42, 57
judicial social policy, 80–81
Justice Department, U.S., 78, 79

Kerner Commission, 202
Kestnbaum Commission, 156
Kuttner, Robert, 88

labor cost reduction efforts, 179–82
Labor Department, U.S., 79
labor market improvement measures, 225–26
Lampman, Robert, 86, 89, 90, 104, 105
"latchkey" children, 200
leadership, tasks of, 283–84
liberals:
  human resource policy, support for, 230
  social policy reform, approach to, 163–65
life expectancy increases, 207
"limited government" philosophy:
  arguments and positions of, 29–30
  as distinctive American viewpoint, 47–48
  federal social role, impact on, 48–49
  individual freedom and, 32
  Jefferson-Hamilton debate on, 32–34
  local government focus, 30, 34
  origins of, 30–31
  persistence of, 48
  Tocqueville's analysis of, 47
limiting factors on the social role, 133–34
  diversity of institutions at federal and local levels, 134–36
  "hard cases" for policy, 151–53
  inclusive political style, 136–39
  individualism, 139–45
  privilege accorded to federal administrators, 151
  privileged institutions, 146–50
Lincoln, Abraham, 20, 230
  activist policies, 36–38
  pragmatism of, 42

Lindblom, Charles E., 146, 147
loan guarantees, 72–73
loans. *See* credit programs
local attachments-national concerns conflict, 48, 49–54
Local Initiatives Support Corporation, 278
local institutions:
  community development and local infrastructure programs, control of, 266, 267–68
  Congress' sympathy for, 148–49
  employment problems, response to, 192–93
  federal government, coordination with. *See* parallel institutions
  human resource policy, possible opposition to, 232–33, 257
  industrial investment, competition for, 150
  initiatives, social role's impact on, 103–7
  "limited government" philosophy and, 30, 34
  privilege accorded to, 146–51
  uniform performance standards, need for, 135
  See also business; division of labor between federal and local institutions
Losing Ground (Murray), 96
Louisiana Purchase, 35
Lowi, Theodore, 137

Madison, James, 53–54, 266
management of programs, problems in, 156–57
manufacturing industries:
  job losses, 171–72
  labor cost reductions, 179
Marshall, John, 44
Masssachusetts, health cost control in, 268

Medicaid, 120, 121–22
children assisted through, 153
comprehensive coverage through,
245, 256
eligibility requirements, 122–23,
266
expenditures on, 64
quality of medical service, variations in, 123
the underclass served by, 206
Medicare, 120, 121
comprehensive coverage through,
245
as contributory system, 140
expenditures on, 62, 209
implementation of, 167
inclusive nature of, 136
limited coverage offered by,
123
nursing home care not covered
by, 124
private supplements to, 111
Melville, Herman, 54
mergers, corporate, 254
middle-class orientation of the
social role, 100–101, 103,
139–40, 145
military spending, economic impact
of, 92
minimum wage, increase in, 252
minority groups as "hard case" for
the social role, 151–52
Mississippi, AFDC payments in,
130
monopolies, legislation on, 38
"moral equivalent of war" concept, 57
mortgage credits, 70–71
Moynihan, Daniel Patrick, 202,
250
Murray, Charles, 96, 97, 98
myths of the social role, 9
bankruptcy of Social Security,
115–18

economy harmed by social programs, 85–92
ineffectiveness of social programs, 92–95
local initiatives discouraged by
the social role, 103–7
poverty, relation to welfare programs, 95–99
privatization, 107–15
winners and losers of social policy, 99–103

National Center for Health Services
Research (NCHSR), 124,
125
National Conference on Social
Welfare (NCSW), 9, 10–11
National Highway Traffic Safety
Administration, 79
national idea of government, 106
nationalism of Americans, 55–56
human resource policy and, 231–
232
political attempts to encourage,
57
National Labor Relations Act
(Wagner Act), 40, 74
National Labor Relations Board, 79
national planning:
absence of, 157
barriers to, 158–59
budget process as mechanism
for, 161
planning mechanism, need for,
160, 161–62
political parties as mechanism
for, 160–61
political reforms to promote, 162
presidency as mechanism for,
160
F. D. Roosevelt's effort, 158
National Resources Planning
Board, 158

nationhood:
  benefits of, 55–56
  growth of, 43–44
needs-based programs:
  argument for, 142
  inadequacy of, 144
New Deal:
  average American family during, 195–96
  employment policy, 221–22
  philosophy of, 39, 106
  social supports, new system of, 39–40
  See also Committee on Economic Security
"new ideas" for social policy, 258
New Jersey, health cost control in, 268
New York Times, 129
nursing home care excluded from health care programs, 124
nutritional programs, inadequacy of, 131

Occupational Safety and Health Administration (OSHA), 79
Office of Management and Budget, 62, 160, 162
oil industry, 187
The Other America (Harrington), 202

parallel institutions, 50
  human resource policy as threat to, 232
  limiting effect on the social role, 134–36
  Madisonian argument for, 52–54
  tax expenditures for, 69
  traditional activist view of, 106
  See also division of labor between federal and local institutions

part-time workers, increase in number of, 180
Pell Grant Program, 83
pension system:
  baby boom generation retirement years, 117, 211–12
  components of, 127
  early retirement trends and, 212–214
  government acceptance of unfunded pension liabilities, 128
  inadequacy of, 127–29, 189
  private pension plans, 127–28
  private savings, 128
  reforms for, 252
  tax expenditures and, 68
  trained and educated children, dependence on, 214–16
  veterans' pensions, 38
  workers excluded from, 189
  See also Social Security
Perkins, Frances, 40
perpetuation of social programs, 137–38
philanthropy, 105, 106–7
Plymouth Notch, Vt., 277–78
political parties, national planning by, 160–61
Polk, James K., 36
poor, the:
  economic profile of, 201–2
  human resource policy and, 226–227
  individualism of Americans and, 143–45
  minimal benefits for, 143
  needs unmet by the social role, 145
  prime-age workers, lack of programs for, 144–45
  See also underclass, the; welfare programs
population aging, 24–25

population aging (*continued*)
    baby boom generation and, 208,
        211–12
    factors affecting, 207–8
    health care concerns, 209–11
    pension-related concerns, 212–
        216
    workforce size reductions and,
        211–12
Portney, Paul, 94
Postal Service, 60
poverty:
    reductions in, 93
    welfare programs, relation to,
        95
pragmatic activism, 29, 41–42,
        45–46
preventive medicine, 126
prime-age workers, lack of pro-
        grams for, 144–45
privatization of technical and sup-
        port functions (petty privati-
        zation), 108–9
privatization of the social role:
    accountability concerns, 113
    adverse selection and, 112
    advocates of, 107–8, 110
    cash transfers, inability to deal
        with, 108
    efficiency issue, 110–12, 114
    guarantees of programs, impact
        on, 113
    insurance functions, 109–10, 111
    means and goals of policy
        changed by, 112–14
    public attitudes toward, 114
    services, 109
productivity increases, 254
Project on the Federal Social Role:
    decentralized plan for, 11–12
    origins of, 9–11
    publications of, 11–12
Public Health Service, 109, 126

public schools:
    enrollment declines, 197–98,
        200
    privatization of, 110
public service jobs, 248, 249–50,
        256

Reagan, Ronald, 17, 41
Reagan administration:
    assessment of, 284
    welfare reforms, 97
recession and employment, 185–86
reform of the social role:
    American political style used for,
        167
    Committee on Federalism recom-
        mendations, 264–72, 273
    conditions for, 166–67
    fiscal capacity grants, 271
    fiscal neutrality of, 271–72
    institutional reform, 273
    crises needed to precede, 157
    managerial problems addressed
        by, 156–57
    national planning focus, 157–
        162
    precedent for, 156
    structure of government foc-
        cus, 162
    job training for welfare clients,
        270
    liberal and conservative
        approaches to, 163–65
    "new ideas" for, 258
    past instances of, 166
    prospects for reform under cur-
        rent conditions, 165–66
    shortcomings of the current sys-
        tem, focus on, 220
    uniform standards for local insti-
        tutions, 135
    See also division of labor
        between federal and local

institutions; employment policy; health care policy, comprehensive; human resource policy
regulation, 61
  administrative agencies for, 76–77
  average American, impact on, 73–75
  of banking industry, 81, 147, 254
  behavioral goals of, 77–80
  business regulations, 78–79
  changes since 1977, 82
  costs of, 80
  of health care system, 246
  inadequacy of, 131
  legislation authorizing, 75–76
  social regulations, 79–80
  of spending and incentive program implementation, 77
  See also deregulation
religion in public institutions, 283
remedial training programs, 225
research and development, expenditures on, 67, 254
retraining of workers, 251
revenue sharing, 271
reverse discrimination, 152
Rivlin, Alice, 162
Robb, Charles S., 11, 264
Roosevelt, Franklin D., 19, 38
  democratic activisim of, 40
  on government's social responsibility, 39
  national planning effort, 158
  pragmatism of, 42
  See also New Deal
Roosevelt, Theodore, 38, 76
  activist philosophy, 17, 19
  on individual autonomy, 230
  pragmatism of, 42

Rural Electrification Administration, 71
rural society, Jefferson's vision of, 31

Salamon, Lester, 111
Sawhill, Isabel, 259
Schlesinger, Arthur M., Jr., 21
school vouchers, 282
Schwarz, John, 93
Securities and Exchange Act, 40, 75
Securities and Exchange Commission, 78
service sector:
  growth of, 172
  jobs and wages in, 176
Shaffer, James C., 178
shared programs, reduction in number of, 264–66
"share-economy," 262
Sherman Anti-Trust Act of 1890, 38, 75
Simon, Paul, 249
slavery, abolition of, 38
small business sector, growth of, 180–81
social safety net, 24
Social Security:
  average annual benefit, 127
  baby boom generation, reforms to deal with, 116–18, 212
  "bankruptcy" of, 115–18
  conservative opposition to, 164, 165
  as contributory system, 140
  early retirements, impact of, 214
  expenditures on, 62
  functioning of, 116
  implementation of, 40, 240
  inclusive nature of, 136
  minimal benefits for the poor, 143

Social Security (*continued*)
national economy's impact on,
116
poverty rate, impact on, 93
public support for, 136
reforms of 1983, 216
retirees' dependence on, 129
success of, 93, 240
taxing of benefits, 257
as welfare program, 65
Social Security Act, 45, 61
Social Security Administration, 77
Social Security Board, 151
South Africa, 279
South Bronx, N.Y., 278
Soviet Union, 50
special interest legislation, 58
spending policies, 61
changes since 1977, 82
diversity of programs, 66–67
for the elderly, 62, 64, 209–11
for health care, 125–26, 209–11
inclusive nature of, 64, 66
regulation of, 77
social spending as percent of
national budget, 59, 62, 63,
65
special groups targeted by, 66
stabilizing effect of, 89
total federal outlays by program
and purpose, 63
welfare spending, 64–65
"welfare state" perspective, 65–
66
See also economic impact of
social spending
SSI. *See* Supplemental Security
Income
stalemate in public policy, 23–24
Stevens, Beth, 104
Stockman, David, 137, 138, 165,
284
student aid system, 71, 72, 243

Student Loan Marketing Associa-
tion (Sallie Mae), 72
Sumner, William Graham, 95
Supplemental Security Income
(SSI), 127, 128
expenditures on, 64
Supreme Court, 44, 45, 80–81
Sviridoff, Mike, 278

tax expenditures:
definition of, 67
history of, 67
individuals targeted by, 68–69
parallel institutions, support of,
69
pension plans, encouragement of,
68
tax reform and, 67–68, 69
tax increase, need for, 92
tax reform of 1986, 67–68, 69
tax system:
dedicated taxes, 138
income tax, introduction of, 36
progressive system, 102
redistributive impact, 101–2
social spending and, 89–90
teen-agers, unemployment among,
174–75, 250
Thoreau, Henry David, 283
Thurow, Lester, 262
Time, Inc., 179
Tocqueville, Alexis de, 47, 54
To Form a More Perfect Union,
264
trade deficit, 171
transitions of worklife, 191–93
Treasury Department, U.S., 162
trust in government, 22, 23
Twain, Mark, 54

UI. *See* Unemployment Insurance
underclass, the, 25

aspirations and values of, 205
as common concern for Americans, 205–6
composition of, 202
federal programs for, 206–7
growth of, explanations for, 204–5
periodic national concern for, 202–3
size of, 203–4
worsening condition of, 203
unemployed population, change in, 25–26
unemployment:
disappearance of jobs, 174
displaced workers, 174, 175
employment policy provisions for, 249–50
"natural rate" of, 260
permanently unemployed people, 174
youth unemployment, 174–75, 250
Unemployment Insurance (UI), 40
as contributory system, 140
expenditures on, 65
inadequacy of, 130–31
inclusive nature of, 136
the poor disqualified from, 144
reform proposals for, 249, 250
unemployment rates, misleading aspects of, 173–74, 180
uninsured population, 121–22, 125
Union, the:
leadership of, 283–84
modern need for, 281
preservation of, 279
strengthening measures, 281–82, 284
threats to, 279–81, 284
United States Employment Service, 190, 250
Urban Affairs Council, 162

Verba, Sidney, 229
Veterans Administration (VA):
civilian workforce, 60
health care system, 120–21
home loan insurance, 72
privatization of health services, 109
veterans' pensions, 38

War on Poverty, 203, 206, 237
Warren, Earl, 44
Washington, George, 35, 56
Washington Post, 129
Webster, Daniel, 35, 36
Weidenbaum, Murray, 80
Weitzman, Martin, 261
welfare programs:
abuse of programs by clients, 96–98, 144–45
criticism of, 65, 95
effectiveness of, 93
expenditures on, 64–65
female-headed households, impact on, 96, 97
illegitimacy, impact on, 96, 97
inadequacy of payments, 95–96
job training for clients, 270
poverty, relation to, 95
Reagan administration reforms, 97
Social Security as, 65
See also specific programs
welfare state:
charter for, 40
spending policies and, 65–66
White, William Allen, 39, 277
WIC program, 94, 131
Wilson, James Q., 229
Wilson, William Julius, 204–5
Wilson, Woodrow, 38, 57, 76
"winners and losers" of social policy, 99–103

women. *See* female single parents; working women

Woodstock, Vt., 279

work effort:
AFDC program and, 98
social spending and, 90

Work Incentive Program (WIN), 190

working women:
as "hard case" for the social role, 152–53

increase in number of, 196
insecurity of employment, 198–199

World War II, 196

Wyoming, Medicaid benefits in, 123

Yankelovich, Skelly and White, 129

youth unemployment, 174–75
measures to deal with, 250